THE LITERARY CRITICS

THE
LITERARY CRITICS

*A Study of
English Descriptive
Criticism*

GEORGE WATSON

Second Edition

THE WOBURN PRESS – LONDON

This edition published in 1973 by
WOBURN BOOKS LIMITED
67 Great Russell Street, London WC1B 3BT

First published by Penguin Books in 1962
Second edition 1973

ISBN 0 7130 0085 6

Printed in Great Britain by
Lewis Reprints Ltd.
member of Brown Knight & Truscott Group
London and Tonbridge.

To Renford Bambrough

CONTENTS

PREFACE TO THE SECOND EDITION

THE opportunity to revise and enlarge this book has been a welcome one, since it remains the only history of English criticism written in this century by a British scholar. But it was written over ten years ago, and a great deal in detail has happened since then: Sidney, Dryden, Addison, Johnson and others have all been edited in new and superior editions, and recent scholarship has thrown light on questions which I once tried to solve single handed. What is more, my own understanding of some of these problems, and especially the more theoretical ones, has been reshaped by writing its sequel, *The Study of Literature* (Penguin Books, 1969), which discusses the nature of critical judgement and its links with linguistics, psychoanalysis, sociology and the history of ideas.

This edition, accordingly, is totally revised, with changes of substance and style in all ten chapters, and some additions further to those in the revisions of 1964. A number of new emphases seem required, and the Bibliography has been extended, though its form remains as it was. Post-Restoration quotations have usually been modernized. I hope the book, so improved, will continue to serve the needs of students and scholars.

The stir the book caused in 1962, when it first appeared, included some helpful and friendly advice from reviewers, along with an attempt on the part of a disciple of one of the critics dealt with in Chapter 9 to force the publisher to withdraw the book. The publisher, I need hardly add, unhesitatingly declined to do so; and I have matched his courage with some of my own by sharpening the account of Eliot's followers in this new edition. The book, as it now stands, owes an infinite deal to many reviewers and correspondents, friendly and hostile alike, as well as to my Cambridge pupils over a dozen years, who have helped me to understand what needs to be said and what may safely be left unsaid. And the dedicatee, a philosopher who is also a colleague, has continued for another decade to justify his place before the contents.

St John's College, Cambridge
June 1971

PREFACE TO THE FIRST EDITION

THIS book, which is a brief history of descriptive criticism in England (and latterly in the United States) from its beginnings some three hundred years ago, is an attempt to show by what stages the art of analysing English literary works has evolved from the early experiments of the seventeenth century into the techniques of the twentieth. In such an argumentative survey, which tries to identify revolutionary figures and to explain the significance of the revolutions they caused, a vast amount of respectable work is bound to be neglected, and major critics themselves are likely to appear in an unfamiliar light as pioneers of a method, or of an influential attitude to the descriptive problem. What *kinds* of questions have the major English critics posed in analysis; and how far, and with what tools, have they succeeded in answering them? The emphasis, in this history, lies squarely on issues like these.

Much of this book began as lectures on the history of criticism delivered in Cambridge during the years 1959 and 1960, and my chief debt is to an audience who, itself the product of the evolution I have tried to describe here, encouraged me by a critical interest in what I had to say. The subject is not much explored. But I hope that, for their sake, I have found some right answers; and that, where I have not, I have at least posed questions in a more precise form than other historians of criticism have done.

St John's College, Cambridge
June 1961

FIRST PRINCIPLES

The Three Kinds of Criticism

SOME things are most readily defined by their contraries, but the ultimate condition of a literature without criticism is one that modern England has happily never known, and we must leave a stranger to speak. These are the words of the Hungarian poet Miklos Gimes, later hanged by the Kadar Government, describing intellectual life in the Socialist countries before the rising of 1956:

Slowly [under Stalin] we had come to believe ... that there are two kinds of truth. If there is a truth of a higher order than objective truth, if the criterion of truth is political expediency, then even a lie can be 'true'; ... and so we arrive at the outlook which infected not only those who thought up the faked political trials, but often infected even the victims: the outlook which poisoned our whole public life, penetrated the remotest corners of our thinking, obscured our vision, paralysed our critical faculties, and finally rendered many of us incapable of simply sensing or apprehending truth.[1]

Criticism, of course, cannot prevent lies from being told. But it does make it its business to see that lies do not establish themselves as truth. It presupposes an open society, and it is one of the conditions by which such a society survives. But English criticism, though prone to sudden convulsions and revolutionary situations, has not suffered much from ruthless authoritarianism. The record is rather one of great revolutionary individuals – their achievement is the subject of this history – who have attacked established

1. *Béké és Szabadsaq* (3 October 1956), quoted in translation by Michael Polanyi, 'Beyond Nihilism' (*Encounter*, March 1960), p. 42.

complacency, dismissed the assumptions of their predecessors, and struck out in new directions.

The second half of the twentieth century marks, in a rather negative sense, a revolutionary phase in the evolution of English criticism, a pause imposed by an access of doubt. The 1950s brought with them a flood of warnings against critical arrogance and a series of demarcation disputes, following upon half a century of unparalleled activity. The very titles of T. S. Eliot's 'The Frontiers of Criticism',[1] Helen Gardner's *The Limits of Literary Criticism* (1956), and John Holloway's 'The New "Establishment" in Criticism' all suggest that caution is in the air. The process of stock-taking, too, is already well under way, and two American histories have already appeared to record at length the progress of the English-speaking, even of the Western, critical tradition. My purpose is more modest, and based on principles that are not theirs. It is to trace one kind of activity only among the many confused under the name of literary criticism as it has been practised in the British Isles, and ultimately in the United States as well, since its emergence some three hundred years ago: descriptive criticism, or the art of analysing works of literature that actually exist.

The oddity is that any historian should ever have attempted in one work to do more. But all previous histories – Saintsbury and Atkins in their day, as much as Wellek and Wimsatt in ours – have assumed that what we call literary criticism is, with some embarrassing exceptions, a single activity, and that its history is the story of successive critics offering different answers to the same questions. We may call this the Tidy School of critical history. Allen Tate has defined its main premiss in an extreme form: 'The permanent critics ... are the rotating chairmen of a debate only the rhetoric of which changes from time to time.'[2]

1. See Select Bibliography, p. 221, for a list of critical studies and histories cited in this chapter.

2. 'Longinus and the New Criticism' (1948), reprinted in his *The Man of Letters in the Modern World* (New York, 1955), p. 192.

Wimsatt and Brooks insist on the principle of 'continuity and intelligibility in the history of literary argument'.[1] I must say at once that the kind of order they see is not visible to me. Where they see a tidy evolution of doctrine, I see a record of chaos marked by sudden revolution. Where they see a continuing debate down the centuries around the same questions, I see a pattern of refusal, on the part of the major critics, to accept the assumptions of existing debate. The great critics do not contribute: they interrupt. Coleridge does not try to answer questions posed by Dryden and Johnson: he poses questions of his own, questions Dryden and Johnson had not thought of and would not have understood. Arnold, again, is not finishing Coleridge's work: there is scarcely a moment in his essays where we are made aware that he has read Coleridge's criticism at all.

More than that, the English critics – like European critics in general – are not all engaged on work of a logically comparable kind. It was Dryden[2] who first used the word 'criticism', in print at least, in the now familiar sense of 'any formal discussion of literature', and so helped to confuse in a single term three kinds of discussion that have nothing in common except a reasoned concern for poetry:

LEGISLATIVE CRITICISM, including books of rhetoric. Such criticism claims to teach the poet how to write, or how to write better. It is the standard – very nearly the only – kind of criticism practised by the Elizabethans, and for half a century after: Sidney apart, nearly all Elizabethan critics directed their remarks to poets rather than to readers of poetry. Their writings, for the most part depressingly uninspired, are the critical equivalent of the recipe-book, and they are based on the master-chef's assumption that any pupil of good intelligence can learn the business if only he

1. W. K. Wimsatt and Cleanth Brooks, *Literary Criticism: a Short History* (New York, 1957), p. vii.

2. In the preface to *The State of Innocence* (1677): 'Criticism, as it was first instituted by Aristotle, was meant a standard of judging well.' But the term 'critic', in a literary application, is at least as old as Bacon's *Advancement of Learning* (1605), I, vii, 21.

is shown how. The imperative, of course, is the characteristic (though not the only) mood of the legislative critic:

Frame your stile to perspicuity, and to be sensible.
> George Gascoigne, 'Certayne Notes of Instruction concerning the Making of Verse', in his *Posies* (1575).

First, ye sall keip just cullouris.
> King James VI of Scotland, 'Ane Schort Treatise conteining some Reulis and Cautelis in Scottis Poesie', in his *The Essays of a Prentise* (1584).

Our proportion poeticall resteth in five points: staff, measure, concord, scituation, and figure.
> George Puttenham (?), *The Arte of English Poesie* (1589), II, i.

Iambick and trochaick feete, which are opposed by nature, are by all rimers confounded.
> Thomas Campion, *Observations in the Art of English Poesie* (1602).

We should not so soone yeeld our consents captive to the authoritie of antiquitie, unless we saw more reason; all our understandings are not built by the square of Greece and Italie. We are the children of nature as well as they.
> Samuel Daniel, 'A Defence of Ryme', a reply to Campion, in his *Panegyrike to the King*, etc. (1603).[1]

These quotations from five Elizabethan critics are all 'legislative', though in ascending order of sophistication: only the first is imperative in syntax, and the last, torn from its context, looks almost modern in its apparent concern for the taste of the reader–until one remembers that Daniel's 'we' refers not to all Englishmen, but to his fellow-poets.

There is no need here to examine the pretensions of legislative criticism. It is dead. In England, indeed in Western Europe, it dominated the sixteenth century and died in the course of the seventeenth, with Dryden representing the point of change. We shall never again see the day when flocks of young poets sought instruction in their craft from rhetoricians. In the whole English-speaking world legislative criticism survives, outside the school-room, only

1. *Elizabethan Critical Essays*, edited by G. Gregory Smith, 2 vols. (Oxford, 1904), I, 53, 212; II, 68, 330–31, 366–7.

in the post-war trickle of handbooks of composition and 'creative writing' assembled by American academic critics for American college students.[1] For the rest, critics are not even the unacknowledged legislators of poets. For three hundred years they have sensibly sought their public not among poets but among readers of poetry.

THEORETICAL CRITICISM, or literary aesthetics. The form first arose in England in the Sidney circle, in the 1570s, under the influence of Spanish and Italian critics such as Vives and J. C. Scaliger. Perhaps the first work in the form by an Englishman was the very derivative treatise by the ex-Jesuit Richard Wills, *De re poetica* (1573). Sidney's own *Apology for Poetry* was written soon after, though it did not appear till 1595, nine years after his heroic death on a Dutch battlefield. To tell the truth, it is not much less derivative than Wills's Latin essay, though Sidney's superior ability in absorbing his continental sources, his decision to write in English at all, and his own distinction as a poet have saved the *Apology* for some sort of immortality. Its intrinsic interest as an original contribution is small. The seventeenth-century critics, such as Dryden, showed a continuing but occasional interest in aesthetics. But by this time most literary forms other than the novel had already won their respectability, and there is certainly no suggestion in Hobbes or Dryden that, as Sidney had once complained, poetry had 'fallen to be the laughing-stock of children'.[2] A new source of theoretical curiosity had to be found. From Hobbes onwards, interest shifts away from such Platonic issues as the nature of poetic truth towards such psychological questions as the nature of the creative act. By the eighteenth century, aesthetics is a mania among the English in an age when, as Boswell shows, the theory of beauty formed part of the small talk of polite London drawing-rooms. From Addison's

1. e.g. Cleanth Brooks and Robert Penn Warren, *Modern Rhetoric* (New York, 1949).
2. *An Apology for Poetry: or the Defence of Poesy*, edited by Geoffrey Shepherd (1965), pp. 96, 145.

essays on the imagination in the *Spectator* of 1712, through the treatises of Lord Kames, Burke's *The Sublime and Beautiful* (1757), and Sir Joshua Reynolds's *Discourses* (1778), the long line comes to an abrupt end in Coleridge's *Biogrcphia Literaria* (1817), largely written in the summer of Waterloo. And there, in England, the story almost ends. The Victorians, repelled by Coleridge's obscurity, and impressed by the rising prestige of historical studies, readily abandoned theoretical criticism to the Germans. There is no Victorian literary aesthetic before Pater and Wilde, and no formal aesthetic of any kind after Coleridge until the work of I. A. Richards in the 1920s and R. G. Collingwood's *The Principles of Art* (1938). In spite of some isolated attempts on the part of British philosophers to interest themselves in the Beautiful,[1] critics and philosophers have drifted further and further apart since the age of Coleridge.

DESCRIPTIVE CRITICISM, or the analysis of existing literary works. This is the youngest of the three forms, by far the most voluminous, and the only one which today possesses any life and vigour of its own. In England it is some three hundred years old, if we confine our attention, as we must, to what survives in print; though it is worth remembering that what remains is the very tiny tip of an impossibly vast iceberg. Verbal (not to say unspoken) comment on poetry must be as old as poetry itself, and in any age the proportion of comment that sees print must fortunately be very small. 'To breathe is to judge' – Dryden's discovery in the 1660s was not that plays and poems are worth discussing, but that they are worth discussing in print. For the rest, we can only guess at the table-talk of English poets before the Restoration about themselves and their fellow-poets – with the unique exception of Ben Jonson, whose comments on his contemporaries, spiteful, bookish, and obviously authentic, luckily survive in a record made by

1. For example, contributions by Stuart Hampshire, Margaret Macdonald, J. A. Passmore, Gilbert Ryle, and others to *Essays in Aesthetics and Language*, edited by William Elton (Oxford, 1954).

his host, the Scottish poet William Drummond, of Jonson's visit to Hawthornden in 1618. Descriptive criticism in English, which is the subject of this history, begins as talk and survives as talk that someone has thought worth writing down. It is the perfect symbol of the way our critical tradition began that the earliest surviving examples occur in Dryden's essay *Of Dramatic Poesy* (1668): for all its stilted contrivance, it is in the form of a dialogue.

I shall try to show that, as anyone might reasonably expect, descriptive criticism begins introspectively, often as self-justification, with poets discussing their own works, as Dryden in his prefaces defended his plays from their detractors. It shelters nervously, at first, behind a respectable façade of legislative or theoretical criticism. But the break is absolute in logical terms. For whereas the legislative critic had said 'This is how a play should be written', and the theoretical critic, like Aristotle in the *Poetics*, 'This is the nature of tragedy in general,' Dryden simply says: 'This is how I have tried to write my play, and why.' Descriptive criticism, uniquely, is particular and, to a unique degree, falsifiable. It is about one thing, a given text to which critic and reader may appeal equally for confirmation.

Whether the achievement of such criticism over three hundred years has been important or not is something that must be allowed to emerge. But a few classic objections to the critical tradition may be answered at once. Some extremists have argued that the very existence of the critic as middleman between poet and reader is an impertinence; or even that the critic is a symptom of a decadent, over-sophisticated civilization. Some literary cultures (e.g. the Indonesian), it is said, are self-explaining, and the profession of critic is unknown among them. But it should be obvious at once that a poetry that does not prompt or demand comment is in its nature trivial. As for the claim that 'there is too much criticism nowadays', it seems to be based on a mere confusion of language. It may be no more true to say that we have too much criticism than to say we have too many novels. Of course there is more of either than any

7

individual can read, and more than is worth reading. But good criticism, like good novels, is in strikingly short supply. It is, after all, immensely difficult. Henry James once noticed how rare the critical talent was, 'that quantity of opinion, very small at all times, but at all times infinitely precious, that is capable of giving some intelligible account of itself'.[1] The gaps, indeed, are startling: there has been no major critical assessment of a novelist as significant as Defoe since Leslie Stephen's essay of 1874; there is still none of many a significant eighteenth-century poet. Shakespeare's imagery remained uninvestigated for more than three hundred years after his death, and to this day much of English medieval poetry awaits its Samuel Johnson.

Again, English criticism has been called derivative and unoriginal. Source-studies have made us conscious of Dryden's debt to Hobbes and Corneille, Coleridge's to the Germans, Arnold's to Sainte-Beuve, Eliot's to Rémy de Gourmont, and so on. There are moments when one feels as if every major English critic has some continental skeleton in his cupboard. But we should remember that original *ideas*, in the strict sense, are not the stock-in-trade of the descriptive critic. Samuel Johnson is a classic case of a great critic of this sort, for it is not clear that he ever had an original abstract intuition about literature in his life. Coleridge is a far greater *critic* than any of the Germans whose ideas he allegedly borrowed. From this point of view – a severely practical one – anyone can have an idea: it is essentially the business of the descriptive critic to perceive connections in terms of actual texts.

Finally, criticism is often condemned as being secondary and parasitic, inferior to what is usually called 'creation'. I do not know what 'creative' means when it is used to include Johnson's *Vanity of Human Wishes* and to exclude his Life of Milton. It is not obvious that these two works are of a different logical order – both, after all, are reasoned statements of experience – and it is premature to assume that

1. From 'The Lesson of Balzac' (1905), reprinted in *The House of Fiction*, edited by Leon Edel (1957), p. 60.

criticism is of a lower order than poetry until we have shown it to be of a different one. Certainly the careers of many of our major poets since Dryden do not suggest that they conceived of criticism as an inferior activity. Johnson, Coleridge and Arnold all abandoned poetry for criticism in early middle age; Dryden and T. S. Eliot have enjoyed long careers as critic–poets, the one concern complementing the other; and Eliot's early essays, collected in *The Sacred Wood* (1920), identify the specific qualities in Renaissance English which he emulated in his own early poems. The very poetry of such poets as these is a critical activity, in that it takes its rise from a will to determine, and perhaps alter, the nature of a given literary inheritance. Again and again, great criticism happens by a similar progress of events: a highly self-conscious, deliberate poet with revolutionary objectives conceives a certain dissatisfaction with his career in early middle age, and attempts in criticism to define more closely what he is about. This recurrent metamorphosis of poet-into-critic, which Eliot has traced in his *The Use of Poetry and the Use of Criticism* (1933), was established in England by Dryden, for whom poets, as he remarked in the preface to *All for Love* (1678), 'make the most proper, though ... not the only critics'. At the moment where '*Kunst wird Kritik*', in Thomas Mann's phrase, where art turns into criticism out of a passion for establishing principles, it is not criticism that the poet feels to be secondary and second-rate. Perhaps, as Baudelaire[1] thought, the crisis is an inevitable one in the career of the conscientious artist. At all events it will hardly do to belittle how much such crises of critical doubt and reappraisal have done for the awareness of Western man.

1. '*Tous les grands poètes deviennent naturellement, fatalement, critiques.*' Baudelaire goes on to speak of '*une crise ... ou [les poètes] veulent raisonner leur art*'. See his review 'Richard Wagner et Tannhäuser à Paris' (1861), posthumously collected in his *L'Art romantique* (Paris, 1869).

Description: its Themes and Languages

This history attempts to trace the development of techniques for describing literary works since, three centuries ago, Englishmen began to take such description seriously enough to publish examples. Nobody can doubt that the story is one of progress in a very simple sense. The average schoolboy of today is probably capable of analysing more closely and more accurately than Dryden or any of Dryden's contemporaries, and the ordinary reviewer often enjoys a similar unearned advantage over the greatest of English critics before the twentieth century. The task is to identify the nature of these advances and to attribute them, where possible, to individuals.

The question might be approached from two points of view, substantive or linguistic. What kinds of question do the major critics attempt to answer in their descriptive criticism? Or, alternatively, in what kinds of descriptive terms does the language of each critic excel? And these, on investigation, prove to be in no sense merely different aspects of the same issue. It may seem natural to suppose that the critic who excels, for example, in the variety and precision of his metrical terms is attempting to answer questions about metre, and so on. No doubt it might ideally be so, and this history would have proved less complicated, and English criticism better, if it had been so. But it is not. On the contrary, criticism has been too idiosyncratic an affair, too subtly interwoven with the careers of critics who are also poets, to allow for any such direct relationship between the special language of criticism and its real subject. Besides, critics commonly inherit their language rather than create it, and though the terminological innovations of Dryden, Arnold, or Richards tell us something significant about their purposes, we cannot expect even the most original of critics to do more than adapt and amplify a language others have made. Dryden's language, for example, is quite unusually rich in terms for describing the parts of the play, and some of them may be his own invention: terms like 'discovery' and 'unravelling' (for *dénouement*), the 'continuity of scenes' (for Corneille's *liaison des scènes*), and so on. But we do not turn to Dryden for technical accounts of the structure of plays, and it is doubtful if anyone ever did; and this because, as I shall try to show, such analysis in Dryden is always patchy and partial, more concerned with self-recommendation or the detection of tricks useful to the working dramatist than with the total anatomy of drama. The question posed by his essay *Of Dramatic Poesy* (1668) is not the nature of dramatic excellence in the abstract, but the prospects for a successful rhyming drama on the French model in the immediate circumstances of Restoration England. In a similar way, Arnold's essays excel in the language and tactics of nineteenth-century biography after the manner of Sainte-Beuve; but I shall indicate, in a later chapter, in what sense Arnold's biographical interests are spurious, and in which other directions his real interests lie. Other critics, such as Coleridge, are bolder and less concessive to popular taste in their procedures. But it will never do to confuse the terminology of criticism with its ultimate purposes.

The record has, in any case, been a conservative one, and no one-man revolutions in critical language have met with much success. Most of Dryden's adaptations from the French failed to take, as Johnson noticed a century later, and Coleridge never found acceptance for terms like 'coadunative' and 'esemplastic', or for his special definitions of 'imagination' and 'fancy'. Certain enrichments of the language as a whole, such as the invasion of Freudian and Marxist terms in the 1930s, have affected the language of criticism along with the rest, but the successful invention of standard terms, like Eliot's 'dissociation of sensibility', is highly exceptional. The fact is that critical terminology has evolved slowly. And it has moved in an unexpected direction. We should have expected it to acquire an increasing number of terms especially suited to literary description in proportion as descriptive criticism itself grew more precise and more fashionable. In fact, just the reverse has happened. English critical terminology has, been steadily impoverished since the sixteenth century, when it stood at its highest point in richness and variety. Puttenham uses far more critical terminology than Dryden, Dryden more than Johnson, and Johnson more than Arnold or Eliot. This may be something to regret, and there will be professional voices raised to demand a new language of rhetoric to replace the disused terminology of the Elizabethans. The fact remains that such special language has been used in English rather for legislative criticism (critic-to-poet) than for analysis (critic-to-reader), and that modern analysis, paradoxically or not, has thrived without it. But this is only part of the answer. To understand how descriptive criticism in English has achieved so much without acquiring or extending a special language of description, one must turn to the first, substantive question: what kinds of question have been posed by critics over the past three hundred years?

On a broadly historical view – that is to say, omitting false starts (like Fielding on the novel) and mere discipleship – several major phases emerge, and it will not falsify the story much if, for the sake of simplicity, we give them the names of Dryden, Coleridge, and Arnold. With Dryden in the 1660s description was practised for the first time in English as a diplomatic compound of formal analysis and self-justification, the critic seeking in his subject – usually a poem or play of his own – the structural origins of its success. This formal school of criticism, which the historians have usually dubbed 'neoclassicism', sets the scene for the great shift of interest on the part of the critic from poet to reader, as in Addison; so that as it draws towards its end, in the final triumph of Johnson's *Lives* (1779–81), it has assimilated both elements: a confident knowledge that the old laws of Renaissance criticism can be usefully turned upon modern vernacular literature, and an awareness that there are thousands of English readers eager to see it done. The second stage, called 'romantic' criticism, with Coleridge, is marked by the discovery that historical information is not a mere accessory to analysis, as in Johnson's *Lives*, but an essential tool to enable the reader to see poems as documents in time or the products of a creative act. As for the third stage, I have called it Arnold, in spite of the grave ambiguities in Arnold's tactics as a critic, because I believe the reactionary anti-historicism of much of English criticism in the early twentieth century, in Eliot, Richards and the early Empson, takes its rise from him.

The subjects of English criticism in terms of literary *genre* evolve less certainly down the centuries and are affected by many conflicting forces. English criticism has often proved itself ill-adjusted to the real literary achievements of its time. In some periods, for example that of the Metaphysical poets, or the first century of the English novel, analysis has simply failed to exist, and several major English critics of later date, including Coleridge and Arnold, have almost ostentatiously abstained from confronting the poetry of their own day. Other critics, such as Dryden and T. S. Eliot, have viewed the contemporary scene only through the distorting glass of their own literary ambitions, so that, if you were to read Dryden's criticism in the 1660s and 1670s as a chronicle of the period, you would imagine the Restoration to be essentially an age of the theatre, while Eliot's essays between the wars tell us practically nothing about Joyce, or D. H. Lawrence, or Auden, or Isherwood. This is not disparagement: critics have no obvious moral duty to talk about the contemporary scene, and the tactic adopted by Dryden and Eliot of using criticism as a preparative to publication – the prefatorial mode of criticism – or Coleridge's passion for ultimate principles, or Arnold's moralism, all have their own justification. The only danger is that they should be mistaken for some other thing, and that we should, for instance, confuse the history of English criticism with the history of English taste. It is worth remembering that the prefatorial critics analyse not so much the poems they have written as the poems they hope to write – hence Dryden's otherwise inexplicable obsession with heroic tragedy, Eliot's with poetic drama, and Arnold's (in the 1853 preface) with the epic. This productive, and perhaps inevitable, distortion of interest through unfulfilled literary ambition has proved fairly general, though there are notable exceptions in the cases of Samuel Johnson and Henry James. The Johnson of the *Lives*, at least, is writing of the age he knows, and he inevitably finds himself discussing the current poetic forms of that age – the verse-satire, the elegy, the classical translation, the ode – largely to the exclusion of drama and the epic. We might not much respect his judgement of either. And James, of course, almost exclusively a novelist, writes almost exclusively about the novel. But such efficient specialization is rare. One may regret it: its rarity makes English the poorer in classic analysis. But English criticism has not triumphed by caution, and nobody who loves the critical spirit can regret that English poets have presumed to explore some areas in which their formal qualifications were uncertain.

In any case it is not, on the whole, so much the vogue of one or another literary form that has provoked analysis, such as that of the novel in the nineteenth century; it has rather been the scope of current analytical techniques. Some techniques are good only for some kinds of literature. The Augustan technique, for example, of identifying the formal 'parts of the poem' in the established terms of classical and Renaissance criticism is useful only for classical forms of literature, notably the epic and the tragedy, and chaos results when some one tries to apply it to *Tom Jones*. Between the wars, both in England and in America, we have seen a similar kind of failure in the neglect of the novel by the New Critics in their marked preference for verbal analysis. It did not matter in the Thirties that the novel was a more important form, both quantitatively and qualitatively, than the short poem. The short poem was 'analysable' by that age in a sense that the novel was not, and it was duly analysed. It was not a matter of private incapacity – Empson, for example, has latterly shown himself a masterly critic of the novel[1] – but of the nature of

1. In his last phase, following his abandonment of verbal analysis; see his article '*Tom Jones*' (*Kenyon Review*, xx, 1958). It is, of course, pos-

the tools to hand. Broadly, then, it has seemed as if the drama and the classical forms of poetry have suited the Augustan mode in criticism best, while the nineteenth century has excelled in the analysis of prose forms, notably the novel, and the early twentieth century in short poems. But this strange evolution has been governed not by one factor but by several, in varying degrees; and some lapses – such as the failure of early Stuart England to analyse its own poetry at all, in spite of the wealth of rhetorical terms left to it by the Elizabethan critics – remain forever unexplained.

But, as I have tried to show, the language of descriptive criticism (if by 'language' is meant the special terms or jargon that distinguish each school) does little or nothing to identify the issues of the great critical schools. Jargon is, in any case, a diminishing element in English criticism, so that what is merely misleading in the writings of the neoclassical critics largely disappears in critical analysis since Coleridge. But there is another sense of 'language' wider and less easily defined than this – so wide, indeed, that to say that the issues of criticism are defined by language in this second sense is almost a tautology. If by 'language' is meant something like 'the total linguistic range' of any given critic (as people speak of 'the language of Shakespeare', or 'the language of the Authorized Version'), then it is self-evidently true that what a critic asserts or implies is contained within such a linguistic pattern. I shall notice such characteristic patterns throughout the course of this history – the special quality of Arnold's urbanity, or Eliot's technique of the parenthetical insult – and such patterns are characteristic in the fullest sense. That is, one cannot remotely imagine similar devices in the mouth of any previous critic: try to

---

sible to expose a brief extract from a novel or epic to verbal analysis: the technique is only unconvincing to the extent that it remains uncertain how far the extract is representative of the whole; see Ian Watt, 'The First Paragraph of [Henry James's] *The Ambassadors*' (*Essays in Criticism,* x, 1960), reprinted in *Literary English since Shakespeare,* edited by George Watson (New York, 1970).

conceive of Eliot's notorious 'not that Montaigne had any philosophy whatever'[1] in the mouth of Dryden, or Addison, or even Arnold. Certainly, in this wider sense of 'language', it may sensibly be claimed that the language of a critic ultimately holds the key to his achievement. And, again in this wider sense, one may sensibly attempt to generalize about the language of description in terms of period, certain (for example) that an extract from an Addisonian analysis could only have occurred in eighteenth-century England, however uncertain one may remain about the reasons for thinking so.

A series of extracts should establish the point at once and offer ground from which to advance the argument a further stage. They are in chronological order.

DRYDEN: I will observe yet one thing further of this admirable plot: the business of it rises in every act. The second is greater than the first; the third than the second; and so forward to the fifth. There too you see, till the very last scene, new difficulties arising to obstruct the action of the play; and when the audience is brought into despair that the business can naturally be effected. then, and not before, the discovery is made ...
>   *Of Dramatic Poesy* (1668)

ADDISON: I look upon the disposition and contrivance of the fable to be the principal beauty of the Ninth Book, which has more *story* in it, and is fuller of incidents, than any other in the whole poem. Satan's traversing the globe, and still keeping within the shadow of the night, as fearing to be discovered by the angel of the sun, who had before detected him, is one of those beautiful imaginations which introduces this his second series of adventures ...
>   *Spectator*, No. 351 (12 April 1712)

JOHNSON: He borrows too many of his sentiments and illustrations from the old mythology, for which it is vain to plead the example of ancient poets: the deities which they introduced so frequently were considered as realities, so far as to be received by the imagination, whatever sober reason might even then determine. But of these images time has tarnished the splendor. A fiction, not only detected but despised, can ever afford a solid basis to any

1. See p. 176, below.

position, though sometimes it may furnish a transient illusion or slight illustration. No modern monarch can be much exalted by hearing that, as Hercules had had his club, he has his navy ...

Life of Waller, from *Lives* (1779–81)

COLERIDGE: A unity of feeling pervades the whole of his plays. In *Romeo and Juliet* all is youth and spring – it is youth with its follies, its virtues, its precipitancies; it is spring with its odours, flowers, and transiency: the same feeling commences, goes through, and ends the play. The old men, the Capulets and Montagues, are not common old men; they have an eagerness, a hastiness, a precipitancy – the effect of spring ...

Lecture 1 (October 1813)

ARNOLD: His expression may often be called bald, as, for instance, in the poem of 'Resolution and Independence'; but it is bald as the bare mountain tops are bald, with a baldness which is full of grandeur. Wherever we meet with the successful balance, in Wordsworth, of profound truth of subject with profound truth of execution, he is unique. His best poems are those which most perfectly exhibit this balance. I have a warm admiration for 'Laodameia' and for the great 'Ode'; but ... I find 'Laodameia' not wholly free from something artificial, and the great 'Ode' not wholly free from something declamatory ...

'Wordsworth' (1879), in *Essays in Criticism: Second Series* (1888)

ELIOT: The wit of the Caroline poets is not the wit of Shakespeare, and it is not the wit of Dryden, the great master of contempt, or of Pope, the great master of hatred, or of Swift, the great master of disgust. What is meant is some quality which is common to the songs in *Comus* and Cowley's Anacreontics and Marvell's Horatian Ode. It is more than a technical accomplishment, or the vocabulary and syntax of an epoch; it is ... a tough reasonableness beneath the slight lyric grace. You cannot find it in Shelley or Keats or Wordsworth ...

'Andrew Marvell' (1921), in *Selected Essays* (1932)

EMPSON (on Donne's 'A Valediction: Of Weeping', st.2, 'On a round ball ...'): The first four lines are defining the new theme, and their grammar is straightforward. Then the *teare* may be active or passive, like the *workeman* or like the *ball*; on the face of it, it is like the *ball*, but *so doth* may treat it as like the *workeman*. For *doth* may be a separate verb as well as an auxiliary of *grow*; while, in any case, *grow* may either mean 'turn into' or 'grow larger' ...

> *Seven Types of Ambiguity* (1930, 1953), ch. iv:
> 'In the fourth type the alternative meanings combine to make clear a complicated state of mind in the author.'

Anyone can see that each of these seven examples of description is intensely characteristic of its own age: an informed reader of English criticism could date all of them without effort, and in most cases he could guess the author too. But suppose he were asked to explain why he is so certain, and suppose that, in answering, he confined himself to the critical substance of each extract. Several conclusions spring to mind at once.

1. The evolution of critical description, as represented here, is almost circular in its concern for what we nowadays call 'close reading'. It has not, as one might first have guessed, evolved in one direction, ever closer to the text: Dryden, after all, is much closer to the text of *The Silent Woman* than Addison is to *Paradise Lost,* or Johnson to any single poem of Waller, or Coleridge to *Romeo and Juliet,* or Arnold to what he thinks are Wordsworth's best poems, or Eliot to the Horatian Ode. Only Empson, in a passage which is a fair run-of-the-mill example of twentieth-century 'verbal analysis', shows himself closer to the text of his choice than Dryden was to his, and it is a closeness of a sort Dryden never attempted. For Dryden's analysis, of course, was not verbal but structural – and so was Rymer's, and so, at times, was Addison's and Johnson's. But Empson's attempt – which would look schoolmasterly if it were not so novel – to explain in detail the meaning of an English poem is more minute and, in principle, more exact than anything before 1930. And to look harder at this nearly circular evolution from Dryden to Empson is to see that the details confirm a first impression of the general pattern. The first three extracts (Dryden, Addison, Johnson) take us further and further from the texts. Addison is admittedly commenting on a specific passage in *Paradise Lost* (ix, 58ff.), but his comment could not be dignified with the term 'analysis',

as Dryden's fairly could – it is rather concerned, like a chairman's remarks, with careless recommendation ('beautiful imaginations'). And Johnson has no text: in the whole Life of Waller he expends only a few sentences on specific poems, and then his comments are only snap judgements ('elegant and happy', 'empty and trifling'), whereas thousands of words are spent in generalizing about Waller's talent and illustrating its characteristic virtues and faults. The next three extracts (Coleridge, Arnold, Eliot) represent a hesitating return to the particular on fresh, historical principles: Coleridge attributes a psychological condition to Shakespeare in one of his plays, Arnold plays amateurishly with a biographical inference concerning a Wordsworthian 'balance', Eliot makes a bold historical generalization, while faintly disparaging the historical method (wit is more than 'the vocabulary and syntax *of an epoch*' – but, presumably, it is that too). With Empson, of course, we have come more than full circle, but Empsonian minuteness is possible only because of nineteenth-century historicism: it devours every kind of historical information in its progress, especially the lexicographical.

2. The terminology of criticism diminishes steeply, and if only an extended example of Elizabethan analysis had survived, the decline would seem even steeper. Dryden's interests in design and structure make a special language indispensable, and the passage quoted is characteristically rich in it: *plot, business* (i.e. dramatic action), *act, scene, discovery* (i.e. *dénouement*). Addison begins in a similarly businesslike style ('the disposition and contrivance of the fable', i.e. the structure of Milton's plot); but he makes the reader feel at once that, unlike Dryden, he is writing for amateurs rather than professionals by explaining his terms in extravagantly – even misleadingly – simple language. Book IX 'has more *story* in it, and is fuller of incidents', which does not, as he seems to suppose, in itself prove its structural superiority. Johnson's terms, such as they are, can hardly be called proper to criticism at all, in the simple sense that Dryden's were: words like 'imagination' and 'reason'

would call for explanation on the part of a conscientious editor only in terms of eighteenth-century philosophy and psychology – they are part of the general current of eighteenth-century debate. Coleridge, in this instance, has no critical terminology, and where he has it is usually self-invented and self-defined – an obvious symptom of the decline of jargon; and much the same is true of Arnold and Eliot. And this decline has proved general. Rhetoric is dead – how many people, offhand, could tell you what 'paralipsis' means, or 'litotes', or 'catachresis'? Words for 'the parts of the poem' have largely disappeared, except for a few indispensables like 'act' and 'scene'. Metrical terms still exist (*sonnet, foot, iambic*, etc.), but under a cloud of unbelief, and phoneticians will tell you that many of them do not correspond to the facts of the language. A few terms in a new rhetoric (*ambiguity, tension, irony*, etc.) do not compensate for a loss which for two hundred years has rendered English criticism less exact but more available.

3. The readership of criticism changes, after Dryden, from poets to readers of poetry, from professionals to amateurs, from producers to consumers; one cause, no doubt, if it is not also the result, of the simplification of the language of criticism I have just noticed. Dryden's remarks on *The Silent Woman* could only be intended for fellow-dramatists – it would be an unimaginably analytical spectator who would want to know about such technical devices as the accelerating tempo by which Jonson's comedy works. But with Addison, the revolution is already complete, and though it is not certain that an Augustan epic-poet like Blackmore might not have learned something from the *Spectator* papers on *Paradise Lost,* it is utterly certain that they were not written for him: the discussion is altogether untechnical in its emphasis, and the critic's function, like a tourist-guide's, is to point out the principal beauties. Johnson is doing the same thing better, Coleridge and Arnold a similar thing differently. But with Arnold one can already sense a new and demanding limitation imposed by intellectual snobbery upon the audience of criticism. It is there in Arnold's de-

precatory tone, based upon a rhetoric which is more complex and more oblique than Johnson's outspoken rigour ('I
find "Laodameia" *not wholly free* from something artificial
...'). And it is there in Eliot's assumption that his readers
are scholars, and not only of English literature; and in
Empson's assumption that his readers are grammarians.

4. The evaluative concern of criticism is a steadily increasing one. This is the more difficult to prove because of
the complicated interrelationship in critical language – as
in most other language – between description and evaluation. No doubt it is easy to think of very simple critical
statements – e.g. '*Paradise Lost* is an epic' – which are
entirely descriptive and in no sense evaluative. But criticism
that counts does not work on this simple level. If some one
were to attempt, in the coldest of cold blood, to describe
what *Paradise Lost* is like above and beyond half a dozen
simple statements – it is an epic, it is long, it is in blank
verse – he should soon find that the language of criticism
did not permit him to describe it without judging it. Even
Dryden, with his wealth of technical terms, is unable to
show what *The Silent Woman* is like without making it sound
like a good play, and if the one frankly evaluative term in the
entire extract, 'admirable' were deleted, it would still be
clear that Dryden is recommending the play as well as
analysing it. And this for two reasons: first, because he has
chosen to describe one of the virtues of Jonson's plot, where
he could as easily have chosen one of its defects; and second,
because his total description is cast in the language of the
exemplary case, as a close examination of its vocabulary
and syntax could reveal. Imagine if, in the last sentence,
you were to substitute for the commendatory phrase 'then,
and not before' another phrase which might fit as well the
objective facts of the play, 'then, at long last'. It is by such
scarcely visible touches that the language of critical description ceases to be pure. Readers who think that Dryden is
overrating *The Silent Woman* cannot usefully charge him
with inaccurate description. The inaccuracies are there, no
doubt, but they are not crucial. The worst they can say is

that Dryden has subtly weighted the evidence, by verbal tricks, for the sake of a favourable judgement.

And here, perhaps, we may identify one of the reasons why the evaluative content of English criticism has risen from age to age. Technical language, as in Dryden, may be used to some evaluative purpose; but *only* a technical language, or a language artificially maintained by a continuing discipline (like the languages of some natural sciences), could in principle be judgement-free. And yet the English critics since Addison have abandoned all prospects of such a technical language in favour of a wider public; and a critical language poor in technical terms is doubly likely to be value-charged. With Addison, recommendation is the explicit purpose of criticism; with Johnson, recommendation and condemnation are elevated into an inquiry of principle. Johnson does not merely blame Waller for his classical references: he uses Waller's mistake of including too many in his poems as a directive to the reader to condemn such excesses wherever they are found ('A fiction ... can *never* afford a solid basis to any position ...'). By the nineteenth century, the question whether the language of criticism is descriptive or evaluative, or in what proportion it is one or the other, no longer makes sense, for the historical method of the romantics so humanized the concept of the poet – Wordsworth's 'man speaking to men' – that we can no longer unpick the elements. In such criticism, all description passes judgement, and all judgement affects to describe. If Coleridge thinks that the 'feeling' of *Romeo and Juliet* is 'all youth and spring', we do not pause to ask ourselves whether this is an objective fact about the play or a subjective experience of Coleridge's. It is both – or, at least, it offers itself as both. And much the same is true of Arnold, Eliot, and Empson, for it is an assumption that what they distinguish for our attention is both there and worth looking at. If Empson were to fail, for once, to discover his ambiguity, we should hardly know where to turn; but he chooses his own examples, justifiably enough, and that is why the effects he admires are there.

So much and a good deal more we might say, faced with seven representative examples of descriptive criticism over three hundred years: that over the centuries English criticism has tended to move away from the text and then back towards it; that it is rapidly and early stripped of all but a few of the technical terms that it inherited from the European tradition; that it began as a dialogue between poets and ends as a demonstration before readers; and that the task of distinguishing the better from the worse has grown more insistent with the generations. It has, in fact, tended to win popularity at the expense of precision, and self-importance at the expense of both.

CHAPTER 2

JOHN DRYDEN

The Precursors

THE first Englishman to attempt any extended descriptive criticism was John Dryden, and this history must begin with him. But it may be useful to emphasize from the start how feeble the Elizabethan and early Stuart inheritance was, and how revolutionary, in their bulk and seriousness of purpose, Dryden's analyses of Ben Jonson, Shakespeare, and his own plays must have seemed.

All English criticism before 1660 was essentially legislative or theoretical, its theoretical content rising steeply in the seventeenth century, notably in Hobbes's occasional interest in the psychology of the creative act. Descriptive criticism before the Restoration is limited to occasional phrases and sentences in essays directed to some other end: the reform of letters, or the continuation of the Platonic argument about poetic truth. These snatches of description, written in an age when description had no purpose and no dignity of its own, read now like extracts from a schoolboy's essay. They are mainly simple evaluative statements, for though the Elizabethan critic inherited the common European stock of *genre*-words (*tragedy, pastoral,* etc.), as well as numerous rhetorical terms for describing figures-of-speech, and a system of metrical description – an immense battery of technical terms, far greater than anything wielded by the twentieth-century critic – he paradoxically inherited no tradition of using them for literary analysis. For him, they simply defined exemplary or cautionary cases. We are left with the embarrassing spectacle of a critic as intelligent as Sidney solemnly telling us that 'Chaucer, undoubtedly, did excellently in his *Troilus and Criseyde*', or that Spenser's

24

Shepheardes Calendar (1579) 'hath much poetry in his eclogues, indeed worthy the reading, if I be not deceived'.[1] George Puttenham (or whoever wrote the 1589 *Arte of English Poesie*) is a legislative critic who, in his vigorous honesty, still impresses us as a good master for a young poet. But a descriptive problem leaves him looking merely flatulent:

Henry Earle of Surrey and Sir Thomas Wyat, betweene whom I finde very litle difference, I repute them (as before) for the two chief lanternes of light to all others that have since employed their pennes upon English poesie: their conceits were loftie, their stiles stately, their conveyance cleanely, their termes proper, their meetre sweete and well proportioned, in all imitating very naturally and studiously their Maister Francis Petrarcha.[2]

There is not much 'cleanely conveyance' here: Puttenham has managed to say nothing except that Wyatt and Surrey are good Petrarchan poets. Perhaps the best thing that can be said for Elizabethan critics, considered in this purely eccentric sense as the pioneers of descriptive criticism, is their clear if rudimentary sense of literary history. There is Sidney's magnificent appeal to Puritanical detractors of poetry, such as Stephen Gosson, to maintain some decent reverence for the past of European poetry, from Homer to Chaucer: 'they go very near to ungratefulness, to seek to deface that which, in the noblest nations and languages that are known, hath been the first light-giver to ignorance.'[3] The first of Puttenham's three books (the second and third are legislative and technical), entitled *Of Poets and Poesie*, recounts in historical order the progress of poetry from its mythical and priestly sources through classical and medieval times. But, like Sidney, Puttenham can only use the historical method, and then fleetingly, for an argumentative purpose, to prove that in most societies 'good poets and poesie were highly esteemed and much favoured of the greatest

1. *An Apology for Poetry*, edited by G. Shepherd, p. 133.

2. *Arte*, I, xxxi; edited by G. D. Willcock and Alice Walker (Cambridge, 1936), p. 62.

3. *An Apology for Poetry*, op. cit., p. 96.

princes'.[1] The Campion–Daniel debate, too, on rhyme (1602–3), calls glibly on ancient and medieval practices to score points in a debate interesting only to fellow-poets.

It would be a fair summary to conclude that there was no Elizabethan tradition in descriptive criticism. There is no surviving Elizabethan analysis of an Elizabethan play, and no contemporary analysis, in the age that followed, of a Metaphysical poem. The nearest approach to Dryden's achievement, perhaps, in the years before the Restoration, is to be found in the critical preface of Sir William Davenant (1606–68), 'A Discourse upon *Gondibert*', published in Paris in 1650 for the exiled Royalist poet before he had written his epic – it was, in fact, never finished – and oddly including an 'Answer' by Thomas Hobbes, who was then completing his *Leviathan* (1651) after a ten-year absence from the England of the Civil War. Davenant's idea of writing serious and extended criticism in prefatorial form looks strikingly like a premonition of the stratagem Dryden was to adopt a dozen years later – especially as Davenant uses the preface, like Dryden after him, for critical self-justification, to defend his poem as an edifying Christian epic. Hobbes's Answer is boldly theoretical, dividing all European poetry into three categories designed for court, city, and country, and each category into the dramatic and the narrative. It is just possible that Dryden took some courage from this early assertion, by two exiled Englishmen, of the usefulness of criticism to defend in advance a poet's reputation. But the *Gondibert* debate of 1650 is not a very impressive example of descriptive criticism, and for a very simple reason: it is about a poem that does not exist, so that the argument is only speciously particular where it is particular at all. In Hobbes's reply, indeed, all pretence at the particular is cast aside: you cannot analyse a poem that is not there. The vacuum may be regarded as fully significant. Dryden inherited from earlier English critics a mass of critical terminology and a few simple notions of poetry as a historical sequence stretching from Homer. But

1. *Arte*, 1, viii; op. cit., p. 16.

he could have found all this, and more, in his continental sources. As for a native tradition in critical analysis, he was forced to start from scratch.

The early Dryden

Whatever is to be made of the elusive achievement of Dryden (1631–1700) as a critic, we can hardly expect our estimate to be one he would have understood himself. For that matter, one can hardly imagine him understanding Johnson's claim, in his Life of Dryden, that he was 'the father of English criticism'. No critic achieves so much with so little sense of his own dignity. He wrote only one work of formal criticism in a crowded literary career of over forty years, the essay *Of Dramatic Poesy* (1668), and all the remaining works of his in which criticism predominates are prefaces, most of them to his own plays and poems. There is no reason to suppose that he thought the function of the critic an important one: one cannot imagine him writing, like Arnold, an essay called 'The Function of Criticism at the Present Time'. And the works of other poets occupy a very modest proportion of his critical interests. And yet he is clearly the founder of descriptive criticism in English. The modern preoccupation with literary analysis emerges, patchily but unmistakably, in his prejudiced and partisan interest in his own plays and poems.

And yet Dryden is a descriptive critic almost without knowing it. Most of his criticism offers itself, in traditional terms, as legislative or theoretical. He never attempted to write anything one could call radically descriptive. The first such work in English is not by Dryden at all: it is Thomas Rymer's *The Tragedies of the Last Age* (1678), an attack upon Elizabethan and Jacobean drama by a learned lawyer, and it is known that Dryden read and welcomed it as soon as it appeared without attempting to emulate it: he had already conceived, and failed to write, such a work himself.[1]

1. See *Of Dramatic Poesy* (1668), 'To the Reader': 'I promise to myself a better success of the second part, wherein the virtues and faults of

On the other hand, he wrote some twenty-five critical prefaces to his own works (1664–1700), three classical lives (Plutarch, Polybius, and Lucian), the dialogue *Of Dramatic Poesy*, and a handful of prefaces to the works of his contemporaries. It is in the prefaces to his own works that the silent transformation of English criticism occurs.

Dryden's first critical essay, the dedicatory letter to his first published play *The Rival Ladies* (1664), illustrates the transition. The young poet is defending the second play he wrote, a rhymed heroic play in the new French mode, against the sort of attacks that new fashions usually provoke. He defends himself in two ways: first, by an appeal to a noble and powerful patron, Roger Earl of Orrery, the first author of such plays in English; and second, an appeal to critical principle in favour of rhyme on the stage. It is only the second part of his preface that concerns us here – though the flattery of the first part is less irrelevant than is usual in the compliments of Restoration poets, since Orrery really was a dramatist as well as a public figure. The second part is an example of descriptive criticism in its most impure form. Dryden is talking about an actual literary work, but it is his own; and though the poet must always be considered an important witness in such a matter, he is also a suspiciously interested one. In any case, the discussion is entirely general: no speech or scene of *The Rival Ladies* is specifically defended, and no aspect of it, apart from rhyme, is really discussed. And much of the defence of rhyme consists of mere appeals to authority. The critical residue, in fact, is extremely small; it is confined to the penultimate paragraph, when we are unexpectedly admitted to the studio and allowed to watch the poet at work:

But that benefit which I consider most in it [rhyme], *because I have not seldom found it,* is that it bounds and circumscribes the fancy. For imagination in a poet is a faculty so wild and lawless that, like

---

the English poets who have written either in this [the dramatic], the epic, or the lyric way, will be more fully treated of.'

an high-ranging spaniel, it must have clogs tied to it lest it outrun the judgment. The great easiness of blank verse renders the poet too luxuriant...

The veil is lifted only for a second. But there, for a moment, is a young poet discussing one of his own problems as a poet. The question whether rhyme or blank verse best suits the stage is a genuinely practical question that the Restoration poet had to face, and the problem of intellectual discipline is one that young poets face in any period. We are within shouting distance of descriptive criticism, near enough to be disappointed that it does not happen. For the advance, from this point, is logical and natural: a poet who is prepared, however briefly, however insincerely, to discuss the psychological processes by which his poems are composed, has reached a point from which he can discuss the faults and virtues of his own work; and, interested as all such discussions must be, they are in turn the starting-point for criticizing of the works of others. It is this path that the greatest of critics have trodden: Coleridge, passing from the authorship of 'The Ancient Mariner' to his notes towards the 1800 preface which seeks to explain and justify such poetry, and so to the Shakespearean lectures and the *Biographia Literaria*; Matthew Arnold, from his own poetry through the 1853 preface and on to the *Essays in Criticism*; or Baudelaire, or T. S. Eliot. Dryden, in his early thirties, stands at the point where art turns into criticism.

The essay *Of Dramatic Poesy* (1668), Dryden's only formal work of criticism – and the only one he ever troubled to revise – can only have been written by a kind of accident. There was no money in criticism in the seventeenth century, and no reputation either, and an ambitious young dramatist like Dryden in the early years of the Restoration would never have allowed precious time on criticism which he could have profitably employed in writing for the stage. But the Great Plague interrupted Dryden's career as a playwright when it was only two years old.

The story, in brief, is this: in June 1665, at the beginning of the Plague, the London theatres closed, and Dryden retired to the country-house of his father-in-law, the first Earl of Berkshire, at Charlton Park near Malmesbury, where he stayed for eighteen months. It seems natural to suppose that the Essay was the first task he set his mind to. It celebrates the naval victory over the Dutch off Lowestoft on 3 June 1665, whereas the poem *Annus Mirabilis* (1667), though published some six months before the Essay, describes the Great Fire of September 1666 as well. And the preface to that poem, addressed to his brother-in-law Sir Robert Howard, discusses the problem of the language of poetry in a way that seems to presuppose much of the debate of the Essay, and contains a brief psychological analysis of the creative act (Invention, Fancy, Elocution), an outgrowth of Hobbes's aesthetics to which, oddly enough, he scarcely returned. There remains a puzzle: the Essay lay unpublished for some two years, and did not appear until August 1667, with '1668' on its title-page. I can only suppose that Dryden guessed how angry Howard would be at this portrait of Crites, and paused to allow the *Annus Mirabilis*, with its complimentary preface, to go on before and smooth the way.

The Essay is a manifesto, a work of legislative criticism, though secreting within itself the first critical analysis of a literary work in English, the examen of Ben Jonson's *Silent Woman*. It is important, however, to appreciate its real nature for what it is before admiring it for virtues which must have seemed to Dryden incidental. His object in the Essay is not, in principle, very different from his object in the prefaces to his plays. It is self-justification. In the preface to *The Rival Ladies* he had defended his first attempt at the heroic play by an appeal to Orrery's example, as he later defended the same form at greater length in the essay 'Of Heroic Plays' prefixed to *The Conquest of Granada* (1672), or his use of blank verse in *All for Love* (1678) in his preface to that tragedy. In the same way, *Of Dramatic Poesy* is a formal and general defence – this time in advance of events – of the kind of play he hoped to write: a recognizably English version of the heroic play, that alien import into Restoration England, which rejects Elizabethan blank verse in favour of rhyme but remains Elizabethan in its variety of plot and temperament. It is about a play he never quite managed to write, as T. S. Eliot never quite managed to write the play foreshadowed in his essay 'Poetry and the Drama' – *All for Love*, the most vigorous and 'English' of Dryden's tragedies, is not in rhyme, and his heroic plays remain stubbornly unacclimatized, redolent of the French inspiration he so often disclaimed. Eliot wrote enthusiastically of the 'almost ideal balance between the critic and the creative poet'[1] that Dryden achieved; and it is the essence of such a balance that the critic should excel at those points where the poet has failed, and feel no special need to exert himself where the poet has succeeded. Dryden's later 'Discourse concerning the Original and Progress of Satire',[2] considering that it is the work of a great satirist in full maturity, is one of the most disappointing essays in the canon of his criticism, while more than two-thirds of his criticism is concerned with the drama, a record of his frustrated ambitions.

Dryden was evidently embarrassed by his legislative intent, and took some trouble to disguise it. The real purpose of the Essay, according to the introductory note 'To the Reader', was historical, 'to vindicate the honour of our English writers [i.e. the Elizabethan and Jacobean dramatists] from the censure of those who unjustly prefer the French before them', and Dryden goes on to confuse the issue still further by denying any intention of influencing the course of Restoration drama: 'This I intimate, least any should think me so exceeding vain as to teach others an art which they understand much better than myself.' All the same, the issues raised in the Essay are argued out as if they concerned all English dramatists of the age; and so, of

1. 'Dryden the Critic, Defender of Sanity', (*Listener*, v, 1931), p. 724. This article has not been reprinted in England; it was revised in his *John Dryden* (New York, 1932), p. 56.
2. Prefixed to *The Satires of Juvenalis Translated into English Verse* (1693).

course, they did. And the Horatian tag on the title-page gives the game away completely: 'I shall play the part of a whetstone, which sharpens steel, though itself incapable of cutting.'

The Essay is in the form of a dialogue among four characters. Eliot compared it to the dialogues of Plato, and its opening to 'the beautiful introduction to the *Theaetetus*'.[1] But the comparison is only illuminating in a negative sense. Dryden cannot possibly be trying to write anything like a Platonic dialogue. He was a professional dramatist, and knew how dialogue was written, but there is nothing here remotely like the cut-and-thrust of a Socratic inquisition, indeed nothing much like any sort of conversation. Nothing, that is, except in the opening pages, where alone conversation among the four characters is allowed to be general, and where a loose definition of a play – '*a genere et fine*, and so not altogether perfect' – is casually accepted without real argument. The rest of the Essay consists of six set speeches, in three pairs: Crites defends the Ancients, Eugenius the Moderns; Lisideius defends the French drama, Neander (Dryden himself) the English; Crites defends blank verse, Neander rhyme. No scheme could be more inflexible, more obviously pre-designed, less 'Platonic'. Argument, under such a plan, obstinately refuses to advance more than a single step at a time. No issue is ever talked out, since the form only allows of assertion and reply: A makes his case, and B answers back. The second speaker in each of the three exchanges is implausibly required to memorize a list of questions raised by the first speaker, and then to reply to them in something like due order. And it cannot be pleaded, in excuse for Dryden, that the dialogue form was in a primitive state in his day: Plato apart, Sir Thomas More, Francis Bacon, Sir Walter Ralegh, Hobbes, and Izaak Walton had all written dialogues which are more convincing as conversation-pieces than this. Evidently the extreme inflexibility of dialogue in the Essay is deliberate – it is more likely to be modelled on the stiff, formal, expository pattern

1. 'Dryden the Critic', op. cit.

of Cicero's *De Oratore* than on anything Platonic, or at least early Platonic – and it is worth asking what Dryden's reason can have been for choosing such a model.

The most probable answer is Dryden's extreme tactical caution as a critic. The note prefixed to the Essay denies any legislative purpose; and his delay in publishing the Essay at all is probably suggestive of caution. Dryden's whole career as a critic is permeated by what might tactfully be called this sense of occasion: Pyrrhonism, or philosophical scepticism, liberated him from the tyranny of the whole truth.

> Dim as the borrow'd beams of moon and stars
> To lonely, weary, wandring travellers,
> Is reason to the soul.[1]

Since no human proposition can ever certainly be true, the poet, in Dryden's view, does not prostitute himself in becoming the paid pen of the Court, and the critic is only showing proper professional caution in refusing to commit himself to ideals he may later find it inconvenient to live up to. Dryden is remarkable as a critic not only for the casual ease with which he contradicts himself,[2] but for the care he takes in advance to ensure that there will not be much in future to contradict. And for this kind of caution the carefully contrived order of the essay *Of Dramatic Poesy* is admirably suited. Dryden does not *want* the argument to advance more than one step at a time. An inference is left – but it is only an inference – that truth, in each of the three exchanges, has the last word, that Dryden is arguing for the Moderns, the English, and rhyming plays against the Ancients, the French, and blank verse. In the second and third controversies, especially, Dryden seems to be speaking in his own person, in the character of Neander, the 'New

1. *Religio Laici* (1682), ll. 1–3.

2. For example, his barefaced reversal of attitude in favour of blank verse in *All for Love* (1678), where he merely notes in the preface: 'Not that I condemn my former way [rhyme], but that this is more proper to my present purpose.'

Man'. But, in reality, he commits himself to nothing. The dialogue form allows him to fly a number of kites, and his self-justification is tactfully semi-anonymous. He is so confident, indeed, of his device that he indulges in his last paragraph in a mild Chaucerian joke at his own expense: he goes on talking after the barge has drawn up at Somerset Stairs, and has to be cut short by his friends.

Where, for all this careful rhetorical contrivance, can Dryden's convictions be said to lie in the essay *Of Dramatic Poesy*? It is surely clear that they are to be found, if anywhere, in the second and third exchanges, when Neander has the last word, and scarcely at all in the introductory conversation, or in the controversy over Ancient and Moderns – a perennial issue of Renaissance criticism which never seems to have interested him much. The introductory passages of the Essay, culminating in Lisideius's bad definition of a play, are superbly contrived, but their excellence is stylistic, not critical; it is notable, for example, that though the definition is not a good one, and though Crites shows that it is not, no attempt is made to arrive at any better: 'A just and lively image of human nature, representing its passions and humours, and the changes of fortune to which it is subject, for the delight and instruction of mankind'. This is an umbrella indeed, and Aristotle had offered a better account two thousand years before – but Dryden's indifference to theory is so deep-rooted that he will not pause to improve his definition. The contrivance of the opening paragraphs is of the same sort. Dryden is only slightly embarrassed by the inconvenient fact that the naval battle which is the alleged occasion of the dialogue is not against the French but against the Dutch, and that in any case it is likely to provoke not bad plays but bad poems. And yet the improbable metaphor is put to good use: the battle is an occasion for general patriotism, a mood later matched by Neander in his abuse of the French dramatists; and Crites arbitrarily limits the dispute to 'dramatic poesy' – by which time we have forgotten how the Dutch got into the story at all. So, by a double somersault, the young dramatist has successfully invoked a great public event (the defeat of the Dutch), and contrived to turn the discussion to his own dramatic art. The effect of this opening is only partly dissipated by the diffuse and derivative exchange that follows on ancient and modern observance of the three unities. Dryden leans so heavily here upon the third of Corneille's three *Discours* of 1660 ('Discours des trois unités'), that he takes trouble to discount any sort of French influence in Neander's first long speech: 'Corneille himself, their arch-poet, what has he produc'd except *The Liar*,[1] and you know how it was cried up in France; but when it came upon the English stage, though well translated, ... the most favourable to it would not put it in competition with many of Fletcher's or Ben Jonson's.' He goes on to defend the Elizabethan drama on contradictory grounds: 'First, that we have many plays of ours as regular as any of theirs [the French] ... and secondly, that in most of the irregular plays of Shakespeare or Fletcher ... there is a more masculine fancy and greater spirit in all the writing than there is in any of the French.' Like many another Renaissance critic, Dryden, when he tries to theorize about poetry, is never so happy as when he eats his cake and has it too: he praises Elizabethan drama for its regularity and for its irregularity alike. But there are better things to follow.

'I will take the pattern of a perfect play from Ben Jonson, who was a careful and learned observer of the dramatic laws, and from all his comedies I shall select *The Silent Woman*; of which I will make a short examen, according to those rules which the French observe.' This passage ushers in three general estimates of Shakespeare, Beaumont and Fletcher, and Ben Jonson, and there follows immediately the first extended analysis of any English poem or play: it is the earliest substantial example of descriptive criticism in the language.

Certain significant facts emerge at once. First, the analysis of *The Silent Woman* is conducted within the framework of a legislative treatise. It is not, like a modern critique,

1. i.e. *Le Menteur* (Paris, 1644), one of his comedies.

gratuitous, in the sense that it is not based on our own assumption that literary works of excellence deserve analysis in their own right. *The Silent Woman* is not just a good play to Dryden: it is 'the pattern of a perfect play', it has secrets to yield up to the modern practitioner of the drama. Second, Dryden himself is aware that there is no English precedent for what he is doing, no native tradition in literary analysis. The very word he uses is scarcely an English one – *examen* – but a Latinism still new to English and probably re-borrowed, for this purpose, from the French of Corneille.

In 1660 Corneille, in reply to attacks made upon him by the French Academy, had collected his plays into three volumes, heading each volume with a '*discours*' or theoreti-cal essay and an '*examen*' of the group of plays included there. The example was a spur to self-criticism. Other European dramatists – Ben Jonson, for instance, and the Frenchman Jean Mairet – had provided some of their plays with critical prefaces. But none had attempted the whole-sale self-vindication of Corneille's *Théâtre* of 1660. Dryden owes Corneille a double debt as a critic: first, he borrows heavily from Corneille's theoretical views, especially from his liberal view of the three unities in the third *Discours*: and second, he takes confidence from Corneille's *examens* to embark on a pioneer attempt at literary analysis of an English poem. There was simply no English source from which he could borrow an example of critical analysis.

The examen of *The Silent Woman* suffers from much of the crudeness and imprecision natural in pioneer work. It would not be acceptable as pass-work in any modern school of English. The patriotic, anti-French bias we may excuse as a peccadillo; but Dryden offends badly in referring the play to a set of criteria – the three unities – which, on his own admission, it is a venial fault to ignore. And he is not very accurate: he even distorts the facts about Jonson's play in order to make his point – a point that, on his own admission, was not worth making in the first place: 'it lies all within the compass of two houses,' he claims, whereas in fact four houses and a lane (II, iv) are mentioned in the text. And his claim that 'the action of the play is entirely one: the end or aim of which is the settling Morose's estate on Dauphine' can only be maintained by juggling with the evidence – there are farcical scenes in the play that relate only faintly to the main plot. Dryden is a radically inaccurate critic when the facts do not suit the story he is determined to tell. And finally, he seems at first obtusely unhistorical in his failure to understand the nature of a Jonsonian humour, and we wonder what kind of a reader of Elizabethan plays could talk like this:

. .. Morose, or an old man, to whom all noise but his own talking is offensive. Some who would be thought critics say this humour of his is forced: but to remove that objection, we may consider him first to be naturally of a delicate hearing . . .; and secondly, we may attribute much of it to the peevishness of his age . . . Besides this, I am assured from divers persons that Ben Jonson was actually acquainted with such a man . . .

This is criticism on the how-many-children-had-Lady-Macbeth principle with a vengeance, and might lead us to think that Dryden supposes a humour to be a character in the naturalistic tradition; but on the next page he surprises with a definition of the humour which a modern literary historian, with his card-index beside him, could hardly improve on:

. .. by humour is meant some extravagant habit, passion, or affection, particular . . . to some one person, by the oddness of which he is immediately distinguished from the rest of the men . . .

Nobody, after that, can say that Dryden is generally deficient in the historical sense, though of course his history is naïve by our standards: he certainly has a real awareness that an Elizabethan play and a Restoration play are governed by different conventions. But his analysis of the plot of the play, though very much the analysis of a professional who has written plays himself and means to write more, is patchy by twentieth-century standards. He acutely notices that the play moves at an accelerating pace:

the business of it rises in every act ... There too you see, till the very last scene, new difficulties rising to obstruct the action of the play;

and he notes that the 'untying', as he calls the *dénouement*, or the revelation that Morose has been married to a boy, is contrived so as to fall upon Morose himself as a shattering discovery. But he is much less satisfactory at doing something where we now expect critics effortlessly to succeed: he does not identify the relationship of the minor characters to the major, or of the sub-plots to the main plot, and contents himself with the vague assertion 'all which persons have several concernments of their own, yet all are used by the poet to the conducting of the main design to perfection'. This is no doubt true – but the exacting modern reader is inclined to ask how.

The chief triumph of the examen lies in its attempt at comparative criticism, in its balancing of the qualities of the English drama against those of the French. It is undeniably the first example of such criticism in English, and among the very earliest in any modern language. Of course it is seriously vitiated by cultural nationalism – Dryden is out to prove that any English play is worth any two by a Frenchman, and he does not much care how he does it. The only reason why the reputation of the English drama has fallen below that of the French, he claims, is the accident of the Puritan revolution:

Be it spoken to the honour of the English, our nation can never want in any age such who are able to dispute the empire of wit with any people in the universe. And though the fury of a civil war, and power for twenty years together abandoned to a barbarous race of men, enemies of all good learning, had buried the muses under the ruins of monarchy; yet, with the restoration of our happiness, we see revived poesy lifting up its head. . . .

These partisan words were published within a few weeks of the appearance of Milton's *Paradise Lost*. And Dryden is unobjective enough to pretend that the feeble English dramatic output since the Restoration – a few plays of Orrery, Killigrew, and himself – 'yield not to those of any foreign nation'. But, though he is unfair to the French drama, he has seized upon the quality that distinguishes it from the Elizabethan – the difference between Shakespeare and Racine. It is the doctrinaire inflexibility and lack of variety of the French:

> If they content themselves, as Corneille did, with some flat design which, like an ill riddle, is found out ere it be half proposed, such plots we can make every way regular as easily as they; but whene'er they endeavour to rise to any quick turns and counterturns of plot ... you see they write as irregularly as we, though they cover it more speciously.... If you consider the plots, our own are fuller of variety; if the writing, ours are more quick and fuller of spirit...

And then, as usual, he goes too far in his attempt to decry the French, and denies that French plays have had any influence on English dramatists: 'We have borrowed nothing from them; our plots are weaved in English looms ...' Dryden had already borrowed a French plot when he wrote that, and was to borrow more. But, deeply biased as the passage is, a new dimension has been added to criticism, that of comparative analysis.

Rymer and Dennis

Dryden's twenty-year obsession with the theatre, hopelessly pursued through more than a score of play-prefaces, culminates in the two essays that accompany *The Conquest of Granada* (1672) in defence of heroic drama, wavers confusedly after the advent of Rymer in 1677, and ends in embittered disillusion with London audiences in the preface to *The Spanish Friar* (1681). It is a record of advance in critical technique and of failure in all else: in dogmatic consistency, in persuasive force, in self-advancement as a dramatist.

We shall probably never know why Dryden took Rymer seriously as a critic. To answer that question, more certain information of Dryden's character than can be derived from his essays would be needed. That character was pragmatic, evidently; evasive on points of principle; easily –

much too easily – impressed by the scholarship and asser-
tiveness of lesser men. 'My chief endeavours are to delight
the age in which I live,' he wrote in his 'Defence of *An
Essay of Dramatic Poesy*',[1] and a poet who can admit that in
public is perilously sensitive to the state of literary opinion.
The writings of Thomas Rymer (1641–1713) represented a
classicizing tendency in English critical thought he may
have felt it imprudent to ignore.

And yet there can be no doubt of the sincerity of Dryden's
admiration for this failed dramatist ten years his junior. In
a private letter to the Earl of Dorset, written late in 1677,
shortly after Rymer had sent him a copy of his *Tragedies of
the Last Age*, Dryden calls the book 'very learned, and the
best piece of criticism in the English tongue ... I think
there is no man will dare to answer him, or can'.[2] Not long
after, he tried to answer Rymer himself, scribbling his first
thoughts into end-papers of his copy – the notes now called
'Heads of an Answer to Rymer'[3] – defending Shakespeare
in the preface to *All for Love* (1678), and ultimately framing
a more formal reply in 'The Grounds of Criticism in
Tragedy'.[4] Both prefaces, like the letter to Lord Dorset, are
oddly respectful of Rymer. In both we await the thunder-
bolt that never falls.

Why is Dryden so respectful? To the modern reader, it is
self-evident that Rymer's attack on the Elizabethan drama
in his first book – he continued it years later in his second,
A Short View of Tragedy (1693) – is not even superficially

1. In the second edition only of his tragedy *The Indian Emperor* (1668),
an angry attack upon his brother-in-law Howard, occasioned by Howard's preface to *The Great Favourite* (1668), itself a reply to Dryden's *Of
Dramatic Poesy* of the previous year.

2. *The R. B. Adam Library* (New York, 1929), 111, 87–8 (with facsimile):
Letters of John Dryden, edited by C. E. Ward (Durham N.C., 1942), no. 6.

3. First published in Jacob Tonson's 1711 edition of Beaumont and
Fletcher, and later, in a different order, by Johnson at the end of his Life
of Dryden. Tonson's version, of which Johnson was unaware, is on the
whole superior. The annotated copy of Rymer's book was destroyed by
fire in 1786 or 1787.

4. In the preface to his adaptation of Shakespeare, *Troilus and Cressida*
(1679).

impressive. And we recall with a start that, where Rymer rushed in, Dryden for ever after refused to tread: in the note 'To the Reader' prefixed to his *Of Dramatic Poesy*, he had already promised a 'Second Part' consisting in a full-scale account, whether historical or not is unclear, of the whole of English poetry for the past hundred years, and if this is what Rymer's book cost us we have a quite unusually good reason for wishing it had not happened. For Rymer is an appalling understudy to a great master. He conforms with alarming precision to the popular image of the critic as the failed writer – his own tragedy, *Edgar,* published later in 1677, was (as Dryden predicted) a total flop, and the feverish pertness of his prose fails to disguise a petulant malice. It looks like a catastrophic beginning to the course of descriptive criticism in English: and yet, after all, it is a beginning of a kind. Rymer's *Tragedies of the Last Age* is the first critical book in English which is altogether concerned with analysing the works of other Englishmen. And its sequel, *A Short View of Tragedy* (1693), is the first pure example of literary history in English. It is an astonishing Double First which the conscientious historian, however regretfully, is bound to record.

Rymer starts his analysis of Elizabethan tragedy without theoretical fuss. This is a remarkable fact in itself: but we should remember that Rymer had already said his say, in the legislative sense, in his first book, a translation of René Rapin's commentary on Aristotle, the *Reflections on Aristotle's Treatise of Poesy* (1674). By 1677, then, the rules may literally be taken as read, and analysis for once has pride of place, though there is still no doubt of Rymer's ultimate legislative intentions: the Elizabethan tragedies are presented as cautionary examples of how tragedy ought not to be written. Still, analysis it is. Disappointed in the company of a London friend, Rymer tells us (for *The Tragedies of the Last Age* is in the form of a Ciceronian, or Senecan, epistle), he has stayed in the country reading, as an alternative to suicide, 'those masterpieces of wit, so re-nown'd everywhere, and so edifying to the stage: I mean the choicest and most applauded English tragedies of this last age'. The inept sarcasm of the opening paragraph establishes the characteristic tone of Rymer's criticism: his will to belittle and to abuse is severely limited by an inadequate vocabulary of invective – Dryden could have helped him here – and an inability, strongly characteristic of young authors who are uncertain of their talents, to take trouble with his writing. He has read six old tragedies, he goes on, and is determined to discuss them all. But by the time he has dealt with the first three on his list, from the supposed canon of the works of 'Fletcher' – *The Bloody Brother*,[1] *A King and No King*, and *The Maid's Tragedy* – he naïvely announces that he finds he already has a volume 'without more scribbling', and ends with a promise to consider the other three plays at some later stage – Shakespeare's *Othello* and *Julius Caesar*, and Ben Jonson's *Catiline* – a few arrogant apologies for his own carelessness, and a vow to attack *Paradise Lost* and the 'slender sophistry' by which Milton had justified his rejection of rhyme. This last impertinence, at least, the world was spared, but not the attack upon Shakespeare and Jonson, which Rymer reserved for the final chapters of his *Short View* a full sixteen years later: surely the most remarkable example on record of a conservation of critical bile.

Rymer had already identified himself, by his translation of Rapin, as an extreme advocate of the literary laws of the French neoclassical critics and of the cause of the Ancients. In Rymer's view, the theatre must be restored to its original condition as a 'School of Vertue', and tragedy to the status of a ' Poem for Kings', an epic on boards. Plot, as in Aristotle, is 'the soul of tragedy', but a soul as brutish among the English as it was reasonable among the Greeks. He then sketches in the prehistory of the drama – a sketch mightily extended for *A Short View*, and a foretaste of Rymer's real historical powers – and proceeds to attack Beaumont and

1. *Rollo: or the Bloody Brother* (Oxford, 1638) is now attributed to John Fletcher, Chapman, Jonson, and Massinger in collaboration, the other two plays to Beaumont and Fletcher.

Fletcher play by play. His analyses are a travesty, but he does analyse, beginning with farcical summaries of the plots ('fables'), which are abbreviated by his sheer impatience to condemn them. His fingers are forever twitching for the black cap: 'Now, if you call this a fable, give me one of old Aesop's. . . . Never were the Muses profan'd with a more foul, unpleasant and unwholesome truth . . .'[1] But he knows how to compare *Rollo* with its source in Herodian, and actually quotes parallel passages to show that while the Greek historian, in his account of the mother's speech, 'seems to show a woman of great spirit, labouring to contain her passion till she may utter her mind', Fletcher's tirade 'seems to present a well-breath'd and practis'd scold'.[2] He is the first English critic to quote abundantly in the course of analysis, and though his comments on quotations are merely generalized insults, they are at least particular in their application. He is capable of raising questions of structure, though not of answering them intelligently, and observes that while the theme of incest is the real plot of *A King and No King*, 'the rest is all episode'. He has, in fact, the astonishing faculty throughout of posing the right critical questions without once getting the right answer to any of them, or even convincing us that he wants a right answer.

Rymer's sequel, *A Short View of Tragedy* (1693), reinforces the impression that his historical sense is his strongest side. It is a history of a literary form, the drama, in eight chapters, beginning with a defence of the Greek chorus, which he believes is about to be revived among the French, followed by a chronological account of tragedy among the Greeks, the Romans, and the early Christians, the contemptible medieval vogue of allegorical criticism, the renaissance of the drama in Italy, France, and England and the refinement of English by Chaucer and Waller, *Gorboduc*, and the early English pre-eminence in comedy. And finally (to show why Elizabethan tragedy will not do), comes the

1. *Critical Works*, edited by C. A. Zimansky (New Haven, 1956), pp. 24–5.
2. ibid., p. 38.

promised damnation of *Othello* at great length, and the dismissal of *Julius Caesar* and *Catiline*.

Rymer's notorious critique of *Othello* follows exactly the lines laid down by his attacks on Beaumont and Fletcher in the earlier volume: its fame derives only from the fact that the target now is a universally respected one. Experience has only taught Rymer greater self-confidence in being silly-clever; the shape of the analysis is unchanged, beginning with an assertion that the source in Cinthio has been abused, and continuing with a derisive plot-summary and a quick, damning value-judgement ('This may be a caution to all maidens of quality how, without their parents' consent, they run away with blackamoors')[1] and a list of Shakespeare's failures in maintaining the true dignity of tragedy based on an inflexible insistence upon character as a pure generality: Othello does not behave like a General, except in his suicide, or Desdemona like a lady.

And yet Dryden was impressed. He was impressed enough, perhaps, to abandon his own thoughts of writing a general study of English poetry He was impressed enough to call Rymer's first book unanswerable, and then, with positively embarrassing humility, to try to answer it himself on three occasions. His notes on the subject, the so-called 'Heads of an Answer', are the most combatively anti-Rymer and anti-Aristotelian of the three. The plot, or 'fable', argues Dryden in his private jottings, is 'not the greatest masterpiece of tragedy' – an audacious attack, this, not only upon Rymer but upon a basic assumption of the whole school of French Aristotelian criticism. And, in any case, he goes on, though Greek plays may be better designed 'to cause terror and pity', there are other ends of tragedy, which the Elizabethans did achieve. In any case – and here Dryden's historical sense shows itself the superior of Rymer's, which limited itself to using historical examples arbitrarily to prove a neoclassical case – Aristotle was writing in ignorance of any tragedies but the Greek, which are inferior to the English in certain respects, in their 'narrowness of plot' and

1. ibid., p. 132.

lack of variety; so that a Greek play, by English standards, is a 'very easy' thing to do. Besides, the English have outdone the Greeks in dealing with several subjects such as love and friendship; and the reformation of many, rather than the moving of pity and terror, is the proper end of tragedy; though perhaps, Dryden adds with very characteristic caution, it all comes to the same thing, since 'pity comprehends this concernment for the good, and terror includes detestation for the bad'. In any case – and here the argument is simply reversed – the Elizabethan plays can be justified on Rymer's principles too. They have certainly pleased, which for Rymer is the prime end of poetry. And (again a powerful historical mind emerges) 'though nature, as he objects, is the same in all places, and reason too the same, yet the climate, the age, the disposition of the people to whom the poet writes, may be so different that what pleased the Greeks would not satisfy an English audience'. English characters, too, are more credible for their imperfections, and the plays of the Elizabethans are 'more beautifully written' than those of the Greeks.[1]

Dryden's 'Heads' show how independent he could be of neoclassical bigotry. The fact that he never published them proves that his independence was a cautious and qualified one. The two replies he did dare to publish, the prefaces to *All for Love* (1678) and to *Troilus and Cressida* (1679), are more diplomatic than the 'Heads', and fail, for this reason, to equal them in interest. Dryden's concern for Shakespeare's reputation is very clear in both, and his lasting contempt for the French theatre:

In this nicety of manners does the exellency of French poetry consist: their heroes are the most civil people breathing; but their good breeding seldom extends to a word of sense.[2]

The essential robustness of the Elizabethan drama is not to be exchanged for a cold correctness, whatever Aristotle

---

1. *Of Dramatic Poesy and Other Critical Essays*, edited by George Watson (Everyman's Library, 1962), I. 211–20.
2. Preface, *All for Love* (1678); reprinted above, I. 224.

may appear to say. The more formal essay, 'The Grounds of Criticism in Tragedy', prefixed to *Troilus and Cressida*, is in part a careful formulation of some of the points listed in the 'Heads' a year and more before, a careful and stylish reconstruction of his objections to Rymer's attack. Aristotle's account of tragedy is conceded at once, for the sake of respectability – the published 'Grounds' is a far less radical document than the unpublished 'Heads' – though the sufficiency of Aristotle's doctrine of pity and terror is again questioned. There is some disagreeable boot-licking of Rymer: 'How defective Shakespeare and Fletcher have been in all their plots, Mr Rymer has discovered in his criticisms: neither can we who follow them be excused from the same or greater errors . . .' Dryden kisses the rod; and, still on his best Aristotelian behaviour, he solemnly tells us that 'Shakespeare generally moves more terror, and Fletcher more compassion'. But a spirit of sneaking rebellion persists, as in the mock-innocence of Dryden's discovery that only one Greek play, the *Oedipus* of Sophocles, actually conforms to Rymer's Aristotelian requirements, or that in *Oedipus Coloneus* the hero ceases to behave like a king:

Sophocles . . . lets fall on purpose his tragic style; his hero speaks not in the arbitrary tone; but remembers, in the softness of his complaints, that he is an unfortunate blind old man.

The sensitive acuteness of the comment leaves us wondering how Dryden can ever have thought Rymer anything better than a bigot and a boor.

The best that can be said for Rymer, perhaps, is that he provoked such replies. *A Short View*, with its more detailed attack on Shakespeare, was answered by John Dennis (1657–1734), like Rymer a failed dramatist, and the first Englishman to earn a living as a literary critic. *The Impartial Critic: or Some Observations upon a Late Book Entitled A Short View of Tragedy* (1693) is a series of five dialogues in which Rymer's points are met after a clumsy fashion, tragedy being conceived as a moral fable and Shakespeare defended as possessing beauties as well as faults, though Rymer's censures are called 'very sensible and very just'. For Dennis's *The Genius and Writings of Shakespeare* his public, if he had one, had to wait till 1712, when they found Shakespeare's genius abruptly tested on Rymer's principle of Poetic Justice, by which all good characters must end happily and all evil characters otherwise. Dennis is no doubt a very slightly better critic than Rymer, on the negative ground that he lacks Rymer's passionate perversity. He is, by the narrowest of margins, the more likely of the two to reach a sensible conclusion. He is none the less impossibly long-winded, a colossal bore, interesting at best for his discipleship to Longinus; at least Rymer's essays have the virtue of brevity. And, like Dryden and Rymer, Dennis never quite liberates himself from the illusion that the critic's chief task is to legislate to poets. The stated purpose of his *The Grounds of Criticism in Poetry* (1704) is not, as its title might suggest, to form a tradition in critical reading, but 'to shew both by reason and examples that the use of religion in poetry was absolutely necessary to raise it to the greatest exaltation of which so noble an art is capable; and, on the other side, that poetry was requisite to religion'.[1] His design, accordingly, is 'to restore poetry to all its greatness, and to all its innocence'.[2]

The later Dryden

The failure of Dryden's contemporaries to create, or even follow, a tradition of critical awareness tempts us to overrate the achievement of Dryden himself. It is, indeed, difficult to credit – almost forty years (1664–1700) of scarcely interrupted activity as a critic. From the appearance of the essay *Of Dramatic Poesy* in 1668 he confined himself to prefaces, usually to his own works, and it is hard now to realize how extravagant this prefatory habit must have seemed to his contemporaries. He had practically no English precedents – only Ben Jonson, among the older

1. *Critical Works*, edited by E. N. Hooker (Baltimore, 1939–43), 1. 325.
2. ibid., 1. 328.

dramatists, had made a practice of justifying himself in prefaces to his own plays, and there was only the 1660 *Théâtre* of Corneille to give him courage. And he failed to establish the practice in England. Dryden's detractors in *The Rehearsal* (1672) make fun of a dramatist who has to explain his plot in printed sheets: 'I have printed above a hundred sheets of paper to insinuate the plot into the boxes,' protests Bayes, when asked if the play will be understood; and Swift, his cousin, probably represents an anticritical majority in his sneer in *A Tale of a Tub* (1704): 'He has often said to me in confidence that the world would never have suspected him to be so great a poet, if he had not assured them so frequently in his prefaces that it was impossible they could either doubt or forget it',[1] or again, in a poem of Swift's last years:

> Read all the prefaces of Dryden
> For these our critics much confide in,
> (Though merely writ at first for filling
> To raise the volume's price a shilling).[2]

To be any sort of critic in England, in the Restoration or long after, was to work against the popular grain. And to write as a descriptive critic, as Dryden intermittently did, was to defy two of the mightiest intellectual fashions of the day.

First, there was neoclassicism. Dryden was lucky to absorb his classical theories, in the first instance, in the dilute and pragmatic form in which they appear in the *Discours* of Corneille, who was profoundly and intelligently aware of the difficulties of practising them; and, as early as the essay *Of Dramatic Poesy*, he quotes with emphatic approval Corneille's dictum in the 'Discours des trois unités': ''Tis easy for theorists to judge severely . . .' By the time the full weight of French neoclassicism fell upon English criticism, in Rymer's *Tragedies of the Last Age*, Dryden – though visibly shaken by Rymer's own speculative

1. Sect. v.
2. 'On Poetry' (1733).

severity – had just enough courage to answer back and go his own way. And Rymer is proof enough that high-flying neoclassical doctrine and critical analysis cannot live together: *any* fiercely doctrinaire theory of criticism, indeed, is likely to reduce the poem to the level of a mere example.

The second intellectual fashion which might have defeated Dryden as a critic was that of experimental science under the influence of Bacon, Descartes, and Hobbes. Dryden was deeply impressed by the new philosophy of science. He was a founder-member of the Royal Society from 1662, and had been made a member of a committee it had created with the object of purifying the language. His prose is abundant in scientific similes and indirect echoes of Hobbes. Aubrey called him a 'great admirer' of Hobbes, and added cryptically that Dryden 'oftentimes makes use of his doctrine in his plays'.[1] Much of the impoverishment of English imagery at this time, and perhaps the death of the Metaphysical style in poetry, must be laid to the door of a generation of scientists who, after Charles II's return, insisted that the language itself must be disciplined to suit the purposes of exact observation. It is worth adding that they were equally philistine in their opposition to history, and must certainly have despised any attempt, like Dryden's, to reinterpret the drama of a past age. Descartes, in the first part of his *Discours de la méthode* (1637), dismisses literary and historical studies in these terms:

But I thought I had given enough time to languages and even to reading old books, their stories and their fables; for to converse with those of other ages is rather like travelling ... When you spend too much time travelling, you become a stranger in your own country; and when you are curious of things done in the past, you usually remain exceedingly ignorant of what is done today.[2]

The New Philosophy was as contemptuously anti-historical as neoclassicism, though for different reasons, and some of

1. *Brief Lives*, edited by Andrew Clark (Oxford, 1898), 1, 372.
2. For a discussion of this passage, see R. G. Collingwood, *The Idea of History* (Oxford, 1946), pp. 59ff.

its contempt for the past undoubtedly rubbed off upon Dryden, especially in his early years. But the severity of the new ideas did not suit his temperament, and the mellow moralism of Montaigne, who provided the chief inspiration of his prose style, superseded them in the classical Lives of Plutarch (1683), Polybius (1693), and Lucian[1] (1711), all prefixed to translations of their works by other hands. History is now the consolation and the guide of the ageing critic: historians 'teach us wisdom by the surest ways', the ways of moral example, and history, he confesses, 'has always been the most delightful entertainment of my life'. In the same Life of Plutarch he uses the word 'biography' for the first time in English, and attempts for the first time the form of the literary life which Johnson was to establish as the chief mode of our criticism a century later, in the *Lives of the English Poets*.

And yet, though his mind, as he grew into 'the tattling quality of age', flowed with increasing ease in unfashionable historical speculations, his critical achievement looks all the more sadly frustrated by his early intellectual interests. Science and neoclassicism had not prevented him from saying important things, but they had prevented him from saying them soon and in formal order. His critical genius lies scattered in several dozens of documents. His perception of the importance of historical affinities in poetry grew stronger with the years, but remained unexplored to the end, a mere passing intuition, as in the priceless hint carelessly dropped in the last of his essays, the preface to the *Fables* (1700):

Milton was the poetical son of Spenser, and Mr Waller of Fairfax; for we have our lineal descents and clans as well as other families. Spenser more than once insinuates that the soul of Chaucer was transfused into his body, and that he was begotten by him two hundred years after his decease. Milton has acknowledged to me that Spenser was his original . . .

The affectionate study of Chaucer that follows in the same preface is richly historical in the same manner:

1. Written in 1695–6, during his work on the translation of Virgil.

He lived in the infancy of our poetry, and ... nothing is brought to perfection at the first. We must be children before we grow men.

A whole tradition of literary history, in such utterances, seems upon the point of being born. But for Dryden it was already too late, and the historical sense in criticism had to wait the greater part of a century, till the literary antiquaries, the Warton brothers and Samuel Johnson, to take deep root in England.

The final estimate of Dryden as a critic must be cautiously stated. 'The favourite exercise of his mind', according to Johnson, 'was ratiocination'[1] – but the use to which he commonly puts his powers of argument is self-justification, almost never the impartial exploration of an idea. Much the greater part of his criticism, the prefaces to his plays and the essay *Of Dramatic Poesy*, represents stages in his career as a dramatist; they are aspects of a continuing literary war that Dryden fought with his own critics, full of the bitter sound and fury of the Restoration theatres and coffee-houses; and his later critical essays, the prefaces to his translations of Juvenal, Virgil, and the *Fables* of 1700, are rather more reflective exercises in the same ephemeral vein. His interest in theoretical ideas is slight, confined almost entirely to the first years of his career, and largely derived from Hobbes. Johnson ingeniously divides his criticism into two kinds, the 'didactic' and the 'defensive', but it is the defensive that predominates at every period of his life except the last ten years. Compared with critics before and after, Dryden is refreshingly egotistical ('he may be thought to mention himself too frequently,' Johnson complained) and free from any legislative intent upon other poets: only in the essay *Of Dramatic Poesy* does he get very near to a general literary manifesto, and he never attempted another. He wrote the first extended examples of descriptive criticism in English – but he analysed, not for the sake of analysis, but in order to generalize afterwards for his own

1. The Life of Dryden, in *The Lives of the English Poets*, edited by G. Birkbeck Hill (Oxford, 1905), 1, 459.

purposes. The logical status of his criticism, then, remains puzzling and ambiguous – it looks backwards to the Elizabethans, and forward to Samuel Johnson, and hardly seems to know itself.

And yet, to repeat, this uncertainty cannot possibly have been present to Dryden himself. No critic, not even Johnson, seems so perfectly sure of himself and of what he is saying at the moment when he says it – and if, a year later, he believes something else, he will say so with the same disarming candour. It is this supreme literary tact, this talent for evasion and equivocation, that allows him to play several critical roles at once. But the cost of such a sense of tact can be crippling: for all the superficial vigour of his prose, real critical assertions are seldom made. (The contrast with Johnson here is sharp, and all in Johnson's favour.) His achievement, ultimately, lies not in analysing much or in doing it well, but in providing the inestimable example of showing that literary analysis is possible at all.

CHAPTER 3

THE AUGUSTANS

Pope

No Augustan criticism looks much like Dryden's, on the face of it. Its style is, in comparison, devitalized. It lacks audacity of judgement – the audacity, say, of Dryden's praise for Shakespeare and Chaucer. It is safe, and the hostilities it risks are personal rather than critical, as in Pope's devastating portrait of Dennis.[1] And yet it accepts and consolidates the revolution that Dryden made, and advances it cautiously on several fronts.

In the first place, the Augustan contempt for French neoclassical authority is much like Dryden's, even in its ambiguities. Dryden, as we have seen in his controversy with Rymer, never attacked the rules frontally: not, at least, in any essay he ever dared to publish. The attitude of the nineteen-year-old Pope, when he wrote the *Essay on Criticism* (written 1705–9), might be Dryden's cultural nationalism put to verse. In so far as the rules are French, Pope argues, they are bad; in so far as they are ancient, and judiciously interpreted by Englishmen, they are good. The Augustan critic, like Dryden, is in the happy position of eating his cake and having it too: his claim is to be more elastic than the French, and more truly classical as well. And admittedly there are sound reasons for claiming something like this: the French neoclassical critics really did misread Aristotle. But the Augustans, like Dryden, quite fail to identify these misreadings, so that their assertions are not much better than bluster:

> But critic-learning flourish'd most in France:
> The rules a nation, born to serve, obeys;

1. The Appius of his *Essay on Criticism* (1711), ll. 584ff.

And Boileau still in right of Horace sways.
But we, brave Britons, foreign laws despis'd,
And kept unconquer'd, and unciviliz'd;
Fierce for the liberties of wit, and bold,
We still defy'd the Romans, as of old.[1]

It is a brave, unsubtle joke, the notion of an uncouth Alexander Pope, painted in woad, throwing back legions of French critics from the shores of England. Pope is evidently a little ashamed of the cultural nationalism he has picked up from Dryden, and his language is defensively jocular. Such moments of disingenuousness are the price, apparently, that Englishmen in the reign of Louis XIV were ready to pay for self-respect.

The second heritage from Dryden is the historical sense. Dryden never wrote a literary history that was altogether his own, or a literary biography of any English poet; but his sense of a historical evolution in poetry intensified with age, and by the end of his life, in the preface to the *Fables* (1700), he demonstrated an untutored but certain conviction that the poetry of different ages calls for different standards of interpretation. Pope and Addison incorporate this radical intuition into their critical attitudes. Pope, indeed, calls for an impossibly high level of literary scholarship to aid the critic, and sets up an ideal of academic severity which, even two and a half centuries later, looks unattainable:

> Know well each Ancient's proper character;
> His fable, subject, scope in every page;
> Religion, country, genius of his age;
> Without all these at once before your eyes,
> Cavil you may, but never criticize.[2]

It is unfortunate for his argument that he should go on to mention Homer, of all poets, and to damn Homeric critics for their anachronistic judgements. Pope, inevitably, committed anachronisms enough when he joined the ranks of Homeric critics himself, in the preface to his own version of the *Iliad* (1715). Of course no Augustan critic can match Dryden for the fineness of his historical taste; but the new

1. ibid., ll. 712–18.   2. ibid., ll. 119–23.

age after 1700 is generally aware that a sense of the past may be a useful part of the equipment of the critic. The work of seventeenth-century antiquaries was beginning to tell, to realize its full popular effect, decades later, in Scott's Waverley novels. But no English critic in the early eighteenth century had the industry or the training to use historical methods fully in the study of English poetry. The hack-writer Gerard Langbaine (1656–92) had regarded source-reading as one of his duties in assembling his encyclopaedic *Account of the English Dramatic Poets* (1691), but only for 'exposing our modern plagiaries by detecting part of their thefts'; and Johnson seems to be speaking the literal truth when he praised his Oxford friend Thomas Warton in a complimentary letter (16 July 1754) on Warton's *Observations on the Fairy Queen*, which had just appeared, for being the first English critic to consider a poet's knowledge of books:

You have shown to all who shall hereafter attempt the study of our ancient authors the way to success, by directing them to the perusal of the books which those authors had read . . . The reason why the authors which are yet read of the sixteenth century are so little understood is that they are read alone . . .[1]

And Johnson adds that he hopes his *Dictionary*, which was to appear in the following year, may remove 'some part of this ignorance'. Of all such sophisticated arts of the literary historian the Augustan critics were still utterly ignorant. Their historical sense is occasional, and hardly aspires to be radical or continuous.

The third debt to Dryden is a more positive one. The Augustans practise descriptive criticism much more casually and naturally than any Restoration critic had been able to do. Swift, in *The Tale of a Tub* (1704), even talks as if, by the end of the seventeenth century, there were already too many critics about in London, and all of them bad[2]; and

1. *The Letters of Samuel Johnson*, edited by R. W. Chapman (Oxford, 1952), 1, 56.
2. Section III, 'Digression Concerning Critics', where Swift complains that commendatory and learned critics no longer exist, but only fault-finders, descended from Momus and Hybris (Censure and Pride).

Pope takes up this complaint – it is the subject of much of the *Dunciad*. Indeed, if we are to believe the youthful Pope of the *Essay on Criticism*, Augustan London was as over-supplied with reviewers as London is today. The *Essay on Criticism* begins with an assertion that there are ten critics for every poet:

> Ten censure wrong for one who writes amiss.[1]

For all our inadequate knowledge of the output of scurrilous literary pamphlets in the period, the claim seems absurd. Pope is surely writing as the anxious young poet, eager to forestall contempt. In fact, the Essay might be read, in its opening section at least, as an attack on any sort of descriptive criticism, a demand for some sort of poetic exemption. Pope certainly poses impossibly difficult conditions, including the ridiculous demand that nobody should be allowed to criticize who has not already established himself as a poet:

> Let such teach others who themselves excel,
> And censure freely who have written well.

This sounds like hurt dignity. And yet, on surviving evidence, the Augustan record in criticism is not much more impressive in its scope than the seventeenth-century one. Pope, Swift, Richardson, Fielding, Defoe all came and went without any memorable critical pronouncement being made upon their work. On the other hand, a tradition of periodical reviewing was in process of creation; and Addison's critical essays on Milton in the *Spectator* of 1712, which were unexpectedly popular, suggest that a new kind of critical audience was growing up, impatient of legislative treatises on poetry and concerned with the useful and the particular. Addison (1672–1719) begins his first essay on Milton in January 1712 with this bracing statement of policy:

There is nothing in Nature more irksome than general discourses, especially when they turn chiefly upon words [i.e. upon the definition of general terms]. For this reason I shall waive the discussion

1. *Essay on Criticism* (1711), l. 6.

of that point which was started some years since, whether Milton's *Paradise Lost* may be called an heroic poem.[1]

And he goes on, in a freshly empirical mood:

Those who will not give it that title may call it (if they please) a Divine Poem. It will be sufficient to its perfection, if it has in it all the beauties of the highest kind of poetry; and as for those who allege it is not an heroic poem, they advance no more to the diminution of it than if they should say Adam is not Aeneas, nor Eve Helen.

This is plain speaking against the whole decaying tradition of the legislative critics with their 'dull receipts', as Pope had recently called them.[2] Dryden's first exercises in literary analysis have, by the new century, partly pushed out the old Elizabethan and neoclassical tradition of considering poems purely in terms of *genre*.

But the Augustans, if they can be called the School of Dryden, are certainly Dryden with a difference. The difference lies pre-eminently in the rise of a new public avid for criticism, a public Dryden never enjoyed. Analysis begins as a fashionable activity in the England of Queen Anne. In these new conditions, descriptive criticism can throw off its disguises and appear for what it is. All of Dryden's analyses had appeared embedded in some other form, and claimed to exist for the sake of some general argument. Pope's *Essay on Criticism* is not very different in this sense, a conservative verse-treatise both in form and content, containing general advice to critics: advice on sins to be avoided being marshalled in Section 2, and the positive advice on critical virtues to be emulated in Section 3. The attitudes are purely Drydenesque, if decidedly more explicit and bold than anything Dryden usually allowed himself; for where Dryden, as a critic, is almost always circumspect and diplomatic, even

1. *Spectator*, no. 267 (5 January 1712), edited by Donald F. Bond (Oxford, 1965), 11. 537–9. The reference is to Dryden's *Discourse Concerning Satire* (1693), where Dryden had doubted if Milton had written a true epic, principally on the ground that it lacks a happy ending: 'his event is not prosperous'.

2. *Essay on Criticism* (1711), l. 115.

sage, the *Essay on Criticism* is the work of a cheeky young poet, brashly confident at having been invited, at the age of fifteen, to mend the verses of the elderly Wycherley,[1] and ambitious to stake out a claim for himself in the domain of poetry and to forestall destructive criticism. Where Dryden tends to let the Ancient-Modern controversy go by default, for example, Pope boldly calls it a red herring:

> Some foreign writers, some our own despise;
> The Ancients only, or the Moderns prize.
> Thus wit, like faith, by each man is apply'd
> To one small sect, and all are damn'd beside . . .
> Regard not then if wit be old or new,
> But blame the false, and value still the true. (ll. 394–407)

Such analysis as Pope does allow himself, like the final review of critics from Aristotle to his own day, is only summary, though his distinction between true wit and false, and his enthusiastic attack on the Metaphysical conceit (l. 289) suggest that only the occasion is lacking for a real critical exercise upon an actual poem. Wycherley was probably well served by this sorcerer's apprentice. And yet it is clear that Pope exploited his critical interests too early to exploit them well, and there are later hints, as in his account of poetic translation in the preface to his version of the *Iliad* (1715), of how his critical sense was to mature. The Essay is clever, but it is the indecent, puppyish cleverness of a precocious boy, and it does not represent an advance on Dryden except in terms of virtuosity.

Addison

Addison certainly does, if we are thinking in terms of a technical advance. His intelligence, beside Dryden's, is mean,

1. Some of Pope's earliest letters to Wycherley and Walsh show how directly the Essay grew out of his commission. Cf. his letters of 26 December 1704, 2 July 1706, and 29 November 1707, where the distinction emerges between true wit ('a justness of thought and a facility of expression' or, later, 'propriety') and false wit ('conceit is to nature what paint is to beauty'); and *Essay*, ll. 289f.

and his careful prose looks flabby when compared with Dryden's modulated gusto and superb variety of pace and mood. But it is clear that, with Addison, something important has happened to English criticism. He may not have fathered much good work, or achieved much himself, but as a symptom he is extraordinary. With him the revolution is complete: a revolution from law to actuality, from interference with the poet in his act of creation to help and advice for the thousands who read. Admittedly, from this concern with actuality, new generalizations arose at once. But they were generalizations about the reader, not about the poet, and it is the reader of poetry who firmly occupies the centre of interest between the death of Dryden and the publication of the 1800 preface to the *Lyrical Ballads*. The Man of Taste is king: the consumer, at last, has won his right of choice. In theoretical criticism – and the eighteenth century is overwhelmingly the age of critical theory – the issue is now joined not on conformity to precept ('Is *Paradise Lost* an epic?'), but on the reader's response. By which of the five senses is the human imagination most gratified? How is true taste to be defined? And if a democracy of taste, a mere counting of heads, is not sufficient, what *does* constitute true taste in reading? These are issues which Dryden never once raises; and Pope raises them for professional critics only. Addison, in the *Spectator* essays, raises them for all polite society.

His programme, at least, is inviting: 'I shall endeavour as much as possible to establish among us a taste of polite writing.'[1] He had already made it clear in the *Tatler* what he thought the trouble with English taste was – people could not see the wood for the trees:

Ned [Softly] is indeed a true English reader, incapable of relishing the great and masterly strokes of this art [of poetry]; but wonderfully pleased with the little Gothic ornaments of epigrammatical conceits, turns, points, and quibbles which are so frequent in the most admired of our English poets, and practised by those who

1. *Spectator*, no. 58 (7 May 1711), edited by Donald F. Bond (Oxford, 1965), 1.245.

want genius and strength to represent, after the manner of the
Ancients, simplicity in its natural beauty and perfection.[1]

This looks sound in principle, even if it is obviously designed
to rule out the densely intellectual effects of the Metaphysical poets: it shows that Addison cares about general
coherence and unity, that he has some interest in the structural properties of poems. And he is equally severe against
the extremes of the procrustean neoclassical critic who,
though he attempts general judgements, does so only by
rule-of-thumb: 'one that, without entering into the sense
and soul of an author, has a few general rules which, like
mechanical instruments, he applies to the works of every
writer'.[2] At this very early stage, we seem to be promised
something subtle and shrewd.

Addison's critical papers in the *Spectator* fall into four
groups, two of them theoretical. First, there are the essays
on 'wit', from April to December 1711 (especially nos. 35,
47, 61-3, 140, 249), where a theory of rhetoric is evolved out
of Locke's distinction between 'wit' and 'judgement' in the
Essay Concerning Human Understanding (1690) (II, xi, 2). It
would be difficult to say whom Addison is addressing in
these papers, whether poets or readers of poetry; but it is
clear that his critical sense is more articulate than that of the
Pope who wrote the *Essay on Criticism*, a poem which appeared in May 1711, while Addison's first critical series
was in progress. True wit, according to Addison, is based on
a 'congruity of ideas', and sometimes on their 'opposition';
false wit on a mere congruity of letters, syllables, and words
(as in anagrams, puns, and figure-poems); with a third
category of 'mixt wit' in between, 'a composition of pun
and true wit' in which Cowley and Waller excelled – a
remarkable identification of the special, alien quality of pre-
1660 poetry.[3] Addison's tolerance of the Metaphysical style
is just wide enough to encourage us to feel that we are al-

1. *Tatler*, no. 163 (25 April 1710).
2. ibid. no. 165 (29 April 1710).
3. *Spectator*, no. 62 (11 May 1711), edited by Bond (Oxford, 1965),
1. 264-7.

ready in a new world where the reader, and not the poet, provides the audience of criticism, for his threefold distinction admits not only of the 'true' and of the 'false', but of a third, historical category as well. He offers reasons for admiring the Metaphysical style without making any attempt to recommend it to living poets. Secondly, there are the two essays of May 1711 on the ballad 'Chevy Chase' (nos. 70, 74), where the shades of the neoclassical critics are adroitly placated by demonstrating that a medieval ballad may reveal Homeric and Virgilian influence and possess the Aristotelian virtues. This clears the way for Addison's work as a critic: he could not have analysed *Paradise Lost* in an atmosphere so free of ancient precept without first poking mild fun at the conservatives. (Dryden, after all, had used a similar strategy against them in his preface to *Troilus and Cressida* (1679) by showing that even Sophocles had broken the rules.) The Chevy Chase issues had a surprising sale, and may have encouraged Addison to undertake the papers on *Paradise Lost*, from January to May 1712.[1] And finally, there is the series 'On the pleasures of the imagination' of June and July 1712 (nos. 411–21), an analysis of taste in poetry, where the pleasures of the imagination are eccentrically defined as 'such as arise from visible objects, either when we have them actually in our view, or when we call up their ideas into our minds by painting, statues, descriptions . . .' (no. 411) – an account that predicts in some measure the relative Augustan neglect, in their poetry, of values other than visual ones.

Addison's analysis of Milton in the *Spectator* achieved notoriety at once, and was collected into a volume as early as 1719, to become the foundation of orthodox views of Milton for the rest of the century, and not only in England. According to Tickell, the materials had been collected over many years, but the success of the first papers evidently surprised Addison himself, encouraging him to expand his scheme to eighteen weekly numbers – six on general ques-

1. *Spectator* nos. 267–369 (weekly), edited by Bond (Oxford, 1965), II.537–III.392.

tions about *Paradise Lost*, followed by twelve papers, one on each book of the poem. Even Addison cannot quite free himself from the seventeenth-century habit of setting up a list of rules by which the poem is to be judged. But at least the rules are Addison rather than 'Aristotle', and the formality merely an opening strategy. Refreshingly, he dismisses the question as to whether *Paradise Lost* is an epic or not at the outset – but goes on to contradict himself by analysing it according to the rules of the epic, calling for a plot of which the action is one, entire, and great. The last of the six general essays (no. 297) lists the defects of the poem: the 'implex' plot, in which the fortunes of the hero, Adam, decline, is 'not so proper for an heroic poem' as for a tragedy such as *Oedipus*; the hero is defeated, which is unheroic of him – but then (striking out boldly in defence of an archaic theory), perhaps the hero is not Adam at all, but Christ; there are too many digressions; the images ('sentiments') are too quaint and punning, the heathen references inappropriate to a Christian poem, and the technical terms indecorous. The book-by-book analysis that follows only confirms how very far from the text Addison is. At a glance, its abundance of quotations looks impressive. But Addison's comments on his quotations have all the vagueness of a schoolboy's ('wonderfully poetical', 'truly sublime'), and he almost never ventures a strictly descriptive or interpretative statement. Casual value-judgments are the only mode of proceeding. For the Augustan Man of Taste, it soon appears, intelligent inquiry concerning the meaning of a passage is barely a possibility. Whatever is obscure is merely bad; the critic's function is simply to point and enthuse: 'to point out its particular beauties, and to determine wherein they consist' (no. 369), as Addison explains in his concluding paper. And 'wherein', for Addison, means only 'under what preconceived category' (the Sublime, the Soft, the Natural). Much of the awful glibness of the Augustan aesthetic, its pathetic readiness to take shelter behind a modish terminology of criticism, is plainly visible in the language of this ambitious but complacent critic.

Fielding

The first century of descriptive criticism in English concerns itself almost exclusively with drama and the epic, and other literary forms are strikingly neglected. One youthful giant, the novel, is largely overlooked until the age of the Victorians. Indeed anyone who still thinks that criticism has regularly existed to serve, as a secondary aid, the cause of literary creation should be invited at once to look at two moments in our literary tradition. The first, in the early seventeenth century, is the Metaphysical poetry of Donne, Herbert, Crashaw, and others. A tradition that dominated English poetry for a good half century and more might be expected to have left some substantial critical comment: the more so since that tradition was complex both in its learning and 'in its logical structure. But not at all. Metaphysical criticism is simply a blank in its own century, and not much better for two centuries after. Indeed hardly anyone thought it worth while analysing a Donne poem until, with Grierson's edition of 1912 and the new Imagist fashion in poetry, the case for analysis suddenly looked urgent. The second negative instance is the rise of the English novel in the decades that followed Defoe's *Robinson Crusoe* (1719), the age of Richardson and Fielding. The novel is an accomplished fact in England by the middle of the eighteenth century; the major form, at least by any quantitative estimate, from Scott's *Waverley* (1814). And yet the mass of novel criticism that, by any naïve expectation, one might look to find in the age of the Georges is simply not there. Richardson's novels provoked a few pamphlets devoted to the question whether they were calculated to corrupt public morals. The anonymous *An Examen of the History of Tom Jones* (1750), by the unknown 'Orbilius', is an abusive attack upon Fielding's moral system innocent of any notion of literary form. The contemporary debate over Sterne's novels was concerned with the propriety of a clergyman writing such works at all; Sterne's technical innovations passed without comment until seized upon by Virginia Woolf in the 1920s. *Illustra-*

tions of Sterne (1798), a study of Sterne's borrowings from Rabelais and Robert Burton by John Ferriar (1761–1815), a Scottish physician in Manchester, remains an exceptional study in the void of eighteenth-century criticism of the novel. Whatever one may think the role of the critic should be, it is obvious that he has not in practice served as the poet's interpreter, forever at hand to inform and explain. The English poet has often been forced to act as his own interpreter, and the circumstances in which he turns critic have been severely limited by his own temperament and by the uncertainties of finding a critical audience.

Criticism of the novel, especially, has proved the slowest of starters, and only Fielding among English novelists before Scott felt the call strongly enough to yield to it. And Fielding's attempt (to face it at once) was something of a false start. His own critical interests diminished during his career as a novelist: he failed to create a tradition, and had as a critic no disciples. For some fifty years after his death in 1754, during the very years in which the novel established itself as a dominant form, criticism returned to poetry (as in Johnson's *Lives*), or expended itself on aesthetic theories like those of Burke and Reynolds. Journals such as the *Monthly Review* (1749–1845) and Smollett's *Critical Review* (1756–1817), it is true, frequently reviewed current novels, but largely in terms of plot-summaries, and though the remaking of literary periodicals early in the nineteenth century improved the situation a little, it is still significant that Jane Austen's novels passed largely unnoticed by the reviewers, apart from Scott's own generous welcome to *Emma* in the *Quarterly Review* (1816). Hazlitt's sixth lecture in his *Lectures on the English Comic Writers* (1819) and Scott's laborious imitation of Johnson in his *Lives of the Novelists* (1821–4) are feeble palliatives. Even the Victorian critics tended to avoid the novel: only one of Arnold's *Essays in Criticism* is about a novelist,[1] and that a Russian. Fielding apart, there is no

1. 'Count Leo Tolstoi', *Fortnightly Review* (December 1887), reprinted in *Essays in Criticism: Second Series* (1888). At the beginning of this essay Arnold talks of the English and French novel as already a thing of the

continuous attempt in England to give the novel a critical respectability until the articles of George Eliot and her companion G. H. Lewes in reviews in the 1840s and 1850s, and nothing that could be called an aesthetic of the novel until the present century, in the prefaces of Henry James (1907–9).

The claim of Henry Fielding (1707–54) to have pioneered novel criticism in English, then, is beyond all challenge. Indeed he is so far ahead of fashion as to be not so much a pioneer as a lost and lonely explorer. This adventurer never returned. His criticism of the novel, which is largely contained in the three prefaces to *Joseph Andrews* (1742) and in the eighteen prefaces to each 'book' of *Tom Jones* (1749), is an attempt, unique in its fullness, to 'respectabilize' the novel by invoking and adapting neoclassical doctrines, like those popularized in England by Rymer and Dennis, in its support. If this attempt to impress educated opinion was a failure – and I think that, by the time he was working on the second novel, it was already clear to Fielding himself that it was – there is something grandiose in the spectacle of this middle-aged magistrate, a full century before George Eliot, attempting to invest so parvenu a form with a classic dignity of its own.

Two great limiting factors prevented a wide success to Fielding's endeavours. The first was his training as a dramatist. His success on the stage cut short by the Licensing Act of 1737, at the age of thirty, Fielding laboriously adapted his talent for farce to the unaccustomed task of writing novels. The adaptation was never complete in the novels themselves, and the theatricality of a good deal of Fielding's fiction clashes oddly with his theories of classic form. You cannot easily indulge a taste for bedroom farce and claim at the same time that a concern for morality and for epic breadth are the motive-forces of your work. Second, Fielding

past: 'The famous English novelists have passed away, and have left no successors of like fame.' This is a fair comment on the immediate situation in the 1880s; but it does not explain why Arnold kept so quiet about Dickens, Thackeray, and George Eliot while they were alive.

suffers from a contemporary incoherence in the European debate over theories of the comic. It is a little hard to call upon the first English critic of the novel not only to advance a coherent account of the novel itself, but to concoct as well an explanation of why people laugh. And yet, if the novel is to be limited by definition, as Fielding limited it, to the *comic* epic in prose, there can be no doubt that some sort of account of the comic is called for. Earlier English critics had not helped much: Dryden's account of what constitutes good satire is exhilarating but not really helpful:

There is still a vast difference betwixt the slovenly butchering of a man, and the fineness of a stroke that separates the head from the body, and leaves it standing in its place. A man may be capable, as Jack Ketch's wife said of his servant, of a plain piece of work, a bare hanging; but to make a malefactor die sweetly was only belonging to her husband.[1]

'Fine raillery', as opposed to old-fashioned 'railing', 'roasting' or mere abuse, was seen as already a fine art when Pope was an infant. And a form of power, too: one remembers Pope's terrible moment of self-congratulation:

> Yes, I am proud; I must be proud to see
> Men not afraid of God, afraid of me.[2]

But it is useless to look to Dryden, or Pope, or Swift, for a realized theory of the comic. Fielding had his continental sources, ancient and modern; but in English terms he was largely forced to start from scratch.

Nothing, he confessed late in his life, is 'so unsettled and uncertain as our notion of humour in general'.[3] That incertainty is based on a Christian charity that held ridicule, unless directed against vicious folly, to violate both the duty of man and the manners of a gentleman.

The deep contradiction in Fielding's theory of the novel

1. 'A Discourse Concerning the Original and Progress of Satire' (1693): in *Of Dramatic Poesy and Other Critical Essays*, edited by George Watson (1962), 11,137.
2. 'Epilogue to the Satires' (1738), ll. 208–9.
3. *Covent-Garden Journal*, No. 19 (7 March 1752).

appears in his first and most ambitious essays, the prefaces to *Joseph Andrews*. No doubt the novel itself has its contradictions: it seems almost torn apart by its social and picaresque elements on the one hand, and its parodic quality on the other, as a reply to (and part-parody of) Richardson's *Pamela* (1740) – the whole overlaid with a thick layer of moralism, largely in Parson Adams's mouth, so that there is rarely any doubt as to what one is meant to think. Without the preface, we could only guess at what went wrong: with it, we know. Fielding has been seduced by the neoclassical doctrine of generality into attempting two irreconcilable objects. On the one hand, the novels themselves suggest that Fielding wants to be what Scott Fitzgerald called a 'Marxian' novelist, or one deeply aware of the social context of the individual. In this sense Fielding is trying to be more of a Defoe than a Richardson, though he is too respectful of established society to explore deep. Against Richardson's conviction of the self-sufficiency of virtue, he insists upon virtue as influenced by circumstance and experience: *Tom Jones* is set against the real and recent fact of the Jacobite Forty-Five, and the title-page insists that it is a 'History'. But, on the other hand, Fielding's use of the word *history* is seriously equivocal:

Is not such a book as that which records the achievements of the renowned Don Quixote more worthy the name of a history than even Mariana's [i.e. a Latin history of Spain (1592–1605)]: for whereas the latter is confined to a particular period of time, and to a particular nation, the former is the history of the world in general...[1]

There is not much use arguing with a critic who will juggle with his own terms. Fielding's ironic proposition in the rest of the chapter – it is entitled 'Matter prefatory in praise of Biography' – is that the novelist is a biographer, or the kind of historian that describes not a whole period, but the life of an individual. Fielding's irony here is laboured and flat, and the biographer-analogy reveals nothing that helps. In

1. *Joseph Andrews* (1742), III, i.

fact, for all his claims to particularity, Fielding is putting a familiar neoclassical case: 'The lawyer is not only alive, but hath been so these 4,000 years ... Mrs Tow-wouse is coeval with our lawyer; and tho' perhaps during the changes which so long an existence must have passed through, she may in her turn have stood behind the bar at an inn; I will not scruple to affirm, she hath likewise in the revolution of ages sat on a throne.' Such lawyers and landladies, existing out of time and place, are no subject for biographers.

Fielding's portentous theory of the 'comic epic in prose', elaborated in the preface to *Joseph Andrews*, is similarly familiar in its assumptions, which are Cervantic[1]; but far more interesting in its conclusions. True, it is not quite consistent either with itself or with the novel it exists to justify. But it is an honest and engaging attempt to define the new dignity of the novel. Fielding is very much aware of his own originality in adopting these arguments into English, and of the probability of being misunderstood. *Joseph Andrews*, he explains in the opening paragraph, represents a 'kind of writing which I do not remember to have seen hitherto attempted in our language'. The epic, he goes on, like the drama, has a comic form as well as a tragic; Homer, according to Aristotle, wrote a comic epic the *Margites* (now lost) as well as the *Iliad*. Further, the epic may be in prose as well as in verse – though verse is natural to the epic. Such a form, the comic epic in prose, is not to be confused with stage-comedy or the serious prose romance. It differs from comedy in that 'its action is more extended and comprehensive, containing a much larger circle of incidents, and introducing a greater variety of characters'; and it differs from the prose romance (and here Fielding lands himself in endless difficulties) in its ludicrous diction and its disposition to parody: 'In the diction, I think, burlesque itself may be sometimes admitted', chiefly in the

1. See E. C. Riley, *Cervantes's Theory of the Novel* (Oxford, 1962), especially pp. 49–57 on theories of the European Renaissance, and notably in *Don Quixote*, to adapt the criticism of epic and romance to justify the novel.

battles, for the delectation of the classical reader. Fielding's love of 'burlesque', or parody, is his besetting temptation. He had learned to love it in his mock-heroic play *Tom Thumb* (1730) before he abandoned the theatre – 'I have had some little success on the stage this way,' he confesses modestly – and he was fatally aware that nothing was better calculated to win a laugh. But, in the novels, it seduces him at times into spoiling effects: he introduces the very sympathetic Joseph Andrews in his eighth chapter with a mock-epic description of night which ruins the entrance of his young hero ('Now the rake Hesperus had called for his breeches ...'); and he treats Sophia Western, the very pattern of feminine perfection, just as badly in *Tom Jones*: 'Hushed be every ruder breath. May the heathen ruler of the winds confine in iron chains the boisterous limbs of noisy Boreas ...' (iv, ii). This is the facetiousness of the hearty classical scholar: Fielding probably felt a gentlemanly contempt for Defoe's demand of historical accuracy in the *Iliad* and for Richardson's priggish dislike of Homer's 'savage spirit'. Fielding calls for readers of stronger stomachs, and his burlesque style in scenes of violence constitutes a kind of toughening course for moral greenhorns – as in *Tom Jones*, v, 8, where the village mob attack a pregnant Molly Seagrim in the churchyard. But parody is a tyrannous master unless, as in Joyce's *Ulysses*, it is skilfully handled within a firmly designed plan. In Fielding's case, only *Amelia* (1751), with its echoes of the *Aeneid*, shows much sign of a structural interest in parody – but by then parody is not consistent enough to count for much. The uncomfortable question remains: is the comic epic essentially a work of literary pastiche, a parody of the classical epic, or is it full-blown moral comedy about a contemporary world? Fielding wants to have it both ways, and in both theory and practice he seems oddly unaware that he cannot.

Fielding's theory of the Comic ('the Ridiculous', he calls it), which forms the second part of the Preface to *Joseph Andrews*, only confirms this sense of confusion. 'The only course of the true Ridiculous', he announces boldly, 'is affectation.' One supposes he cannot have read *Joseph Andrews*. The funniest character in the novel is beyond all question Parson Adams, whose simple-minded sincerity is unqualified. As a matter of fact, Fielding's honest characters are often more ridiculous than his affected ones: Adams is much funnier than the nymphomaniac Lady Booby, who pretends to a niceness of chastity she cannot live up to, and is rather frightening in the process. Jonathan Wild, too, that prince of hypocritical scoundrels, seems too terrible to be genuinely ridiculous, though other readers than myself have been drawn to laughter. Fielding goes on to propose a further distinction that does not work:

Now affectation proceeds from one of these two causes: vanity or hypocrisy. For as vanity puts us on affecting false characters, in order to purchase applause; so hypocrisy sets us on an endeavour to avoid censure, by concealing our vices under an appearance of their opposite virtues.

But, as he frankly adds, we tend to be hypocritical because we are vain, so that the distinction does not amount to much. And, in any case, it is not observable in his novels, where hypocrites abound and mere vanity is scarcely ever in question.

No wonder Fielding's own critical certainties, as represented by the *Joseph Andrews* prefaces, seem to have crumbled in the seven years that divide this novel from *Tom Jones*. True, there is more criticism in the second novel, quantitatively, than in the first – all eighteen books lead off with a critical chapter. But it is all occasional. The *Tom Jones* prefaces make no attempt to erect a system. They occasionally make a gesture of acknowledgement to the old epic theory of the novel – 'prosai-comi-epic writing', Fielding calls it in Book v – but they make no attempt to defend or elaborate abstract issues in which the novelist seems to have lost interest. And they diminish fairly steadily throughout the novel, both in length and in substance. By Book v – the most interesting of all in its preface – Fielding seems ready to throw in his hand, and few of the remaining prefaces are better than jokes. They are only there at all, Fielding explains in his fifth preface, for an effect of contrast with the comedy of the novel itself:

These soporific parts are so many scenes of Serious artfully interwoven, in order to contrast and set off the rest ... In this light, then, or rather in this darkness, I would have the reader to consider these initial essays.

Fielding's defensive facetiousness fails to obscure the truth: by now he is finished with criticism. And yet his new distaste for analysis, as revealed in *Tom Jones*, is based upon an acute intuition that English criticism in his age is on the wrong track. The legislative role of criticism, as he insists, is an illusion, in so far as the neoclassical critics base their rules on observation of an alien literary tradition. The dramatic unities are a mere shibboleth, he contends, sixteen years before Johnson's Preface to Shakespeare (1765) exposed the same fallacy, and modern critics offend in that they 'adhere to the lifeless letter of law and reject the spirit'. 'We have not the profoundest veneration', he goes on, for 'the authority of *ipse dixit*.' This is spirited language, even when one grants that Fielding failed to devise a mode of analysis to compete with the arbitrary system he had grown to hate. His theories of the Comic and of the Novel-as-History are incoherent, and have little influence; his grandiose attempt, in *Joseph Andrews*, to give the novel classical status by re-defining its *genre* in terms of the epic is impressive only in its recognition that the novel needed status, and deserved it. No wonder, after such a false start, if the novel had to wait for a century or more before it found a critical tradition worthy of itself. But Fielding's attempt to explain and justify his own fiction in prefaces, as Dryden had sought to justify his plays, still looks audacious and brave. The silence all about it is so very profound.

CHAPTER 4

SAMUEL JOHNSON

WITH Samuel Johnson (1709–84), English criticism achieves greatness on a scale that any reader can instantly recognize. *The Lives of the Poets* stand four-square as the foundation-stone of our critical tradition, and they need no concessive defence of an historical kind: the Life of Pope, for instance, is still the best general account of Pope in existence. The task is not to justify or recommend – Johnson's *Lives* need to be recommended about as much as the Odes of Keats – but rather to defend Johnson from his own fan-club of devotees. For in spite of several notable calls-to-order, the Johnson of the Johnsonian's imagination can still exert more influence than the Johnson of the *Rambler*, or even of the *Lives*: a burly, irreverent iconoclast, half Falstaff, half Winston Churchill, shouting down the pedants in the cause of common sense and seeking (as one American critic has put it) 'to subvert accepted critical dogmas and to deliver literature from the fetters of prescriptive criticism'.[1]

This does not sound remotely like the Johnson of *Rambler* no. 92:

It is ... the task of criticism to establish principles, to improve opinion into knowledge, and to distinguish those means of pleasing which depend upon known causes and rational deduction from the nameless and inexplicable elegancies which appeal wholly to the fancy ...

The tone of voice is positively schoolmasterly. And not only the tone: the sense, too, is deeply prescriptive or legislative. Johnson certainly believed that the object of

1. W. R. Keast, 'The Theoretical Foundations of Johnson's Criticism' in *Critics and Criticism Ancient and Modern*, edited by R. S. Crane (Chicago, 1952), p. 393.

criticism was, in a very literal sense, to lay down the law, to ascertain and apply general principles of poetic excellence.

Nor does the man-in-the-street image of Johnson, or that of the common man raised to a higher power, find much support in the texts. Boswell reveals one of his terrors – that of death – and Reynolds another which we might have guessed from Boswell, and indeed from his very association with Boswell: his terror of loneliness.[1] And Johnson's neurotic sensibility is a significant element in his perception of literature. Boswell tells how 'he read Shakespeare at a period so early that the speech of the ghost in *Hamlet* terrified him when he was alone',[2] and it is at first tempting to dismiss the story as a childish phase. But some of Johnson's most mature criticism is conducted just this side of screaming-point. He is the only editor of Shakespeare one can imagine writing a note like this on the fifth act of *Othello*: 'I am glad that I have ended my revisal of this dreadful scene. It is not to be endured.' Such sensitivities do not make Johnson a better critic: they merely make him a more interesting 'case'. But they help to dispose of the *persona* which deceived few of his intimates.

Other misconceptions are more subtle. It is not much use, for example, to read Johnson in search of evidences for 'close reading'. It may be true that, of all eighteenth-century critics, he gets closest to his texts. He quotes liberally – so did Addison in his Milton papers, and to small purpose – and he can actually comment upon quotations in language which is sometimes descriptive enough to admit of real distinctions. Still, it should be clear that Johnson would not shine in the more restricted versions of a modern practical-criticism class. His mind does not settle: it darts. In his passion for knowledge, including remote and useless knowledge, he is more of a Saintsbury than an Empson. On entering a strange house, Boswell relates, he went straight

1. Sir Joshua Reynolds, *Portraits* (New Haven, 1952), p. 68: 'Solitude to him was horror . . . Any company to him was better than none.'
2. *The Life of Samuel Johnson* (1791), (the year 1729).

to the bookcase and read the backs of books; and, antiquary-like, he recognized that knowledge was of two kinds: 'We know a subject ourselves, or we know where we can find information upon it.'[1] It was the second order of knowledge he excelled in. 'From his earliest years', Boswell tells us, 'he loved to read poetry, but hardly ever read any poem to an end,'[2] and he once asked an acquaintance incredulously: 'Sir, do *you* read books *through*?'[3] This is not the language of the close critical analyst. It suggests virtues of quite another kind: momentary but brilliant insights, a gift for perceiving relationships, certainty of judgement, breadth. And these are pre-eminently the virtues of Johnson's criticism.

And finally, Johnson is an unambiguously historical critic, and the true father of historical criticism in English. In him, Dryden's faint intuition of a historical order of 'schools' and 'influences' in English poetry is solidly realized. It would do Johnson a resounding injustice to suppose that his greatest talent was for conversation. Above all, he was a scholar. Oxford's honorary doctorate was no accident: Johnson designed his career after arriving in London in 1737, after the first dreary years of hack work, to pivot upon the *Dictionary* of 1755, the greatest work of English literary scholarship before the Victorian philologists; and he confirmed his reputation as a scholar ten years later, with the edition of Shakespeare (1765), an edition which arose directly out of his lexical interests. Even in the *Dictionary* his purpose was a critical one, as he explained to Warton,[4] and its full title reveals how: *A Dictionary of the English Language: in which the words are deduced from their originals, and illustrated in their different significations by examples from the best writers.* This is a programme for editors; it opens out into vast inquiries involving textual criticism, source-studies, semantics. Not that Johnson himself foresaw all these possibilities,

1. *Life of Johnson* (18 April 1775).
2. ibid. (1729).
3. ibid. (19 April 1773).
4. Quoted p. 55, above.

though the latter part of the preface to Shakespeare is an astonishingly comprehensive account of the duties of a critical editor. But a literary career that begins with the first historical dictionary in English, establishes itself with an annotated edition of Shakespeare, and ends with a collection of literary biographies, has about it an air of positively formidable solidity, and one wonders how Johnson's triumphs as a historical critic come to be mentioned so seldom. The answer, this time, is not only Boswell, though Boswell is always a large part of the answer to any question concerning the Johnson myth. The responsibility for this conspiracy of silence must rest squarely with critics of our own age. They have used Johnsonian criticism as if it were a schoolboy's idea of *Hamlet*, a ragbag of quotations to be discussed, at the point of an imperative, by hapless examinees. The sweep and scholarship of any critic would vanish under so selective a neglect.

So much for the myth. But certainly oddities in Johnson's career remain, such as may justifiably diminish any tendency towards 'prescriptive reverence'. The first is his laziness. This is not much in doubt: one thinks of the carelessness of detail in his scholarly works, justifiable as it may be by its scope and scale; the significant silences (years long) in his career, and the bland facility of many of the lesser *Lives*. In one of his last letters to Langton he talks of 'that voluntary debility' or indolence which 'will, if it is not counteracted by resolution, render in time the strongest faculties lifeless ...' (12 July 1784); and he confessed to himself in his diary in 1781, on finishing the *Lives*, that he had written them 'in my usual way, dilatorily and hastily, unwilling to work and working with vigour and haste'.[1] Johnson, it is true, had the wonderful ability to cultivate an indolence that did not kill his talents, but merely held them in suspension. His finest criticism was written in the last seven years of his life, after a writing silence of a dozen years. But again and again (and especially in the *Lives*,

1. *Diaries, Prayers and Annals*, edited by E. L. McAdam jr (New Haven, 1958), pp. 303–4.

which were written at speed) it is easy to remark in the loose ends of his arguments the price that he paid.

And then there is his early record as a poet, notably in the verse satires *London* (1738) and *The Vanity of Human Wishes* (1749). Johnson's career is in the right order, in Baudelairean terms: his poetry turned to criticism. But whether it 'turned' in any very creative sense, as it did with Coleridge and Eliot, one may reasonably doubt. I cannot see that Johnson's early years as a poet taught him anything that was critically useful to him: the very faults of his own poems, such as their excessive generalization, are among his own blind-spots as a critic in middle and later life. This failure may help to account for, but not altogether excuse, a certain unctuous severity that occasionally reminds one of Rymer, and a very general lack of intimacy with the creative act. Whether Johnson praises or blames, he sits remotely in judgement, and everywhere except in the *Life of Richard Savage* (1744) we feel that his early literary struggles have been willingly forgotten. Admittedly, his criticism gains thereby in dignity: Johnson is the first English critic to write as if he were the equal of the greatest of modern poets. But dignity is no good substitute for sympathy.

Johnson's criticism, which was all written after the age of forty, falls into four groups. First, there are the periodical essays of his middle years, where the critical interest is largely concentrated in a dozen papers in the *Rambler* (1750–2).[1] Second, there is the *Dictionary* (1755), itself a critical endeavour as well as a programme and aid for future criticism. Thirdly, there is the edition of Shakespeare (1765), preceded by the *Proposals for Printing the Dramatic Works of Shakespeare* (1756). And fourthly and most substantially, there are the *Lives* of 1779–81, which crown his career. This progress reveals a certain symmetry which is partly deliberate. The *Rambler* papers contain Johnson's

1. The principal critical papers are nos. 37 (on the pastoral), 92 (on onomatopoeia), 125 (against tragi-comedy), 156 (against some dramatic rules), and 158 (on the authority of the Ancients).

critical theory: here, if only for a moment, he joins in the Augustan and post-Augustan battle of aesthetics, but in his own sceptical vein. The *Dictionary* and the Shakespeare preface establish his more original pretensions to be not merely a man of taste but a literary scholar. And in the *Lives* he exploits his learned reputation to evaluate the English poets of the past hundred years: an inquiry into taste, but in no ordinary Augustan style, since taste is founded now upon sound scholarship and wide reading. Johnson's ordering of his career is so good that it would be impertinent to depart from it.

First, the *Rambler*. After one or two occasional papers of a critical interest (such as no. 37, where his account of the pastoral is a good deal more sympathetic than in the Life of Milton, a quarter of a century later), Johnson enters the lists of the aesthetic battle with no. 92 (2 February 1751). The search for good taste, he insists, can only be considered historically and relatively: what is beautiful to one generation is ugly to the next.

Beauty ... is relative and comparative ... and therefore Boileau justly remarks that the books which have stood the test of time ... have a better claim to our regard than any modern can boast, because the long continuance of their reputation proves that they are adequate to our faculties, and agreeable to nature. It is, however, the task of criticism to establish principles ....[1]

Certain major elements in the Johnsonian aesthetic emerge at once. First, Johnson accepts the Augustan revolution whereby, as in Addison's Milton papers of 1712, criticism is openly designed for the reader rather than for the poet; like the Augustans, he regards the formation of public taste as his first duty. Secondly, he is sceptical of current theoretical criticism in its attempt to define good taste. His argument, on this level, is impatient and dismissive: good books are books which have survived. It is not we who sit in judgment over great literature, but great literature – signalled by its lasting power – that sits in judgment over

1. The quotation is continued on p. 72 above.

us. To ascertain the essence of the Beautiful, he continues with airy scorn, 'would perhaps require a very great part of the life of Aristotle and Plato'. The general cast of Johnson's mind is vigorously anti-theoretical. 'Definitions are hazardous':[1] such sentiments are in sharp defiance of an age much in love with abstract critical terminology. This is not to say that Johnson does not have his critical theories. But he is impatiently averse to arguing them at length.

Johnson's theory of literary excellence, which we are obliged to snatch at as he runs, claims as its foundation the practice – but only the practice – of the Ancients. The authority of classical *criticism*, i.e. Aristotle, is largely dismissed. Ancient literature, simply by virtue of its survival, is a court of appeal of ultimate excellence, and laws of excellence are to be deduced from it by the conscientious critic. Moreover, whatever falls outside such laws is probably bad. Johnson does not even pretend to be a liberator from the critically prescriptive. Some laws, admittedly – such as the limit of two or three actors upon the stage at any one moment – are silly and ought to be discarded: Johnson is very hot against 'literary dictators', 'blind reverence',[2] and some aspects of 'the tyranny of prescription'. 'Many rules', he complains in no. 156, 'have been advanced without consulting nature or reason.' But 'nature' means the practice of the ancient poets, and 'reason' the historical sense that enables the informed critic to interpret their practice in the light of existing conditions. Johnson is very far from seeking an end to rule. His object, as a theoretical critic, is not to repeal the neoclassical laws, but to amend them. The alternative to rule is, for Johnson, merely awful: 'the anarchy of ignorance' and 'the caprices of fancy'.[3]

But the theory, tight and coherent as it looks, contains at least two escape-clauses, of which Johnson avails himself often in the Preface to Shakespeare and in the *Lives*:

　1. The effective survival of ancient poetry is a debatable

---

1. *Rambler*, no. 125 (28 May 1751).
2. ibid., no. 158 (21 September 1751).
3. ibid., no. 92 (2 February 1751).

issue. Can the pastoral be said to have survived? In *Rambler* no. 37 Johnson believes it has, and suggests how ancient practice should be interpreted by the modern poet, and in what sense Spenser in the *Shepheardes Calender* has taken a false path:

In writing or judging of pastoral poetry, neither the authors nor critics of later times seem to have paid sufficient regard to the originals left us by antiquity but have entangled themselves with unnecessary difficulties by advancing principles which, having no foundation in the nature of things, are wholly to be rejected . . .

Nature, as usually in Johnson, equals the Ancients; but the passage certainly suggests the modern pastoral is a viable form. A quarter of a century later, in the Life of Milton, *Lycidas* is roundly condemned for its pastoral frame: 'Its form is that of a pastoral, easy, vulgar, and therefore disgusting.' Evidently the survival of ancient practice is an issue where Johnson allowed himself a certain latitude.

2. The tradition, with its roots deep in classical poetry, is itself subject to alteration. 'Every new genius produces some innovation which, when invented and approved, subverts the rules which the practice of foregoing authors had established.'[1] Without this escape-clause, Johnson would indeed be in an embarrassing position in his defence of the Augustan poets: there is nothing much like Pope's *Rape of the Lock* in the literature of the Ancients. And certainly the concession is sensible. Too sensible: it admits exceptions vast enough to destroy any usefulness the original principle may have had.

Johnson's critical theory, conscientious and scholarly as it looks, is not in fact much better than an umbrella to shelter under in showery weather. It allows Johnson to praise what he likes, and condemn what he does not like. But this, after all, is precisely what it is right to demand of a critic, especially of a critic whose intuitions are as just as Johnson's. And, moreover, it is a theory which leads him directly into descriptive criticism. Poetry is an evolutionary stream, a

1. *Rambler*, no. 125 (28 May 1751).

'tradition': it invites examination as such. *The Lives of the Poets* only occurred at all by a happy publishing accident, but they do arise naturally out of Johnson's abstract convictions concerning the progressive nature of art.

So, of course, does the *Dictionary*. Johnson would not have understood the early twentieth-century battle between the conservatives who hold linguistics to be a prescriptive discipline, and the radicals who insist that it is a descriptive science. For Johnson, lexicography is both, and it is only one because it is the other. Of course usage varies from age to age, argues Johnson, and his *Dictionary* is proudly the first historical dictionary of English: 'As by the cultivation of various sciences a language is amplified, it will be more furnished with words deflected from their original sense,' he explains in his preface. But, like the critic in search of principles, the lexicographer selects as well as reports. 'I applied myself to the perusal of our writers,' he tells us, but in a critical spirit, and 'found our speech copious without order, and energetic without rules'. The *Dictionary* seeks to tidy up – there was 'perplexity to be disentangled, confusion to be regulated'. It illustrates by quotations, but only quotation from the 'best', so that it does not aspire to the impartiality of the Oxford English Dictionary. A word means, not what most men suppose it to mean, but what the finest authors have made it mean. Like his critical theory, Johnson's theory of language is only superficially democratic: it is not content to count heads.

The edition of Shakespeare (1765), arising out of early lexical interests and long delayed by them, was embarked upon in 1756, as soon as the *Dictionary* had been dismissed into the world 'with frigid tranquillity' – Johnson's incomparable phrase to describe his final emotions as a lexicographer. It must have been far more congenial work, though less important for his age, and the style of the *Proposals for Printing the Dramatic Works of Shakespeare* (1756) and of the 1765 preface suggests a certain gusto of mood. Johnson's Shakespeare is the seventh edition since the early folios – the others were by Rowe, Pope, Theobald, Hanmer, and Warburton – and Johnson followed his predecessors closely in form and even in substance. All wrote prefaces, which Johnson reprinted in his own edition (with Rowe's preface in Pope's revision). In his own preface, Johnson follows them in insisting on his own labours in collating texts – there is nothing new in this pretension – and in praising Shakespeare's genius as a sport of nature. But Johnson's preface is syncretic only in a respectable sense: we expect an editor to have studied his forerunners, and to have learned from them.

The preface is in essence a brilliant exercise in descriptive criticism – Johnson's first extended attempt at the form – with a major essay in theoretical criticism, the refutation of the unities of time and place, inserted mid way, and along appendix on editorial method. It falls, fairly clearly, into seven parts: Shakespeare considered as a poet of nature, followed by a defence of his tragi-comedy, his 'central' style, his defects, the general attack upon the unities, the historical background, and editorial method. The preface is firmly grounded, in its opening pages, in Johnsonian theory: Shakespeare happily occupies a classic position, like an Ancient, by virtue of his relative antiquity and 'continuance of esteem'. He *must* be great. (Johnson even dares speak here of 'prescriptive veneration'.) And his greatness is of a familiar neoclassical kind, a mastery of generality: his characters are not 'individuals' but 'species'. All this is much of a piece with the earlier *Rambler* essays: 'Poetry cannot dwell upon the minuter distinctions ...'[1] But, familiar as it all looks, Johnson has some odd cards up his sleeve, and he will not scruple to play them, even at the cost of compromising his general strategy.

Three major inconsistencies emerge from the preface as a whole, though they are inconsistencies which, like the antitheses for which Johnson's syntax is famous, seem not so much defects as sources of energy – they provide power by which the argument moves vigorously on. First, tragi-comedy is justified on conflicting grounds. This, the second

1. *Rambler*, no. 36 (21 July 1750); see *Rasselas* (1759), ch. x.

section, is one of the most original parts of the preface. Dryden too had occasionally defended mixed plays, but only as the occasion suited: he had condemned them too. And given that the neoclassical critics had abandoned, or forgotten, the Renaissance distinction between tragedy and comedy, it must indeed have seemed important to justify Shakespeare's mixture of 'crimes' and 'absurdities'. But it will hardly do to justify tragi-comedy on Dryden's grounds that contraries set off each other, and then to excuse 'the rules of criticism' on the grounds that 'there is always an appeal open from criticism to nature', and that 'the mingled drama' can be shown to have instructed as well as pleased: this is a characteristically Johnsonian use of the escape-clause. Second, the extravagant (or at least unqualified) praise of Shakespeare as supremely 'the poet of nature' in the first part of the preface seems discredited in the light of some of his disparagements towards the end: 'As we owe every thing to him, he owes something to us; ... we fix our eyes upon his graces, and turn them from his deformities, and endure in him what we should in another loath or despise ... He has ... perhaps not one play which, if it were now exhibited as the work of a contemporary writer, would be heard to the conclusion.'[1] This has the ring of sincerity: but, if sincere, it makes the veneration of the opening pages look prescriptive indeed. And finally, Johnson's somewhat Coleridgean praise for Shakespeare as the poet of the 'central' style, 'probably to be sought in the common intercourse of life, among those who speak only to be understood, without ambition of elegance', seems out of tune with the attack that follows, in the list of Shakespearean defects, upon his 'tumour', his weak declamation, his 'unwieldy sentiment'. More than once, the preface seems torn apart by Johnson's failure to qualify either his praise or his blame or to relate one to the other. But there are moments of scintillating perception. The refutation of the unities of time and place, though not strictly unprecedented in English, with its assertion of the special status of dramatic illusion,

1. *Johnson on Shakespeare* (Oxford, 1908), pp. 40–41.

is a model of logical demonstration, and rich in those effects of mock-simplicity which Johnson loved to affect:

It will be asked how the drama moves, if it is not credited. It is credited with all the credit due to a drama. It is credited, whenever it moves, as a just picture of a real original.[1]

So he kicked the stone for Boswell to refute Berkeleian idealism. The exposure of the unities that follows, 'not dogmatically but deliberately written', as he magnificently excused his own temerity, is one of the great moments of liberating intelligence in English criticism. And there is a superb historical understanding implied, not only in the exposition of editorial principles with which the preface closes, but in the constant appeals to the study of background as an antidote to mere rule-of-thumb:

Works tentative and experimental must be estimated by their proportion to the general and collective ability of man, as it is discovered in a long succession of endeavours.[2]

Every man's performances, to be rightly estimated, must be compared with the state of the age in which he lived, and with his own particular opportunities ... Curiosity is always busy to discover the instruments, as well as to survey the workmanship, to know how much is to be ascribed to original powers, and how much to casual and adventitious help.[3]

Most nineteenth-century historical criticism, in its characteristic excesses as well as in its characteristic triumphs, seems foreshadowed here. However naïve Johnson's particular historical judgements ('The English nation, in the time of Shakespeare, was yet struggling to emerge from barbarity,' he goes on), there can be no doubt of his profound determination to view poetry as a tradition or evolution, 'a long succession'.

The *Lives of the English Poets*[4] (1779–81), a collection of

1. ibid., p. 28. 'Moves' = moves emotion in the audience; 'credited' = believed to be real.

2. ibid., p. 10.

3. ibid., pp. 30–31.

4. So called since the second edition of 1781. The original title was *Prefaces Biographical and Critical to the Works of the English Poets.*

fifty-two literary biographies, is a fitting climax to the career of our first great scholar-critic. It is a belated achievement – Johnson was sixty-eight when he began work on the *Lives* – but beyond all dispute his most brilliant. Boswell could hardly contain himself in his enthusiasm over the collection: 'the richest, most beautiful, and indeed most perfect production of Johnson's pen'.[1] 'Perfect' is an odd description: the *Lives* were written in haste, in the confidence of a great reputation, and there is a good deal in them that is formula-ridden and inconclusive. Their 'charm', as Boswell predicted in a letter to Johnson, justly owes something at least to 'the *magnum nomen*'[2] on the title-page.

In 1777 a committee of some forty booksellers determined upon a new and superior collection of the works of the major English poets from Chaucer to their own times, and a deputation called upon Johnson to invite him to undertake the prefaces. He accepted promptly, but on his own terms. The whole of medieval, and almost the whole of Renaissance poetry, was eventually cut from the publishers' scheme and, of the fifty-two Lives that Johnson wrote, all but two – Milton and Cowley – are of post-Restoration poets. There is nothing to regret here. The Life of Cowley shows how alien pre-Restoration poetry was to Johnson, and if we could choose we should choose very much what we have – a review of the body of English poetry during the century that had elapsed since 1660, the period where Johnson is king.

Within four years the *Lives* were written – an average rate of about one Life a month, and surely a terrible pace to maintain. Not enough thought, perhaps, has been given to the cost of this haste. It is clear, for instance, that Johnson felt obliged to adopt a formula to save himself time. In his Advertisement to the first edition, he speaks of having first planned to write an 'advertisement' for each poet like those in what he calls the '*French Miscellanies*'. Sir John Hawkins, in his *Life of Johnson* (1787), identifies the source:

When Johnson had determined on this work, he was to seek for the best mode for executing it. On a hint from a literary lady of his

1. *Life of Johnson* (May 1777).　　2. ibid. (24 April 1777).

acquaintance and mine [probably Charlotte Lennox] he adopted for his outline, that form in which the Countess D'Aunois has drawn up the memoirs of the French poets, in her *Recueil des plus belles pièces des Poètes François*;[1]

and he adds that 'the foundation of his work', i.e. his chief sources of information, were the biographical dictionaries of Winstanley, Langbaine, and Jacob (1660, 1691, 1719). Hawkins is right about the *Recueil* (1692), though in attributing it to Mme d'Aunois he was misled by the title-page of an early edition ('Amsterdam', 1692). An early biographer of Fontenelle[2] concludes that Fontenelle himself was probably the author of the *notices biographiques*, or biographical introductions, in the *Recueil*; and since these *notices*, and no other biographical model before Johnson, use the characteristic structure of Johnson's own *Lives*, it seems likely that Fontenelle was Johnson's source here.

In planning the *Lives*, however, the ageing Johnson can hardly have needed any advice. His hackwork in literary biography during his first and neediest days in London, between 1738 and 1756 – prefaces to booksellers' reprints, written on fee, and commissioned articles in the *Gentleman's Magazine* and elsewhere – had already taught him Fontenelle's formula, and how to use it. Two of the Lives, indeed (those of Roscommon and Savage), were written during these grim years and resurrected forty years later for insertion in the *Lives*. The anonymous 'Life of Dr Herman Boerhaave of Leyden',[3] for example, written by Johnson in his thirtieth year, already reveals the characteristic structure of a Fontenelle *notice*.

1. 'The Life of Samuel Johnson', in *The Works of Johnson* (1787–9), 1, 532–3. For the suggestion of Mrs Charlotte Lennox (1720–1804), who translated several memoirs from the French, I am indebted to Hawkins's latest editor, Bertram H. Davis (1962), p. 301.

2. N. C. J. Trublet (1697–1770), *Mémoires pour servir à l'histoire de la vie et des ouvrages de M. de Fontenelle* (Amsterdam, 1759) (second edition corrected), p. 72. Trublet knew Fontenelle as an old man, and his biography is generally reliable.

3. *Gentleman's Magazine* (January–April 1739).

That structure is a tripartite one: biography, character, criticism. A Fontenelle Life, like a Johnsonian, begins with a severely chronological account of the poet's life – ancestry, birth, education, and so on; in both critics, this is commonly by far the largest section. The second section, always the shortest, is a brief 'character' of the poet – his appearance and temperament. The third is purely critical, and usually of middling length. Digressions are admitted. But, on the whole, the formula is as rigorously applied by Johnson as by Fontenelle. Twenty-four of Johnson's fifty-two Lives, indeed, observe the tripartite arrangement absolutely, but even this figure gives an inadequate impression of the uniformity of his practice. Literally all of the Lives, for example, begin with biography, and all but four (Dryden, Smith, Halifax, and Hughes) end with criticism. Moreover, the divisions in Johnson are perfectly clear-cut. There is no question of over-simplifying his design: it really *is* simple. One striking aspect of the *Lives*, indeed, is the total absence of bridge-passages (which might have been easy enough to invent) connecting the two major sections, the biographical and the critical. The character-section, for instance, might have been used as a link, as Fontenelle had sometimes done, but Johnson makes no effort to use it for this purpose. He is writing to a recipe, and he does not stir his ingredients.

Not that a Johnson Life is much like one by Fontenelle except in its bare bones. The French Lives are much shorter than any but the very shortest of Johnson's – often only a matter of several hundred words. Johnson's immense facility, once the initial impulse had been supplied, must have led him astray here, and may account for the fact that the English Lives, unlike the French, were published as a separate collection. They are much too weighty to be considered as mere introductions. Moreover, Fontenelle's criticism (his third section) is always far sketchier than Johnson's; it is often confined to a few valedictory phrases, and painfully general phrases at that. His criticism of Belleau may be taken as representative:

Ronsard l'appelloit· le poète de la nature, parce que la nature règne dans tous ces ouvrages, qu'elle y peint et anime tout (1.267).

Johnson, in fact, expands the Fontenelle scheme generously, especially in its critical conclusion. His achievement is to turn the literary life into a vehicle of criticism.

An odd vehicle, none the less, and plainly a top-heavy one. Why does Johnson spend well over half his space on pure biography? And why does he throw up his formula in the face of his reader, neglecting every opportunity to disguise it? It would be tempting to argue, in the face of Johnson's reputation as a scholar-critic, that in the *Lives* he is creating the foundations of the nineteenth-century school of historical criticism by elevating the literary life to a new critical eminence. But Johnson is not a very biographical critic. His point of departure, it is true, is invariably in the poet's life, but he makes singularly little attempt to exploit biography for critical purposes. His notion of the creative act is not so much naïve as non-existent. He seems surprisingly indifferent to the paradox (for Johnson as a royalist) that Milton, with his outrageous republican sentiments, wrote the greatest of the English epics, and his formula allows him to evade this issue in a few dismissive phrases. His treatment of Gray, again, shows the opportunities he missed. The biography shows Gray leading the life of a Cambridge scholar, the character reports him to be 'the most learned man in Europe', and he is then appropriately rebuked for his unscholarly 'Ode on Spring': 'I was sorry to see, in the lines of a scholar like Gray, "the *honied* Spring".'[1] That the virtues and failings of Gray's poems might be more closely defined by using the biographical evidence he has just rehearsed does not occur to Johnson. In modern terms, the *Lives* fall badly between two stools: those who, like the New Critics between the wars, prefer their criticism devoid of biography, will complain that Johnson is largely biographical; and those who accept the critical relevance of some biographical facts will wonder why Johnson uses his facts so little.

1. *Lives*, edited by Birkbeck Hill, 111, 434.

It should be obvious, then, that Johnson is not at all a biographical critic in a manner that foreshadows Sainte-Beuve. He is rather one who has discovered that criticism may usefully be practised as an appendage to biography. Johnson's explicit interest in biography, like Dryden's before him, is moral and cautionary.[1] The image of Gray's tranquil Cambridge existence really does reveal a quality, and a lack, in his verse – but only, so far as Johnson can see, by a kind of accident.

The Life of Milton is a monumental example of the characteristic triumphs and failures of Johnson's historical sense. Its design is as formal as any – biography, character, criticism – except that the middle section contains some oddly irrelevant material, including an account of Milton's family. On this occasion, however, the two principal sections of biography and criticism are in full collision: the biography goes far beyond an attack upon Milton's political views to the point of personal vindictiveness. Mere Toryism would hardly account for Johnson's jibes against Milton's work as a schoolmaster after his return from Italy in 1639: it is the nastiest passage in the Lives;[2] though such real targets as Milton's egotism and his easy talent for self-justification are surprisingly overlooked. Animus, again, is the dominating mood of the early passages in the critical section: the short poems are 'distinguished by repulsive harshness'[3] and the celebrated denunciation of 'Lycidas' along with all modern pastorals fails to notice that most of the poem is scarcely pastoral at all. The progress of 'Lycidas' from the feebly particular to the magnificently general, from the dead youth to the Poet in his cosmic setting, is all dismissed by Johnson as an 'inherent improbability' polluted by 'irreverent combinations'.[4] He is not much more sympathetic to Comus and Samson Agonistes, but there are early signs of recovery in his critique of 'L'Allegro' and 'Il

1. See Rambler, no. 60 (13 October 1750).
2. Lives, 1, 98.
3. ibid., 1, 162.
4. ibid., 1, 163, 165.

Penseroso', where he expertly recognizes the purely formal nature of Milton's distinction, designed to show 'how, among the successive variety of appearances, every disposition of mind takes hold on those by which it may be gratified.'

Johnson's critique of *Paradise Lost*, sixty years later than Addison's, is so far its superior that it is worth posing the contrast in reply to any question that seems to challenge Johnson's powers as an analyst. It is obvious that he is vastly nearer to Milton's text than Addison is, and worth noticing, at the same time, that he contrives to be so almost without quotation, 'because of selecting beauties there had been no end'[1] – there is only one in his whole account of the poem – whereas Addison loads his pages with extracts from the text. But Addison is concerned only with judgement, and snap judgement at that. Johnson attempts descriptive distinctions, even if by modern standards they are usually over-bold. The following passage, even to its initial hint of biographical intrusion, is a representative one:

He had considered creation in its whole extent, and his descriptions are therefore learned. He had accustomed his imagination to unrestrained indulgence, and his conceptions therefore were extensive. The characteristic quality of his poem is sublimity. He sometimes descends to the elegant, but his element is the great. He can occasionally invest himself with grace; but his natural port is gigantic loftiness. He can please when pleasure is required; but it is his peculiar power to astonish.[2]

One asks oneself, as so often in Johnson, just what the limiting factor in such language is. The set of antitheses upon which such a description of Milton's poetic talent is built (learning-provincialism; imagination-restraint; sublimity (*or* greatness, *or* loftiness) -grace; astonishment-pleasure) are by no means without their force. But their force would be the greater for precise illustration. And when Johnson does illustrate, he seems unwilling to test his principles closely in quotation. The following example is unusually precise in its language:

1. ibid., 1, 180.   2. ibid., 1, 177.

His similes are less numerous and more various than those of his predecessors. But he does not confine himself within the limits of rigorous comparison: his great excellence is amplitude, and he expands the adventitious image beyond the dimensions which the occasion required. Thus, comparing the shield of Satan to the orb of the Moon, he crowds the imagination with the discovery of the telescope and all the wonders which the telescope discovers.[1]

Milton's imagery, in fact, is sparser than that of Shakespeare and the Metaphysicals, and more readily extended in epic similes; Johnson oddly omits to mention the Homeric and Virgilian models that Milton copies in his effort to attain epic dignity. The comment is just: but, as so often in Johnson, there is an absolute failure to reconcile theory and practice. Is 'amplitude' in imagery, or the extension of the image beyond the limits of comparison, a virtue or not? Johnson's language suggests he has his doubts: the image in *Paradise Lost*, 1, 284 passes 'beyond the dimensions which the occasion required'. But the fault may be a generous one ('He does not confine himself . . .'). The diagnosis is admirably just, but in his conclusion Johnson fumbles and fails. And yet this, after all, is vastly superior to the far commoner offence of eighteenth-century criticism, where judgements often arose from no analysis at all.

Here, and often elsewhere, Johnson is clearly embarrassed by his own 'laws'. The ambiguity of his judgements, and the force that 'prescriptive veneration' of established masterpieces always held for him, emerges almost as clearly in the Life of Milton as in the Preface to Shakespeare. Johnson writes of *Paradise Lost* as if the poem were a visit to the dentist, or a regrettable aspect of Sunday observance like church-attendance. His analysis is an act of self-persuasion, and one unconvincing and unconvinced reason after another is advanced why the epic has to be praised:

Every line breathes sanctity of thought . . .
Of human beings there are but two; but those two are the parents
of mankind . . .
The poet, whatever be done, is always great . . .

1. ibid., 1, 179.

There is ... little opportunity for the pathetic; but what little there is has not been lost ...[1]

until, at last, the truth is out: Johnson is determined, both as a patriot and a Christian, to assert a judgement he cannot feel; to 'lessen the reputation of Milton', as he confesses, might be to 'diminish in some degree the honour of our country',[2] and the fatal flaws in Milton's conception are finally conceded with an awful clarity:

The man and woman who act and suffer are in a state which no other man or woman can ever know ...
These truths [of sin and redemption] are too important to be new ... They raise no unaccustomed emotion in the mind; what we knew before, we cannot learn; what is not unexpected, cannot surprise ...
The good and evil of Eternity are too ponderous for the wings of wit ...[3]

The essential ambiguity of the attitudes to Milton – a bored and disingenuous reverence – is sufficiently represented by these two groups of quotations. As in the Preface to Shakespeare, Johnson has not played quite fair with us. But the wonder is not that critics who, like Johnson, are at once patriots and Christians should feel obliged to relax their critical vigour before *Paradise Lost*, but that one of them contrived to define his objections so much more simply, more baldly, and more convincingly than Milton's modern detractors have done. If any modern readers still find the peom a bore, it seems likely to be for something like Johnson's reasons. For better or worse, many twentieth-century readers are simply not curious to know the answer to the questions that Milton poses in his greatest poem.

The Life of Milton shows Johnson uncomfortably poised upon a double contradiction: he respects Milton's poetry more than Milton himself, and he respects it without loving it. The Life of Cowley, for all the notoriety of Johnson's attack upon the Metaphysical style, is a happier

1. ibid., 1, 179–80.
2. ibid., 1, 181.
3. ibid., 1, 181–2.

example of his genius for distinction. The knockabout abuse of the Metaphysical poets, so familiar in quotation, does not represent Johson's purpose fairly:

The Metaphysical poets were men of learning, and to shew their learning was their whole endeavour; but, unluckily resolving to shew it in rhyme...[1]

Johnson will have his little joke, and one of his favourite jokes is to pretend he cannot see beyond the end of his nose. We read on, happily eager to see him make more of a fool of himself: so certain, when he quotes (or misquotes) Pope's dictum on wit, that this must be the limit of his horizon too:

What oft was thought, but ne'er so well expressed.

In the next two paragraphs he offers us two further accounts of 'wit', and in a moment we are panting to keep up with him:

that which, though not obvious, is, upon its first production, acknowledged to be just...
a kind of *discordia concors*; a combination of dissimilar images, or discovery of occult resemblances in things apparently unlike...[2]

Here is not one definition of wit, but three. And it is by the second test of the three that the Metaphysicals fail – their thoughts are 'not obvious, but neither are they just'. By the third definition, they triumph, though their victory (in Johnsonian terms) hardly seems justifiable: 'the reader commonly thinks his improvement dearly bought and, though he sometimes admires, is seldom pleased'. But the *nature* of the Metaphysical achievement is in large part clearly defined, whatever we may think of Johnson's view of it:

The most heterogeneous ideas are yoked by violence together; nature and art are ransacked for illustrations, comparisons, and allusions: their learning instructs, and their subtlety surprises ...

1. *Lives*, I, 19.
2. ibid., I, 20.

This is an admirable account, in general terms, of Donne's *Songs and Sonets*; and so is the lively sequel, framed as it is as a rebuttal:

> Their attempts were always analytic; they broke every image into fragments, and could no more represent, by their slender conceits and laboured particularities, the prospects of nature or the scenes of life, than he who dissects a sun-beam with a prism can exhibit the wide effulgence of a summer noon.

Johnson is seeking in poetry something few readers now want; but only a very perceptive reader of Cowley could have offered such an analysis at all, and the concessions he is ready to make to the Metaphysical mode are wide and generous.

> If they frequently threw away their wit upon false conceits, they likewise sometimes struck out unexpected truth: if their conceits were far-fetched, they were often worth the carriage. To write on their plan, it was at least necessary to read and think.[1]

But the *Lives* are essentially a study of the Augustan mode in English poetry, and the Lives of Dryden and Pope are its real glories. At last the greatest of the English neoclassical critics finds his own level: at last he speaks, and at length, of what he knows and loves. To read these Lives is to realize how aberrant was the task he had set himself in the Preface to Shakespeare and in the Life of Milton. With them, his best endeavour was to justify and excuse; with Dryden and Pope, he needs no longer to defend. He is advocate; at times, he is almost mouthpiece. In Johnson the Augustan poets found the most perfect of exponents: it is as if Donne had written a treatise on the comedies of Shakespeare, or Andrew Marvell a critique of *Paradise Lost*. No doubt so total a sympathy can be a positive nuisance in a critic: you do not explain what you know in your bones, and occasionally, it might be objected against the Life of Pope, enthusiasm supplants discrimination. But not often: Johnson is the kind of critic who hates to seem anyone's fool. He loves the qualifying phrase. The most rapturous paragraphs,

1. *Lives*, I, 20–21.

such as those that conclude the critical section of the Life of Pope, are always balanced by a hint of detraction. A eulogy beginning:

Pope had, in proportions very nicely adjusted to each other, all the qualities that constitute genius . . .

may end:

The construction of his language is not always strictly grammatical; . . . nor was he very careful to vary his terminations or to refuse admission at a small distance to the same rhymes.[1]

The ferrule is always to Johnson's hand, ready for use. And, in any case, his enthusiasm for Dryden and Pope is limited to their technical achievement: he is no more impressed by their attitudes than the next man. They 'reformed our numbers' – but the 'metaphysical morality' of Pope's *Essay on Man* is relentlessly deflated: 'Never were penury of knowledge and vulgarity of sentiment so happily disguised.'[2] Dryden purified our diction and versification; but *The Hind and the Panther* is based on a fable 'full of absurdity', and though *Absalom and Achitophel* possesses, as a political poem, 'all the excellences of which the subject is susceptible: acrimony of censure, elegance of praise, artful delineation of characters . . .', yet its construction is beyond repair:

We are alarmed by a faction formed out of many sects various in their principles, but agreeing in their purpose of mischief, formidable for their numbers and strong by their supports, while the king's friends are few and weak. The chiefs on either part are set forth to view; but when expectation is at the height, the king makes a speech . . .[3]

The critical balance, in the Lives of Dryden and Pope, seems just right: a total sympathy with the artistic ends of the two poets, and a shameless scepticism concerning everything else.

Johnson's *Lives* mark the end of an era – an era that began with Dryden's essays of the 1660s, and which shared some

1. ibid., III, 247, 249.
2. ibid., III, 243.
3. ibid., I, 436–7.

common assumptions about the nature of poetry which are called neoclassical. But the more talk there is about neoclassicism, the less interesting Dryden, Addison, Pope, Fielding, and Johnson will look. A common denominator of doctrine – any doctrine – is always likely to be uninteresting. It is, in any case, hardly more than a historian's tool: no European critic can be produced who believed in the whole of neoclassical doctrine as scholars now expound it. And, ultimately, it does not matter whether Dryden, or Johnson, believed in it or not: the critic's strategy in the field, like any good general's, is likely to vary with the needs of the moment, and the study of theory is more likely to reveal his characteristic manner of excuse and justification than to produce any other result of intrinsic interest. Criticism is incurably pragmatic: Dryden will write blank verse if it suits him to do so, and Addison's love of *Paradise Lost*, or Johnson's admiration for the *Rape of the Lock*, is instinctive rather than principled. And, of course – overwhelming objection – theory has no future. The elaborate psychological and physiological theories of the Augustan aestheticians concerning the nature of beauty have now only the melancholy interest of deserted ruins. They are not even worth contradicting, for the most part, and (for the most part) no one in print ever troubled to contradict them. An occasional law, like that of the unities of time and place, finds its refutation, but on the whole Augustan aesthetic debates are neither talked out nor talked down: they simply fail to generate debate at all. For the solid achievement of this first continuous century in the English critical tradition, one must surely look beyond theory altogether.

That achievement may best, perhaps, be described as a historical one. Before Dryden, formal literary analysis had no purpose and therefore no existence, but Dryden's realization that an English tradition of poetry existed as a court of appeal against foreign laws, at a moment when French literary influence was almost overpowering, made criticism useful: his analysis of Jonson's *Silent Woman*, and his defensive prefaces, are stages in a literary war in which the chief prize is the English past, 'the giant race before the flood'. The assertion, once made, started a debate, and by Addison's time analysis had become almost a habit. The second stage, marked by the career of Johnson, is historical in a more precise sense: the endeavour now is a scholarly one.

Johnson dominates this stage so completely that it is easy to forget he is not the whole of it, or even (in a strict sense) the pioneer. His *Dictionary*, and his editorial labours upon Shakespeare, are both deeply derivative. Thomas Warton's *Observations on the Fairy Queen* (1754) had, on Johnson's own generous admission, shown him the importance of the poet's background in its analysis of Spenser's Arthurian and (in its second edition of 1762) of his Italian sources. *An Essay on the Writings and Genius of Mr Pope* (1756–82), by Thomas's elder brother Joseph Warton, headmaster of Winchester College, was a laborious, poem-by-poem analysis of Pope's works on Longinian principles, devoted to the absurd task of showing that, if 'the sublime and the pathetic are the two chief nerves of all genuine poesy', then Pope does not belong to the highest rank of poets – a conclusion implicit in the premiss, if conclusion ever was, but curiously attractive in its naïve solemnity. Johnson, no doubt seriously, called this schoolmasterly undertaking 'a book which teaches how the brow of Criticism may be smoothed, and how she may be enabled, with all her severity, to attract and to delight'.[1] From the 1750s onwards, the emotional as well as the sheerly cognitive foundations of historical criticism are rapidly laid: nostalgia for the past, as in Richard Hurd's *Letters on Chivalry and Romance* (1762); biography and gossip, in Horace Walpole's *Catalogue of the Royal and Noble Authors of England* (1758), and Johnson's *Lives*; edited texts like Bishop Percy's *Reliques of Ancient English Poetry* (1765), Thomas Tyrwhitt's *Canterbury Tales* (1775–8), and Malone's Shakespeare (1790); and full-scale literary history in Thomas Warton's *History of English Poetry* (1774–81) which, unfinished as it is, carries the story through three bulky volumes from the eleventh

1. ibid., III, 236.

century to about 1600. And the Rowley controversy occasioned by Chatterton's *Poems* (1777), like the Ossian controversy of the 1760s, shows that for Johnson's day the poetry of the Middle Ages had become as disputed as Elizabethan poets had been for Dryden and Rymer. The historians have happily labelled these names – Hurd, Walpole, Percy, the Wartons, Macpherson, and Chatterton – as 'transitional' or 'pre-romantic'. But is it so clear that their attitude to medieval poetry, at once affectionate, hesitant, and condescending, is in *any* way different from that of Coleridge in his loving parody of the ballad 'The Ancient Mariner', or of Keats in buying his 'black-letter Chaucer', which he at once determined to have 'bounden gothique'?[1] Percy is utterly at one with Coleridge when he presents his ballads, in the dedication to his *Reliques*, 'not as labours of art but as effusions of nature, shewing the first efforts of ancient genius, and exhibiting the customs and opinions of remote ages' (p.vi): he even interpolated modern, literary ballads into his collection, to make his medievalia tolerable to polite readers. Such precautions are as much 'romantic' as 'pre-romantic', and persisted well into the nineteenth century, until overtaken by German research techniques of history and the Higher Criticism. The great document of eighteenth-century medievalism, Gibbon's *Decline and Fall* (1776–88), lies outside our subject but belongs utterly here in terms of chronology, and in terms of ethos too.

In face of such dates, Johnson's claim to be a pioneer of the historical method in criticism is thin indeed, and he never attempted to make it. But his is the only formidable critical intelligence in this parade of names. The writings of the Warton brothers, to whom he avowedly owed much, seem desperately lacking in intellectual pressure. Thomas Warton's *History* is just the kind of book a man does not finish, and it is no wonder either that his elder brother Joseph, who outlived Thomas by ten years, failed to finish it for him. They may have discouraged as well as provoked

1. Letter to J. H. Reynolds (3 May 1818).

originality. Thomas Gray[1] in the 1750s had planned to write a history of English poetry with his friend William Mason, and even detailed his plan in a letter to Thomas Warton (15 April 1770), based upon the Drydenesque theory of 'schools' of poetry – three 'Italian' schools of Chaucer, Spenser, and Donne, and the 'School of France' initiated by Waller and Dryden – rather than upon Warton's chronological scheme, and the loss seems nearly as great as the earlier loss of Dryden's history in favour of Rymer's. *The Observations on the Faery Queen* retains, it is true, a certain pallid interest in its laborious attempt to create a sense of intellectual background, and it explains what would otherwise be unexplainable – how the nineteenth century came to see Spenser as a romantic, visionary poet, Coleridge's 'mind constitutionally tender, delicate, and . . . effeminate',[2] before C. S. Lewis, in his *Allegory of Love* (1936), restored to us a poet of rugged Protestantism and almost muscular Christianity. 'Sensibility' is simply a quality invented by Thomas Warton and later romantic critics to justify Spenser's lack of architectonics:

> Spenser, and the same may be said of Ariosto, did not live in an age of planning. His poetry is the careless exuberance of a warm imagination and a strong sensibility. . . . Exactness in his poem would have been like the cornice which a painter introduced in the grotto of Calypso. Spenser's beauties are like the flowers of paradise.[3]

This is nonsense, and the wonder is that anyone can ever have read the *Faerie Queene* for long without realizing it to be nonsense. And yet there is no doubt that Warton has read the poem, and marshalled its qualities under such general

---

1. *Correspondence of Thomas Gray*, edited by Paget Toynbee and Leonard Whibley (Oxford, 1935), pp. 1122–5. Gray admits to Warton that his scheme is based on 'a scribbled paper of Pope' discovered after his death by his friend Warburton, who sent it to Mason. Warton, in the preface to his *History* (1774), calls Gray's sketch 'that of Mr Pope, considerably enlarged, extended, and improved'.

2. *Biographia Literaria* (1817), ch. 2.

3. *Observations*, sect. 1.

headings as 'Of Spenser's stanza, versification, and language', where he is notably severe upon the Spenserian stanza, which 'led our author into many absurdities'.

Only two other eighteenth-century critics seem worthy of notice, and they are both Shakespeareans. Maurice Morgann (1726–1802) is credited, for his *Essay on the Dramatic Character of Sir John Falstaff* (1777), with the creation of the school of character-analysis in Shakespearean criticism later consummated in Bradley's *Shakespearean Tragedy* (1904). The title certainly belongs to Morgann more naturally than to Coleridge, whose claim to be a character-critic is based on a few familiar quotations torn out of context. And Morgann, in his pleasant, amateur fashion – the *Essay* was written for a dare, and apologetically offered to the reader as a 'mere experiment' and a 'novelty' (pp. 7–8) – is an impressive analyst of character, well aware (like Bradley) of the pitfalls of his own technique:

But what have we to do, may my readers exclaim, with principles so latent, so obscured? In dramatic composition the impression is the fact; and the writer who, meaning to impress one thing, has impressed another, is unworthy of observation (p. 4).

This is a welcome assurance: but it is none the less true that Morgann's demonstration of Falstaff as no 'constitutional coward' offends precisely in this way, by supposing the revealed facts about Falstaff's career to be more important that the impression of what happens on the stage.

The other Shakespearean is at once more interesting and more obscure. Walter Whiter (1758–1832), Fellow of Clare College, Cambridge, and later a dissolute Norfolk clergyman, was a critic whose claim to be considered the founder of imagery-analysis might be called unassailable, if it were not for the known fact that his work passed unnoticed until the present century. Coleridge, and G. Wilson Knight and Wolfgang Clemen in our own times, seem to have owed nothing to him,[1] though they might have owed the very

1. The references to Whiter in the revised, English edition of Clemen's *The Development of Shakespeare's Imagery* (1951) (pp. 13, 74n.) are late ad-

principles of their procedures. Because of this neglect – a neglect that Whiter himself bitterly resented – his 'Attempt to Explain and Illustrate Various Passages on a New Principle of Criticism, Derived from Mr Locke's Doctrine of the Association of Ideas'[1] is now merely a curiosity. Whiter's thesis was brilliantly original. It was that Locke's theory of association in the *Essay Concerning Human Understanding* (1690) provided a technique for interpreting and emending the text of Shakespeare:

Ideas ... always keep in company, and the one no sooner at any time comes into the understanding, but its associate appears with it...[2]

Shakespeare's images, as Whiter shows by example upon example based on Malone's edition of 1790, are linked by just such subconscious associations. Hanmer, Johnson, Steevens, and Malone, for example, had all preferred the emendation 'mossed' to 'moist' in Apemantus's speech in *Timon*, IV, iii:

> What, think'st
> That the bleake ayre, thy boysterous chamberlaine,
> Will put thy shirt on warme? Will these moyst trees
> That have out-liv'd the eagle, page thy heeles
> And skip when thou point'st out?

But, argues Whiter, '*warm* and *moist* were the appropriate terms in the days of Shakespeare for what we should how call an *air'd* and a *damp* shirt ... Can the reader doubt (though he may perhaps smile at the association) that the image of the Chamberlain putting the shirt on *warm* impressed the oppos-

---

ditions, and are not to be found in the first, German edition of 1936. Wilson Knight does not mention Whiter at all. His effective rediscovery can be attributed to Professor J. Isaacs in *A Companion to Shakespeare Studies* (Cambridge 1934), pp. 312–13, 320, and to a leading article in *The Times Literary Supplement*, (5 September 1936), after the first studies by Wilson Knight and Caroline Spurgeon had appeared.

1. The second part of *A Specimen of a Commentary on Shakespeare* (1794). The first part of the book is a commentary on *As You Like It*.

2. Locke, *Essay* (1690), 11, 33.

ite word *moist* on the imagination of the poet? Though he was himself unconscious how he came by it . . .'[1] For some two hundred pages Whiter pursues his point with pedantic zeal: one can only wonder how different nineteenth-century Shakespearean criticism would have looked if Coleridge had read this book. But his refinement of the historical imagination, which almost involves the critic in the psychoanalysis of his poet, came too soon and fell dead from the press.

1. *A Specimen of a Commentary on Shakespeare*, edited by Alan Over (1967), pp. 71–2.

CHAPTER 5

WORDSWORTH AND COLERIDGE

THE achievement of Coleridge is rightly held to be supreme among the English critics, but no one seeking to expound it can face his task with much confidence. Existing expositions, often by the most influential of modern critics, bear so little resemblance to one another that it is difficult to believe they are about the same works, and the most famous of them all, I. A. Richards's *Coleridge on Imagination* (1934), seems to bear little relation to any text of Coleridge. And no wonder, since his criticism is only now in process of being adequately edited for the first time. Meanwhile, Professor Wellek has reconstructed the evidence for maintaining that few, if any, of the philosophical doctrines on which Coleridge based his aesthetic were original to him, and that his chief importance is as a 'mediator' between Germany and England.[1] And worst of all, the very nature of Coleridge's texts forever defies clear analysis: of the seven major series of lectures he is known to have delivered, only three or four have substantially survived, and those in texts which he did not himself prepare for the press; his notebooks suffer from the usual confusions of notebooks; his first major critical essay (if one may so describe Wordsworth's 1800 preface to the *Lyrical Ballads*) was written by somebody else; and the only critical book which appeared in his own lifetime, the *Biographia Literaria* (1817), is so discursive and so sporadic in its arguments as almost to merit its subtitle 'Biographical Sketches'. It is really not at all surprising if the commentators have failed to agree. The intriguing aspect of the mystery is that, while they have failed to agree on what Coleridge actually said,

1. René Wellek, *A History of Modern Criticism* (New Haven, 1955–), II, p. 151.

they are nearly all agreed that it was of the first importance.

Coleridge himself would have sympathized with the principle that the inductive process is an illusion, that one must begin with an affirmation. For all the diversity of Coleridge's criticism, it is safe to begin by asserting that its object is not analysis, but a theoretical certainty – 'to reduce criticism to a system', as he put it in a letter to Byron (15 October 1815), 'by the deduction of the causes from principles involved in our faculties'; or, again, in the *Biographia Literaria*, 'to establish the principles of writing rather than to furnish rules how to pass judgement on what has been written by others' (ch. 18). This is the language of a theoretical critic – of one, indeed, operating on a level of abstraction remote even by the ordinary standards of aestheticians. For Coleridge, ultimately, only a theory of poetic creation matters: he analyses, not so much poems as they exist, but the creative act that made them what they are.

Now this is an interest of revolutionary significance. No English critic since Dryden had much concerned himself with the question of the poetic process, and Dryden's interest had been little better than a passing one, based on his acquaintance with Hobbesian psychology.[1] For eighteenth-century critics, a poem is simply there, and it is the variety or uniformity of human reactions to it that is worth discussing. But with Coleridge, by contrast, creation is central. In his criticism there is no hypothesis of the ideal reader, or of the average reader corresponding to Johnson's consensus of informed opinion down the ages. There is just Coleridge. Whether he is reading Shakespeare or Wordsworth or Jeremy Taylor, we are frankly invited to see in them what Coleridge sees in them. There might be no 'problem of the reader' at all, so unaware is he of any such thing. But then, for Coleridge, a poem is not a machine, and you cannot

1. It is confined to three texts, two of them very early: the prefaces to *The Rival Ladies* (1664) and *Annus Mirabilis* (1667), and the 'Parallel betwixt Painting and Poetry' prefixed to his translation of Fresnoy's *Art of Painting* (1695).

write it off, as Johnson or I. A. Richards might do, by taking it to pieces and showing that it does not work. It is, for better or worse, evidence of a historical event, tempting inquiry into origins and sources. The question of values is scarcely a prominent aspect of his criticism, and Coleridge hardly ever tells you whether he thinks a poem good or bad. The nearest approach he is ready to make is to discuss some issue of category, such as in the eighteenth chapter of the *Biographia Literaria*, where he debates whether a mere 'metrical composition' is indeed a poem or some other thing; or in his celebrated argument in the same book on the superiority of poems of imagination over poems of fancy.

Coleridge, then, unlike Johnson, is essentially a critic who practises descriptive criticism primarily as illustration. His analysis of Wordsworth's poems in the second half of the *Biographia Literaria* is not gratuitous in the sense that Johnson's analysis of *Paradise Lost* in his Life of Milton might be called gratuitous: it is not, that is, based on any Johnsonian assumption that the analysis of existing works of literature might be usefully pursued for its own sake. I shall try to show later that the lectures on Shakespeare too have an ulterior, theoretical purpose; though they were delivered on commission, and suggest some concessions to the demands of an audience. If this is right, it might easily be argued that Coleridge's criticism represents a regression in the history of descriptive criticism in English. It certainly represents an interruption, and it should be honestly admitted at once that the interruption did not have very fruitful consequences. There is no immediate School of Coleridge among the English critics. The young men who crowded to his house in Highgate in the last years of his life, among whom (according to Carlyle) he enjoyed the reputation of a sage, sought wisdom of a kind too generalized and too occult to turn them into good critics – indeed, into any kind of critic. The Victorians could not be expected to understand what in his criticism he was talking about: some of his texts had not been printed, most had not been edited, and his criticism was nearly all of an order that would respond only to close and concentrated exegesis. Coleridge's influence is largely a twentieth-century one. He is a whole movement in himself, the first and last of his line, the one English critic to try, and to go on trying, to apply Kantian aesthetics to the past and present of English letters.

For Coleridge, then, right theory is a cause – *the* cause. The great defect of English criticism, he insists again and again, has been its lack of fixed standards, and his repeated attacks on the reviewers, tedious and self-interested as they undeniably are – the uncertain logical progressions of the *Biographia Literaria* is held up several times because Coleridge cannot stay away from the subject – have some justification when we remember that the personalities in which journalists indulged were at the far pole to his own critical ideal: 'Reviews are generally pernicious, because the writers determine without reference to fixed principles;.. because they teach people rather to judge than to consider, to decide than to reflect.'[1] That is a very Coleridgean emphasis: he saw himself surrounded by impetuous dabblers eager to know which were the good books and which the bad; whereas his own method presupposed a delicate and inquiring reverence for all of man's creation, and a passionate curiosity to explore its depths.

At its fullest extent, the whole body of Coleridgean criticism stretches over a period of more than thirty years, from the notes he scribbled in the autumn of 1800 for a preface to the second edition of the *Lyrical Ballads* down to the last note made by his nephew H. N. Coleridge of his conversation shortly before his death in 1834. The beginnings sound uncertain, but there can be little doubt that the inspiration of the 1800 preface was Coleridge's. Wordsworth, years later, insisted it was so, and Coleridge, in a letter of 1802, talks of having turned over his notes for the preface, which he had originally intended to write himself. One of his notes, indeed, survives, containing the phrase 'the recalling

1. *Shakespearean Criticism*, edited by T. M. Raysor (Cambridge, Mass., 1930), 11, 57–8.

of passion in tranquillity'[1] evidently the ancestor of the most famous phrase of the preface, 'emotion recollected in tranquillity'. On the other hand, there can be no doubt that Wordsworth was the actual author of the 1800 preface. Its language is of a plushiness, a rotundity, that is eminently Wordsworthian, and utterly different from the feverish, button-holing intimacy of Coleridge's prose. (It is one great rhetorical defect of the preface that, whereas its argument assumes prose to be stylistically more commonplace than verse, its own prose is of polished stateliness that is the child of Johnson and Gibbon.) And in any case – final proof of Wordsworthian composition – it concerns itself solely with Wordsworth's own contributions to the *Lyrical Ballads*. To read the 1800 preface, you would never guess that the collection to which it is prefixed contains 'The Rime of the Ancient Mariner'.

There is no need, however, to father upon Wordsworth the logical incongruities of the 1800 preface. Coleridge's own thinking about aesthetics was confused in much the same way, as his early letters show, and the preface is as likely to be a distorting mirror of his own confusions as an example of Wordsworth's inability to theorize. It is, in all probability, both: Coleridge would never have tolerated such a formulation as this:

Poetry is the spontaneous overflow of powerful feelings: it takes its origin from emotion recollected in tranquillity: the emotion is contemplated till, by a species of reaction, the tranquillity gradually disappears, and an emotion, kindred to that which was before the subject of contemplation, is gradually produced, and does itself actually exist in the mind.

The idea of a double creative process could easily be Coleridgean, but the 'is' of the first sentence is utterly Wordsworthian – the verb 'to be' holding a fascination for him that

1. *Notebooks*, edited by Kathleen Coburn (New York, 1957–), no. 787 and note. L. A. Willoughby has shown that the phrase echoes one by Schiller in an early review of 1791; see *German Studies Presented to H. G. Fiedler* (Oxford, 1938), pp. 443f.

was sometimes fatal[1] – and, in combination with the word 'spontaneous', it leads the reader into endless difficulties; for, in the light of the claims that follow, 'is' must equal something like 'is the final product of', and 'spontaneous' must indicate something unforced, and yet paradoxically deliberated. Wordsworth is badly out of his depth as a critic here: to a mind so forcefully bent upon human observation, the writing of the preface, as he later protested, must have been a most uncongenial distraction.

The movement of the 1800 preface is essentially a three-fold one, though Wordsworth's revision and expansion for the third edition of 1802 introduces a fourth element – ('What is a poet?') – between the first and the second, and indeed a fifth in the form of an Appendix. First comes the notorious theory of the diction of poetry as 'a selection of language really used by men' – a cautious restatement of the phrase in the introductory note or 'Advertisement' to the first edition of 1798, which was almost entirely absorbed into the 1800 preface, 'the language of conversation in the middle and lower classes of society'. The history of this revision, from 1798 to 1800 to 1802, is one of increasingly defensive vagueness and, alas, of increasing logical incongruity: Wordsworth, in trying to extricate himself, only succeeds in getting in deeper and deeper. For his theory of language leads him into a discussion of metre which, he is forced to admit, is a merely 'superadded' and 'adventitious' attraction, exposing himself in an assertion as vulnerable as critic ever made: 'There neither is, nor can be, any *essential* difference between the language of prose and metrical composition.' From this the preface moves into the third most positive, and (perhaps) most Coleridgean section: an attempt to analyse the creative act of the poet. But by now the difficulties of reconciling the parts of the argument are

1. cf. his 1800 note on 'The Thorn': 'Poetry is passion: it is the history or science of feelings'; or, magnificently from the 'Song at the Feast of Brougham Castle' (1807), ll. 163–4:
The silence that is in the starry sky,
The sleep that is among the lonely hills.

so vast that it seems embarrassing to begin to pose them: in what sense, for example, can the process of linguistic selection which Wordsworth began by recommending be reconciled with the rapt condition he now suggests as proper to the poet? Coleridge's attack on the preface, culminating in chapters 17–20 of the *Biographia Literaria*, seems graceless in its determination to pursue its quarry to the end: the more so, when we remember that Coleridge had been its chief begetter. But his careful and sensible insistence upon the differences that properly distinguish the language of poetry, and his call for 'a certain aloofness', is all fumblingly anticipated by Wordsworth himself in his revision of 1802. The Appendix completes the drift away from the purely imitative, almost photographically naturalistic, theories of the Advertisement in its self-contradictory admission that 'the first poets . . . spake a language which though unusual was still the language of men.' (But if men really spoke it, in what sense was it unusual?) Wordsworth knew that something had gone wrong, and he attempted criticism again only in the three *Essays upon Epitaphs* of 1809–10 and in the 1815 preface to his poems, with its 'Essay Supplementary'. These complete the defensive withdrawal from 'the language of conversation'. After 1815 there is no more. He may also have sensed, and rightly, that it was not his fault. After all, he had never wanted to be a critic.

Coleridge's *Biographia Literaria* (1817), hastily written in the summer of 1815, is a summary attempt to marshal objections against the preface that had been growing up in his mind over the past fifteen years, and to provide criticism with a systematic basis of its own. Its curious structure – largely metaphysical in its first half, largely critical in its second, and (in spite of its title) only sporadically autobiographical – may be accidental, or the result of a hasty decision: but at least it has the merit of balancing the two great interests of his career, philosophy and poetry. Indeed, the structure of the book might have been its greatest triumph, if only the connection had been well and truly made between the two sections, at chapters 12 and 13. As it is, Coleridge fails to make clear the vital link between Kantian meta-physics and his distinction between imagination and fancy; and when he takes up the story again, in Chapter 14, with an account of the genesis of the *Lyrical Ballads*, its 1800 pre-face, and the ensuing controversy, the reader may be forgiven for failing to grasp where the connection lies. Chapter 13, indeed, is the Waterloo of English aesthetics – oddly enough, it was probably written within a few weeks of the battle – in that, at the very moment when Coleridge is pro-pounding his theory of 'counteraction', he breaks off in mid-sentence and calls off the chase with a childish joke: a pretended letter from a friend urging him not to publish the present chapter in the *Biographia* at all, but to hold it over for some later work. And the result, of course, was that it was never written at all.

Still, it seems unjust and unwise to lay the emphasis else-where, and to read the *Biographia* primarily for its *obiter dicta* or its occasional biographical revelations. There is no doubt that, for Coleridge, the heart of the book lay in Chap-ter 12 and its ten 'theses', and a reconstruction of his argu-ment in this neglected chapter will carry us further towards the heart of his critical preoccupations than anything else. The movement of his argument is away from an initial, ten-tative dualism, much of it based upon his study of Schelling. 'All knowledge,' he begins, 'rests on the coincidence of an object with a subject ... The sum of all that is merely objec-tive we will henceforth call *nature* ... The sum of all that is subjective we may comprehend in the name of the *self* or intelligence.' But this assertion, common to much eight-eenth-century aesthetics and indeed to all Cartesian logic, is set up only to be knocked down. For if truth presupposes a knower and a known (Thesis I), it is also clear that many truths, far from being immediate and original, are derived from others (II). There must, he suggests rather hastily, be an ultimate truth, 'self-grounded, unconditional, and known by its own light' (III), and it must be unique (IV). Neither objective nor subjective, it is a fusion of both (V), a fusion Coleridge calls the Self or I AM (VI), which has a will to act (vii) and is neither finite nor infinite (viii).'In the reconciling and the recurrence of this contradiction', Coleridge goes on, 'consists the process and mystery of production and life.' At this point philosophy passes into religion (ix), a theism based on the conviction that the individual can only be a modification of a higher consciousness (x).

Theses i–iv, then, are the philosophical groundwork of the system, ix–x a religious superstructure that does not concern me here. Theses v–viii, however, are a revealing summary of Coleridge's view of the creative act. They show that, for him, the truth that the poet seeks is neither objective nor subjective; that is to say, it exists neither in the mind of the poet nor in what he sees about him, but in 'the identity of both', the one acting upon the other in 'a perpetual self-duplication'. 'The spirit, in all the objects which it views, views only itself', or, as he had put it in erse a dozen years before:

> O Lady! we receive but what we give,
> And in our life alone does nature live:
> Ours is her wedding-garment, ours her shroud![1]

This Kantian 'counteraction' of forces, as Coleridge calls it – the poet informing nature, even as he is informed by it – is driven or guided by the imagination, that 'essentially vital' force which, unlike the fancy, 'dissolves, diffuses, dissipates' the world around it.

The achievement of Kantian aesthetics, of which Coleridge is the one considerable English spokesman in his age, was to convert our notion of the creative act from the poet/nature dualism of eighteenth-century aesthetics and the 1800 preface into a puzzlingly circular process of endless counteraction. It follows, for Coleridge, that the outcome of such a process, the poem itself, is of a bafflingly difficult logical status. Coleridge, in the fragmentary Chapter 13, calls it a '*tertium aliquid*', being neither subject nor object but 'an interpenetration of the counteracting powers, partaking of both'; it is neither a thought nor a thing, but what Cole-

1. 'Dejection: an Ode' (1802), stanza iv; see *Notebooks*, no. 921.

ridge later called 'a middle quality'[1] between the two. By the very equivocation of its status, it is unique, answerable to no laws but its own.

In all this the debt to Kant is clear, and yet it does not amount to a case for denying Coleridge his originality as a critic; a reading of Kant, which he probably did not begin until his visit to Germany in 1798–9, only helped him to formalize his deepest intuitions concerning poetic creation. The evidence for saying so is in the *Biographia* and in the poems. According to his own account of his school-days, he learned as a boy from his schoolmaster that 'poetry . . . had a logic of its own as severe as that of science; and more difficult, because more subtle, more complex, and dependent on more, and more fugitive, causes'.[2] And 'Kubla Khan', probably written in May 1798, and surely the greatest triumph in English of what Mr F. W. Bateson would call 'the Critical Muse', shows how far a pre-Kantian Coleridge had already felt his way towards this revolutionary position. For the Khan too, like the poet, is intent on reconciling a contradiction, and the pleasure-dome that he decrees lies within 'twice five miles' of ordered gardens which yet contain a 'deep romantic chasm', where the river Alph is paradoxically forced, for all its violence, into a decoration for a despot:

> A mighty fountain momently was forced:
> Amid whose swift, half-intermittent burst
> Huge fragments vaulted like rebounding hail . . .

The roar of the 'fountain' and the caves is tamed into the 'mingled measure' of a work of art. The equation with poetry, in the last stanza, is almost explicit:

> I would build that dome in air,
> That sunny dome! those caves of ice!
> And all who heard should see them there . . .

1. 'On Poesy or Art' (lecture XIII, 1818), reprinted in *Biographia Literaria*, edited by J. Shawcross (Oxford, 1907), II, 254.
2. *Biographia Literaria* (1817), ch. I.

Unlike the Khan, the true poet certainly re-creates, in some sense, the objects which he sees and hears, and in a sense which Coleridge already felt to be unusual and terrifying, like the madness of the Platonic bard:

And all should cry, Beware! Beware!

The mass of descriptive criticism – notes, lectures, and published works – that Coleridge erected upon this grandiose theoretical foundation are less impressive, in themselves, than has sometimes been claimed, and hardly intelligible when divorced from his theory. Many an innocent reader, directed to read 'Coleridge on Wordsworth' or 'Coleridge on Shakespeare' as major texts of illumination, must have left them with a sense of puzzlement. What has all the fuss been about? How has such a discursive and inconclusive analyst of poetry won the reputation of the greatest English critic?

The answer is that Coleridge's descriptive criticism has too easily been divorced from its foundations, studied as if it were something other than variations upon a given theme, and not unnaturally found to be disappointing. The task of seeing it steadily within its framework of theory is not easy, and could not be easy even if Coleridge had left his writings in a final form. As it is, problems of transmission complicate a task which is already complicated in its nature.

Coleridge's descriptive criticism, in terms of subject, falls into three groups. First, there is the confused body of his Shakespearean criticism, principally in the 1811–12 lectures on Shakespeare and Milton, as well as various marginalia and notes; together with Chapter 15 of the *Biographia Literaria*, largely a revision of one of his lectures of 1811–12 and entitled 'The specific symptoms of poetic power elucidated in a critical analysis of Shakespeare's *Venus and Adonis* and *Lucrece*'. Second, there is the critique of Wordsworth in the *Biographia Literaria*, chapters 14, 17–20, and 22. And third, there is a vast miscellany of comments on various poets, mainly of the English seventeenth century, in lectures, marginalia, notes, and even formal treatises, such as the tribute to Samuel Daniel in the eighteenth chapter of the *Biographia*, or to Herbert's *Temple* in the nineteenth. The modern reputation of these, and some other, poets stems from such passing recommendations, though it is worth noticing at once that Coleridge is not much more sympathetic to the Metaphysical style than Johnson had been: the Herbert he discovered and loved is a 'well-bred gentleman' in his expressions whose language possesses a 'simple dignity', in spite of a 'too frequent quaintness of the thoughts'. Characteristically, Coleridge does not recommend the older English poets for their own virtues; his concern, as he explains at length in the sixteenth chapter of the *Biographia*, is to unite their 'characteristic merits' with those of his own age to form an ideal poetic language.

Coleridge's view of Shakespeare survives, unfortunately, mainly in the form of lecture-notes of varying authenticity. His whole career as a lecturer deserves a quick review. He is known, for certain, to have delivered seven major series (or groups) of lectures, of which only three or four substantially survive. The first, delivered in Bristol between January and November 1796, on historical and political questions, survives only in notes. The second, given in London at the Royal Institution from January to June 1808 and entitled 'Principles of Poetry', being mainly on Shakespeare and Milton, is largely lost: a profoundly complicating factor, since A. W. Schlegel was delivering his own course on the drama in Vienna at the same time, and the loss leaves the question of Coleridge's alleged plagiarism of Schlegel forever uncertain. The third course (18 November 1811 to 27 January 1812) is the chief single source of our knowledge of Coleridge's Shakespearean criticism, being delivered near Fetter Lane, in London, under the inaccurate title 'Shakespear and Milton in Illustration of the Principles of Poetry, and their Application as Grounds of Criticism to the... Later English Poets'; it has survived in two reports by members of his audience. As in 1808, he hoped to reach the poets of his own age and, as in 1808, he failed to do so. Fourthly, Coleridge gave at least two series of lectures in the course of

1812 on classic and romantic drama, largely lost. Fifthly, he gave several courses in Bristol in 1813 and 1814 on Shakespeare, Milton, and various political issues, of which we have only newspaper reports. Sixthly, from January to March 1818 he delivered, again near Fetter Lane, a course which remains our chief source of his non-Shakespearean criticism, a survey of English poetry from the Middle Ages to the Restoration, which survives in autograph notes and in reports. And seventh, from December 1818 to March 1819, in the Strand, he delivered a course of lectures on the history of philosophy, which has survived in shorthand notes,[1] and, concurrently, two successive literary courses that have not survived at all.

We are fully entitled to feel confused. In spite of the efforts of his nephew Henry Nelson Coleridge, and of his daughter Sara, to collect such material and render it continuous, and in spite of the more scrupulous efforts of modern editors, the form in which Coleridge's analysis of Shakespeare and other poets has survived does not invite. It is not surprising if a good many strange notions are abroad concerning the nature of this material, based on repetitious quotations of a few extracts. Coleridge has commonly been called a character-critic, a follower of Maurice Morgann and an ancestor of A. C. Bradley, based on his famous remark, 'I have a smack of Hamlet myself, if I may say so.' More recently, an attempt has been made to represent him as an ancestor of G. Wilson Knight and the post-1930 school of imagery-analysis.[2] The second is certainly nearer the mark, but Coleridge, though interested in imagery, can hardly be said to analyse it; he never examines the text of an entire play or poem with a view to isolating single images or systems of imagery. As for character-analysis, the claim is evidently absurd. The general temper of Coleridge's mind was too

1. First published as *Philosophical Lectures*, edited by Kathleen Coburn (1949).
2. Barbara H. Hardy, 'A Smack of Hamlet', *Essays in Criticism*, VIII (1958), and M. M. Badawi, 'Coleridge's Formal Criticism of Shakespeare's Plays', ibid., X (1960).

abstract to encourage him to suppose that the motives of others – whether those others were real or fictional characters – were worthy of extensive analysis. Besides, Bradley's style of criticism was based upon an assumption that Shakespearean characters are as naturalistic as the characters of nineteenth-century novels; and if there is one species of literature Coleridge is not interested in, it is the novel. All the novels of Jane Austen and Walter Scott appeared during his working life, and yet there is only the barest comment on them in all his books and lectures. The whole quality of his mind was too abstract and too humanly disinterested to make it imaginable for him to pose any such question as 'How Many Children Had Lady Macbeth?' (Bradley, to do him belated justice, was well aware of the absurdity of this question, and said so.) The essential nature of Coleridge's Shakespearean criticism defies classification in terms of the great modern schools. It comes near to defying it in any terms, but if sense is to be made of it at all, it can only be in terms of Coleridge's own aesthetic principles.

The 1811–12 lectures on Shakespeare are a very explicit attempt to illustrate the principles of 'counteraction' and 'organic growth' in relation to the greatest of all the English poets. The poet, in Coleridge's view, does not create – he becomes; and a poem is not created – it grows, like a tree, as if with an inner life of its own. Shakespeare's works are handled as a vast illustration of the failure of Aristotle's principle of art as an imitation of nature, and the theoretical foundations are firmly laid before the illustrations are offered. This is what he is reported to have said in Lecture III:

Of Shakespeare he had often heard it said that he was a close copier of nature, that he was a child of nature, like a Dutch painter[1] copying exactly the object before him. He *was* a child of nature, but it was of human nature and of the most important of human nature. In the meanest characters, it was still Shakespeare: it was not the mere Nurse in *Romeo and Juliet*, or the Dogberry in *Much Ado about Nothing*, or the blundering Constable in

1. 'Dutchified' is a term of contempt in Coleridge for an excess of poetic detail. See *Shakespearean Criticism* (1930), 11, 174.

Measure for Measure, but it was this great and mighty being changing himself into the Nurse or the blundering Constable that gave delight ... Compare it to Proteus, who now flowed, a river; now raged, a fire; now roared, a lion ...

The attack here upon the whole neoclassical tradition of Shakespeare criticism, and especially upon Johnson's 1765 preface, is as plain as can be – upon Johnson's assertion that 'Shakespeare is, above all writers ... the poet of nature; the poet that holds up to his readers a faithful mirror of manners and of life.'

The most sustained attempt to analyse a Shakespeare play according to the new mode is to be found in Coleridge's account of *The Tempest* in the ninth lecture of the 1811–12 series. This lecture, in Collier's report, is a comprehensive attack on neo-Aristotelian dramatic criticism, including the three unities; and especially against the French neoclassical critics, such as Voltaire. 'These creatures,' Coleridge observes acidly, 'have informed us that Shakespeare is a miraculous monster, in whom many heterogeneous components were thrown together, producing a discordant mass of genius – an irregular and ill-assorted structure of gigantic proportions.' He then turns to *The Tempest* 'by way of example'. It proves to be an example of 'organic', as against 'mechanic', regularity – Coleridge is, of all the English critics, the fondest of abstract distinctions – and this distinction is very like the one R. G. Collingwood was to draw, more than a century later, between 'art' and 'craft'; for while a mechanic object is moulded in identical form to its prototype, an organic one, such as a Shakespearean character, conceals 'a law which all the parts obey, conforming themselves to the outward symbols and manifestations of the essential principle'. A Shakespearean character, in fact, is not pre-determined: it shapes itself according to circumstances, and the poet acquires knowledge of how his puppets would react by an act of empathy. Gonzalo's surprisingly moderate reaction to the Boatswain's rudeness during the storm in the first scene of the play, Coleridge continues ('I have great comfort from this fellow ...'), shows how Shakespeare 'transports himself into the very being of each personage', and so does Miranda's first sight of the ship ('A brave vessel, Who had, no doubt, some noble creature in her, Dash'd all to pieces'), since Shakespeare has felt his way into the mind of an unknowing girl who has seen only Prospero and Caliban. This is the characteristic tactic of analysis of Shakespeare's plays and poems, and his conclusion may be simply stated. It is that Shakespeare's supremacy among the English poets lies, not (as Johnson supposed) in the richness and detail of his observation – no 'mere observation' of old women, he concludes, could in itself have produced the portrait of the garrulous Nurse in *Romeo and Juliet* – but in the wide sympathy that enables him to identify himself at will:

The great prerogative of genius . . . is now to swell itself to the dignity of a god, and now to subdue and keep dormant some part of that lofty nature, and to descend even to the lowest character – to become everything, in fact . . . (Lecture VII, 1811–12)

Everything 'but the vicious', Coleridge adds, with an unexpected intrusion of simplicity. It is easy to forget that he believed in his theory of counteraction in a literal sense, and not as metaphor.

Coleridge's aesthetic might have been expected to find its ideal illustration in the critique of Wordsworth that dominates the second half of the *Biographia Literaria*, following immediately upon the most comprehensive account he ever wrote of that aesthetic in chapters 12–13. He has a perfect – indeed, all too easy – target in the 1800 preface, where neo-Aristotelianism achieves its final *reductio ad absurdum*. And the poetry of Wordsworth lends itself to the kind of distinction-making in which Coleridge delights. Its inequalities provoke a reasoned explanation, and the Imagination/Fancy distinction defined in Chapter 4, and again in Chapter 13, was never used to better purpose than here:

I challenge for this poet the gift of imagination in the highest and strictest sense of the word. In the play of fancy Wordsworth, to my feelings, is not always graceful, and sometimes recondite. The likeness is occasionally too strange, or demands too peculiar a point of view, or is such as appears the creature of predetermined research rather than spontaneous presentation (ch. 22).

This account seemed just, when were call that, whereas the imagination is given to 're-create, ... idealize, ... unify', the fancy 'has no other counters to play with but fixities and definites' and is a mere 'mode of memory' (ch. 13). Here, indeed, are the two Wordsworths, and Coleridge was the first critic to demonstrate how oddly they coexist, and how intimately:

> 'Once I could meet with them on every side,
> But they have dwindled long by slow decay;
> Yet still I persevere, and find them where I may.'
>
> While he was talking thus, the lonely place,
> The old man's shape, and speech, all troubled me;
> In my mind's eye I seemed to see him pace
> About the weary moors continually,
> Wandering about alone and silently.[1]

It is the leech-gatherer who speaks, and the first stanza is 'fanciful' indeed, the merest reportàge. The second stanza, as Coleridge notes, belongs to another order of experience.

Still, the entire critique suffers in the end from its status as a mere illustration. The stylistic theories of the 1800 preface are efficiently exploded, indeed, and the case is made in chapters 19 and 20 for a new poetic diction, based upon a study of some of the older poets, notably Chaucer, Daniel, and Herbert: a diction based on a *lingua communis* or 'neutral style' of English, which is 'natural', 'unstudied', and 'logical'. For a moment Coleridge flirts with a legislative purpose in his criticism. But the role of an arbiter of literary fashion was never a congenial one to him, doomed to unsuccess as he felt himself to be, and his repeated failure in lectures to consider the state of contemporary poetry surely suggests a strong distaste for the part. And descriptive criti-

1. From 'Resolution and Independence' (1807), quoted in ch. 22 of the *Biographia*.

cism, too, is sent to the tradesmen's entrance. For an analysis of Wordsworth's verse as such, we have to wait till Chapter 22, with its long catalogue of Wordsworth's 'defects' and 'beauties'. And even here, the approach is abstract: poems are marshalled under eleven heads – five defects and six excellences – and provided with illustrative texts from the *Lyrical Ballads* and the poems of 1807 and 1815. Only this chapter, in the whole book, deserves the title of extended analysis, and it is the longest single analysis that Coleridge ever ventured.

Hasty as its composition evidently was, and extravagant in its wealth of quotation, the critique of Wordsworth is scattered with evidences of an analytical delicacy and insight that deserve the title of greatness, though they are too occasional and too sporadic to unite into a major critique. Coleridge's rich capacity for perceiving and identifying distinctions is at last directed to a particular end, though his judgements are still more generalized than we should think natural today – no less generalized, indeed, than Johnson's had been. The five defects, and less clearly the six excellences, are ranged in ascending order of generality: both lists begin with the questions of style, and end with questions of subject, so that the very ordering of Wordsworth's trial, admirably inclusive as it is, is weighted in favour of a certain kind of philosophical amplitude. Not that Coleridge overvalues the philosophical element in poetry: he is almost uncharitably funny about his old friend's endless solemnity when he protests that

the feelings with which, as Christians, we contemplate a mixed congregation rising or kneeling before their common Maker, Mr Wordsworth would have us entertain at all times, as men and as readers.

But he is eager to make the case for the unique intellectual task of a poet who, when he can forget his pettier preoccupations, is fully capable of raising poetry to the function of original thought. The five defects are 'inconstancy' of style, 'matter-of-factness' (or a 'laborious minuteness of detail), 'an over-fondness for the dramatic form', 'an intensity of feeling disproportionate to such knowledge and value of the objects described as can fairly be anticipated' or 'verbal bombast', and 'thoughts and images too great for the subject' or 'mental bombast'. It does not matter that the list of Wordsworth's excellences that follows contradicts much of this indictment; Coleridge's whole case is based on the conviction that there are two Wordsworths, and that his poems are marked by incongruity on every level. 'An austere purity of language' is the first, followed by 'a correspondent weight and sanity of the thoughts and sentiments', 'the sinewy strength and originality of single lines and paragraphs', 'truth of nature in his images and descriptions', 'a meditative pathos', and 'the gift of imagination'. The scheme allows him opportunities for closer analysis than one might expect: not, in general, in the wealth of quotations, which are offered merely as illustrative of general qualities, but in Coleridge's loving concern for the quality which distinguishes a Wordsworthian poem from any other:

a sympathy with man as man; the sympathy indeed of a contemplator, rather than a fellow-sufferer or co-mate,... but of a contemplator from whose view no difference of rank conceals the sameness of the nature; no injuries of wind or weather, of toil or even of ignorance, wholly disguise the human face divine...

It is difficult to summarize, in historical terms, the achievement of a critic whose influence had been as delayed, and as problematical as that of Coleridge. His overriding interest in the creative process was one which later nineteenth-century critics did not share, and it is not clear that, in our own century, he has taught such modern admirers as I. A. Richards, T. S. Eliot, or G. Wilson Knight anything as critics which they would not have thought of for themselves. Most modern parallels are decidedly *post facto*: the alleged likeness of Coleridge's Shakespearean criticism to the modern school of imagery-analysis was not suggested until nearly thirty years after the appearance of *The Wheel of Fire* (1930). Coleridge's aesthetic could not appeal to a generation of Victorians to whom no system of aesthetics was of much interest. As a descriptive critic, his achievement is brilliant but sporadic, and offers no single example worthy to be advanced as a model. If his criticism survives, as it vigorously does, it is not by virtue of what it demonstrates but by what it abundantly suggests, for no English critic has so excelled at providing profitable points of departure for his succeeding century. Perhaps there is something perverse about a professional sage who had so little to say that was comprehensible to his own century; but, a hundred years later, his manuscripts, as they belatedly see print, seem among the richest of our capital treasures. They are the relics of a mind passionately in love with free inquiry, concentrated and disciplined in its determination to decipher the secret of poetic discourse. The obsession is an eccentric one, in English terms: a culture as intensively literary as that of England has little reason to pose questions about literature which are as abstract and as sceptical as those which Coleridge, for thirty years, struggled to answer.

CHAPTER 6

LAMB, HAZLITT, DE QUINCEY

THERE is no School of Coleridge in nineteenth-century English criticism, and the achievement of Charles Lamb (1775-1834), Coleridge's friend since their schooldays at Christ's Hospital, suggests in its minor distinction how difficult and confusing a master Coleridge must have seemed. Lamb's criticism, almost all descriptive apart from a late essay on 'Stage Illusion', is tiny in its scope. It could be collected – and has been collected[1] – into a slim volume of less than fifty thousand words, and survives as something altogether desultory, scattered through his letters, the apparatus of the *Specimens* (1808) and other editions of his favourite authors, the monthly and quarterly reviews, and of course *The Essays of Elia* (1823-33). Unmistakably Coleridgean in its subject-matter – it concerns itself overwhelmingly with such favourite subjects of Coleridge's as Elizabethan and Jacobean drama, the prose of Sir Thomas Browne, Jeremy Taylor, Fuller, and Walton, and contemporary romanticism – it looks timid and cautious when set beside the revolutionary assertions of some of his contemporaries. Everything points to a lack of confidence. But Lamb is one of those rare authors who can make a virtue of timidity and amateurishness. Throughout his long clerkship in East India House (1792-1825) he would never have pretended to be an 'important' critic, and only asks that he should be seen lucidly for what he is: a good friend and a good disciple whose critical intuitions possess, at the best, a delicacy unknown to more vigorous and ambitious intelligences than his own.

There are moments, none the less, when we feel that Lamb's real mentor is not Coleridge but Samuel Johnson, and it comes as a start, in view of Lamb's reputation as

1. *Lamb's Criticism*, edited by E. M. W. Tillyard (Cambridge, 1923).

leader of the nineteenth-century vogue for the quaint and
the baroque, to watch him inveigh as heavily as Johnson
might have done against medieval and Tudor extravagan-
ces, both literary and moral. The following judgement
against Marlowe could easily belong to some neoclassical
critic:

Tamburlaine ... comes in, drawn by conquered kings, and re-
proaches these 'pampered jades of Asia' that they can 'draw but
twenty miles a day'. Till I saw this passage with my own eyes, I
never believed that it was anything more than a pleasant burlesque
of mine ancient's. But I can assure my readers that it is soberly set
down in a play which their ancestors took to be serious.

and

Barabas the Jew, and Faustus the conjurer, arc offsprings of a mind
which at least delighted to dally with interdicted subjects.[1]

Only the 'quaint' reference to 'mine ancient' belongs to
the beloved Lamb of the Elians, forever tolerant and (in
spite of personal tragedy) forever good-humoured. The
sentiments belong to the world of Johnson's sound Anglican
moralism that makes no bones about being shocked and will
have no truck with the fanciful. There is much more of this
sort of thing in Lamb than is commonly remembered. The
moral assumptions of his criticism are not exactly stern. But
they are conventional, a part of that continuum of English
prudery that has its roots in eighteenth-century piety and
looks forward to the great Victorian self-censorship. The fact
is that his taste for Renaissance quaintness is only a degree
or two more developed than Johnson's, and hardly different
at all from that of the Wartons or of his friend Coleridge. It
is rather a symptom of the growth of popular historicism, of
the vogue for the 'Gothic' past, than of any determined
critical analysis. Lamb's taste for the seventeenth century is
sentimental, and scarcely more than sentimental: he could
no more abide the Metaphysical conceit than Coleridge
could, and preferred Wither, who 'lays more hold of the
heart', to Quarles's 'wretched stuff":

1. ibid., pp. 16, 17 (from the *Specimens* of 1808).

Religion appears to him no longer valuable than it furnishes matters for quibbles and riddles; he turns God's grace into wantonness. Wither is like an old friend . . .[1]

On the other hand, he can see virtues in Renaissance poetry less baroque than the imagery of Quarles, and yet too particular to have appealed to Johnson. Sidney's sonnets struck the mean that he loved best, 'full, material, and circumstantiated', in healthy contrast to late eighteenth-century verse, where there are too many 'vague and unlocalized feelings'.[2] Poetry *may* number the streaks of the tulip, in Lamb's view – perhaps ought to do so. The Johnsonian term 'Nature' resounds through his criticism, but it is a Nature strangely elastic in its scope, and includes even the matter of visions and of waking dreams. Where the poet

seems most to recede from humanity, he will be found the truest to it. From beyond the scope of Nature if he summon possible existences, he subjugates them to the law of her consistency. He is beautifully loyal to that sovereign directress, even when he appears most to betray and desert her . . . Caliban, the Witches, are as true to the laws of their own nature (ours with a difference) as Othello, Hamlet, and Macbeth.[3]

This is to liberalize neoclassicism out of existence. But it is very characteristic of Lamb that, in offering his own version of the Coleridgean doctrine of organic growth, he should clothe it in the familiar if incongruous language of eighteenth-century aesthetics.

A sound Johnsonian critic, then, partly romanticized by his reverence for Coleridge: this seems an apter summary of Lamb's quality as a critic than any view that conceives of him as the perfect prototype of the romantic critic. Wordsworth, Coleridge, Hazlitt, and De Quincey are all more romantic critics than Lamb, and all of them reject more firmly than he did the 'Aristotelian' criteria of critical

1. ibid., p. 67 (letter to Southey, 8 November 1798).
2. ibid., p. 13 ('Some Sonnets of Sir Philip Sydney', in *Last Essays of Elia*).
3. ibid., p. 5 ('Sanity of True Genius', in *Last Essays of Elia*).

judgement. Compared with them, Lamb's position seems wavering and uncertain, and his belief in a clear, moral light and his affection for the obscure and Cavalier are often in mild, unworried conflict. But he is not the kind of critic who takes himself seriously or thinks consistency to be any sort of virtue, and the doubleness of his vision is on the whole a matter for complaisant pride. His attitude to Restoration comedy provides a perfect illustration. He has no doubt that, ultimately, it deserves the moral condemnation it had already received ('The business of their dramatic characters will not stand the moral test'). But, on the other hand, 'I am glad for a season to take an airing beyond the diocese of the strict conscience . . . I come back to my cage and my restraint the fresher and more healthy for it. I wear my shackles more contentedly for having respired the breath of an imaginary freedom.'[1] The spiritual tourist is all the better for his little spree, though even on his day out he observes some essential rules, abandoning himself to Congreve and drawing the line at Marlowe. Such tolerances would not have been admitted by Addison or Johnson: but they have a future, they make sense in Victorian terms, in the liberal morality of Leslie Stephen, Walter Pater, and the Bloomsbury Group.

Lamb's attraction to Jacobean tragedy, which he sought to revive through the slightly bowdlerized *Specimens of English Dramatic Poets Who Lived about the Time of Shakespeare* (1808), is all of a piece with this readiness to enjoy new and alien experiences. The attraction is one of opposites. Lamb's very gentleness is drawn to the Webster of *The Duchess of Malfi*:

To move a horror skilfully, to touch a soul to the quick, to lay upon fear as much as it can bear, to wean and weary a life till it is ready to drop, and then step in with mortal instruments to take its last forfeit: this only a Webster can do.[2]

1. ibid., p. 75 ('On the Artificial Comedy of the Last Century', in *Essays of Elia*).
2. ibid., p. 23 (from the *Specimens*).

The distance between Lamb and Webster is so vast that it is surprising he can see him even with a telescope; yet he describes Webster's essential quality with notable accuracy, if by generalities. Lamb's analysis is rarely more particular than this, and its chief virtue is the virtue of sound charaterization. He loves to tell you, in a few phrases, what a whole author is like. And the taste that moves him is conservative but self-indulgent, in love with quaintness if it is not too quaint, and romanticism if it is not too romantic, but above all impressed by the abiding worth of sober virtue. The middle-aged critic who welcomed Wordsworth's *Excursion* (1814) in the *Quarterly Review* for its devotional seriousness rejected much of the work of the second generation of romantic poets, including all of Byron and Shelley, and much of Keats. 'They are for younger impressibilities. To *us* an ounce of feeling is worth a pound of fancy.'[1]

The criticism of William Hazlitt (1778–1830) is at once more ambitious and less satisfying than Lamb's: it is not content to be judged as minor. Hazlitt is the first English writer to make a major career out of descriptive criticism; following upon the double failure of his early career – after declining to follow his father into the Unitarian ministry, he tried to be a painter, and then a philosopher, and did not satisfy himself in either part – his concern is uniquely with the English poets past and present. His criticism is purely descriptive, with no motive beyond analysis and judgement: or rather judgement and then analysis, for he understood perfectly what some later critics have laboured to deny, that evaluation is rather the starting-point of criticism than its aim and object. If you are any sort of reader (let alone a professional critic) you begin with an opinion – it is nonsense to talk of 'arriving at' one: 'to feel what is good, and give reasons for the faith that is in me', as Hazlitt defined his task. He was, at any rate, good at getting his priorities right.

To feel well, however, implies a wide and delicate sensitivity, and to give reasons that matter calls for analytic gifts.

1. ibid., p. 110 (from the review of *Lamia*, *New Times*, 19 July 1820).

Hazlitt's criticism has enjoyed a sizeable reputation for more than a century, but it is doubtful if it will bear examination on either of these counts. For sensitivity, he possesses only a familiar clutch of *a priori* notions of a romantic radical born a little too late; and since he never pursues analysis beyond a few phrases, it is in no way certain that he was capable of it.

The range of his interests is at first sight impressive. At the age of thirty-eight he turned to criticism with a study entitled *Characters of Shakespear's Plays* (1817), in which he attempted to 'vindicate the characters of Shakespeare's plays from the stigma of French criticism', allowing some credit to August Wilhelm Schlegel as a precursor. But Hazlitt's account of Shakespeare is as simple as his title suggests, and he commits the elementary offence of detaching figures from their dramatic contexts, as Schlegel and Coleridge rarely do. In the same year appeared a collection of essays entitled *The Round Table*, including his review of Wordsworth's *Excursion*, and in 1818 a collection of his dramatic reviews, *A View of the English Stage*, and the eight *Lectures on the English Poets*, a synoptic view of the major poets from Chaucer to the contemporary scene. In 1819 the *Lectures on the English Comic Writers* were published, mainly on eighteenth-century literature, and in 1820 the *Lectures on the Dramatic Literature of the Age of Elizabeth*; and finally, after the period of his marital crisis of 1823–4, *The Spirit of the Age*, or essays on writers of the previous half century, which appeared anonymously in 1825. The achievement is no doubt deliberately comprehensive; so far as verse and drama are concerned, little or nothing that he valued highly in modern English escapes this battery of essays and lectures, all composed in the last fifteen years of his life.

And yet, when all is said, what are the merits of it all, beyond a few telling phrases? Hazlitt's language has at times a certain splendour, but a splendour flyblown and empty of significance, like a schoolboy in a hurry with his homework anxious to impress a master with a taste for rhetoric. His language abuses meaning: look, for instance, at the famous 'general notion' of poetry in the introductory lecture of

1818, 'On Poetry in General': 'the natural impression of any object or event, by its vividness exciting an involuntary movement of imagination and passion and producing, by sympathy, a certain modulation of the voice, or sounds, expressing it'.[1] There are grave confusions here – whose impression (poet's or reader's?); and how does anyone's impression 'produce' modulations? Or consider the pompous claims for poetry in the paragraphs that follow, father to so many confusions; 'wherever there is a sense of beauty, or power, or harmony, as in a motion of a wave of the sea ... Fear is poetry, hope is poetry ...' Does 'is' mean 'equals', or 'is the subject of'? But no use the machinery of siege – there is nothing in all this to be taken. Hazlitt, in such instances, is not saying anything: he is simply making a noise to suggest that he is, or has been, excited about something. He is eminently the kind of descriptive critic who flaunts his own personality at the expense of his subject, and finds in poetry an admirable and infinitely various excuse for a favourite exercise of self-exposure. He is the father of our Sunday journalism. It is a pursuit of nothing to ask for evidence and elucidation of his impression of Chaucer, which (as it happens) looks just enough – 'his poetry reads like history. Everything has a downright reality' – or of Spenser, which is riotous nonsense – 'In reading the *Faery Queen*, you see a little withered old man by a woodside opening a wicket, a giant, and a dwarf lagging far behind, a damsel in a boat upon an enchanted lake, wood-nymphs, and satyrs ...'[2] His quotations, which (as in many of our early critics) are nearly all misquotations, do not illustrate passages before or after, and De Quincey was surely justified in condemning as 'indolent' and 'dishonest' his habit of using quotations and misquotations in irrelevant abundance to advance his own argument.[3] His criticism is void of scholarship even in the most elementary sense, and he com-

1. *Complete Works*, edited by P. P. Howe (1930–34), v, 1.
2. ibid., v, 35–6.
3. *North British Review* (November 1848), reprinted in *De Quincey's Literary Criticism*, edited by Helen Darbishire (Oxford, 1909), p. 256.

mits, as a professional critic, elementary errors (such as attributing the Spenserian stanza to the Italians) [1] which we should hesitate to forgive in the hurried work of such good poets as Dryden and Coleridge. It is easy to guess what the biographers' evidence confirms to the hilt: that Hazlitt's criticism is not about the English poets, but about Hazlitt's memory – years, sometimes decades, old – of the English poets as he first knew them. A friend reports that 'unless what he was employed on was a review, he never had a book or paper of any kind about him when he wrote', [2] and his confessions in *The Plain Speaker* that 'I hate to read new books', and that 'books have in a great measure lost their power over me' [3] is one of the frankest statements of incompetence in the record of literary journalism. 'I know how I should have felt at one time', was his sad comment on Keats's 'Eve of St Agnes'. [4] And at no time did he have patience for difficulties. 'Of Donne,' he wrote in the fourth lecture of 1818, 'I know nothing but some beautiful verses to his wife, dissuading her from accompanying him on his travels abroad, and some quaint riddles in verse which the Sphinx could not unravel.' [5] This suggests a mind already closed to critical endeavour. The contrast with Coleridge's sensitive, compassionate regard for what is strange, as in his hesitating but just recommendation of Herbert's *Temple* in the nineteenth chapter of the *Biographia Literaria*, seems unchallengeable. Unless one looks to criticism for a few portable phrases – such phrases as Dryden's 'magnanimity of abuse', or Scott's 'pleasing superficiality' as a poet – Hazlitt is not useful as a critic of English. His gustiness and vigour may, as rhetoric, approach the virtues; but they also serve to mask a coarseness of apprehension and a con-

1. *Complete Works*, v, 43.

2. Quoted by P. P. Howe in his *Life of William Hazlitt* (1947) (new edition), p. 259.

3. *Complete Works*, xii, 220, 225 ('On Reading Old Books'), first published in *London Magazine* (February, 1821), rather *early* in Hazlitt's career as a critic.

4. ibid., xii, 225.

5. ibid., v, 83.

servative hatred of ideas which the nineteenth-century reader tolerated with alarming readiness. Only Leslie Stephen, in a brilliant essay on Hazlitt, has troubled to expose his philistinism: 'He recognized and denounced, but he never shook off, the faults characteristic of small sects,' he pointed out, concluding: 'To claim to have learnt nothing from 1792 to 1830 is almost to write yourself down as hopelessly impenetrable.'[1] Hazlitt may not have been hopelessly impenetrable. But the obstinacy of his Bonapartism long after Napoleon's crimes had been exposed to Europe, and his stubborn refusal to reread and reappraise English poetry, are lamentably alike.

The youngest of the three, Thomas De Quincey (1785–1859), suffered from no such intellectual obstinacy. He is, in fact, the most impressionable, and impressionistic, of all the English romantic critics, and marvellously retained a sense of enthusiasm and wonder for what he loved best in English poetry – the Elizabethans and Wordsworth – until the last, poverty-stricken years of a long life. His faults are not the faults of the doctrinaire, but simply those of a good man in a hurry, anxious to be fair, remarkably judicious, but too eager for his monthly cheque to be careful of fact and detail.

De Quincey's discipleship to Wordsworth was the starting-point of his critical career – the *Lyrical Ballads* appeared when he was only thirteen years old, and he settled in Grasmere eleven years later, in 1809; and though it grew discriminating with the years, and though his friendship with the older man ceased with De Quincey's unworldly marriage in 1817, it was a discipleship that never wavered in its ultimate loyalty. The final measure of excellence in all De Quincey's criticism, which is contained mainly in periodical essays of the 1820s and 1830s, is the 'moral sublime' of the poet whom, as late as 1845, he called 'not only supreme, but unique'.[2] De Quincey is the most Wordsworthian of critics. He is, in a way, more Wordsworthian than Wordsworth

1. *Hours in a Library: Second Series* (1876).
2. *De Quincey's Literary Criticism*, edited by Helen Darbishire (Oxford, 1909), p, 221 (*Tait's Magazine*, September 1845).

himself, whose 1800 preface owes too much to Coleridge to
fit the quality of his genius, as De Quincey saw, or to be
anything better than a 'needless embarrassment'[1] to the
Wordsworthians. De Quincey's rebuttal of the 1800 theory
of diction is intellectually almost as impressive as Coleridge's,
and leaves a much better taste in the mouth. It is full of
eloquent sympathy for a great poet who is out of his depth:
'How *could* a man so much in earnest, and so deeply interested in the question [of poetic diction], commit so capital
an oversight?' he exclaims in affectionate indignation at
Wordsworth's failure, half a century before, to cite examples
of which past styles in English poetry he was for, and which
against. As it is, he goes on, in a memorable passage that
might stand as an epitaph on many controversies in aesthetics,

no man, in this dispute, steadily understands even himself; and, if
he did, no other person understands him, for want of distinct illustrations. Not only the answer, therefore, is still entirely in arrear,
but even the question is still in arrear: it has not yet practically explained itself so as an answer to it could be possible.[2]

Most of De Quincey's criticism, hasty and sporadic as it all
is, looks like an attempt to rectify Wordsworth's unfortunate
'oversight' in failing to be a great critic as well as a great
poet. His critical essays are mostly about his contemporaries,
the romantic poets, rich in reminiscence and unreliable
anecdotage. Their quality is not easy to describe. They
appear in a relaxed, playful, exuberant prose that none the
less allows for strict organization and a firm, argumentative
pressure. There is an underlying austerity in De Quincey's
criticism, a faculty for reasoning at length of which Wordsworth and Hazlitt were utterly innocent, and a conscientious determination to get the right answer which Hazlitt
did not share at all. His most famous critical essay, 'On the
Knocking at the Gate in *Macbeth*', which appeared in the
London Magazine as early as October 1823, not long after the

1. ibid., p. 225.
2. ibid., p. 226.

successful series *Confessions of an English Opium Eater* (September–October 1821) that made his reputation, is as neatly organized a demonstration as the logician could wish, beginning with a posing of the question which looks chatty and is in fact wonderfully precise:

> From my boyish days I had always felt a great perplexity on one point in *Macbeth*. It was this: the knocking at the gate, which succeeds to the murder of Duncan, produced to my feelings an effect for which I never could account . . .

and proceeding by way of a 'digression' which is nothing of the kind towards a finely perceptive conclusion:

> In order that a new world may step in, this world must for a time disappear. The murderers, and the murder, must be insulated . . .; we must be made sensible that the world of ordinary life is suddenly arrested – laid asleep – tranced – racked into a dread armistice; time must be annihilated; relation to things without abolished; and all must pass self-withdrawn into a deep syncope and suspension of early passion. Hence it is, that when the deed is done–when the work of darkness is perfect, then the world of darkness passes away like a pageantry in the clouds: the knocking at the gate is heard; and it makes known audibly that the reaction has commenced; the human has made its reflux upon the fiendish; the pulses of life are beginning to beat again . . .

De Quincey has posed a question and then answered it with telling accuracy. But in a way, the question is more original than the answer. No doubt it is modishly suspect, and modern critics who worry about something they call 'the Affective Fallacy', or the 'confusion between the poem and its results' are certain to be embarrassed by De Quincey's excellence as a critic – no critic could be more frankly 'affective' – and certain too to be puzzled why it is that *Macbeth* does not 'tend to disappear'[1] under such analysis. But the problem has been falsely defined. Certainly the affective reactions of some critics to some poems may be too

1. W. K. Wimsatt and Monroe C. Beardsley, 'The Affective Fallacy', *Sewanee Review*, lvii (1949), reprinted in Wimsatt, *The Verbal Icon* (Lexington, Kentucky, 1954).

eccentric and too extravagant to be worth analysing; and again, an irresponsible critic may tiresomely insist upon his own emotional response to a given poem to the extent of neglecting or denying its intelligible content. Both offences arise from a failure in the critic's historical sense, and both can be rebutted, if at all, only by an appeal to history. (Swinburne's impressionistic *Study of Shakespeare* (1880), for example, calls for the expert historical study of Elizabethan theatrical convention to prove that Swinburne is writing not so much about Shakespeare as about himself.) But to admit all this is not to admit that it is wrong for the critic to analyse his own emotional reactions. In a sense, there is nothing else he can ever do. It is simply to insist that such reactions should be historically informed as well as deeply experienced. Much of De Quincey's criticism shows how good 'affective' criticism can be: he feels Wordsworth to be the greatest of contemporary poets, and then seeks reasons for his unique quality. He feels the knocking on the gate in Macbeth to be magnificently theatrical, and twenty years later he discovers why. To pose such questions at all, and so frankly, is to make descriptive criticism one degree more honest, more penetrating and more sane. The danger of eccentricity, in principle, remains – what if a reader were to object that he felt nothing of De Quincey's 'peculiar awfulness and depth of solemnity'? Such a critic can only help to sharpen the reader's own reactions to a given work – he cannot create a reaction out of nothing. And yet, given the sharing of a premiss, his analysis is likely to reveal more of Shakespeare's stagecraft than the remoter generalizations of many of his predecessors. It is the great merit of De Quincey as a critic that he trusts his own instincts enough to test them rigorously; and though he is modern enough to think analysis worth doing for its own sake, his favourite form of criticism begins in description and ends in generality. A beam of light touches the poem, and passes through it; and, for an instant we see its strange transparency, and understand in some part how it came to be made.

CHAPTER 7

MATTHEW ARNOLD

... the method of historical criticism, that great and famous power in the present day ... The advice to study the character of an author and the circumstances in which he has lived, in order to account to oneself for his work, is excellent. But it is a perilous doctrine that from such a study the right understanding of his work will 'spontaneously issue'.

THIS quotation from one of the last and best of the critical essays of Matthew Arnold (1822–88)[1] suggests at once how untypical a Victorian critic he was, and how proudly he knew it. The 'great and famous power' of historical criticism, against which no other Victorian critic before the nineties raised his voice, seemed to him implausible and overrated almost before it had established itself. 'The old story of *the man and the milieu*' – that is how, in the same essay, he dismisses by misquotation the grandiose theories of Taine concerning 'race, milieu, moment' as the occasion for creative energy.

Each civilized age has its favourite discipline from which special enlightenment is expected to flow. Today it is sociology; for Arnold's age it was undeniably history, and the new techniques of historical research summed up for the heroine of George Eliot's *Middlemarch* (1871–2) by the dread word 'German'. The amateur English tradition of Gibbon and Hallam had fallen back before the systematic researches of Niebuhr and Ranke; techniques of the new scientific criticism of texts ('the Higher Criticism', as it came impressively to be called) had invaded the study of the Bible, and with the publication of seven *Essays and Reviews* in 1860 was shown to have established itself inside the

1. 'A French Critic [Edmond Scherer] on Milton' (*Quarterly Review*, January 1877), reprinted in his *Mixed Essays* (1879).

Church of England. For the President of Mark Rutherford's nonconformist seminary in the 1850s the word 'German' was 'a term of reproach suggesting something very awful, although nobody knew exactly what it was'.[1] Germany led: France followed only a little behind. A French reviewer confidently wrote as early as 1825 that the absolute study of texts was already dead in French criticism, and the day of historical criticism at hand:

After long considering literature as something invariable and absolute, capable of submitting itself to prearranged forms, criticism now regards it as the variable and changing product of its own society.[2]

That was written when Arnold was three years old; in France, at least, the battle for history was already won. But England was submitting very fast. G. H. Lewes (1817–78) hailed the new 'scientific' historiography in his articles in the *Westminster Review* in the 1840s as the foundation of a future 'science of man'.[3] The Utilitarians were among the most enthusiastic claimants for the new historiography of France and Germany as the basis of all future humane studies, and the early *Westminster Review* is full of such assertions. The battle was soon won. 'From this time,' wrote John Stuart Mill twenty years later, on Comte's sociological discoveries, 'any political thinker who fancies himself able to dispense with a connected view of the great facts of history, as a chain of causes and effects, must be regarded as below the level of the age'.[4] Years later, in a lecture delivered at St Andrews University in 1887, Leslie Stephen (1832–1904), whose long, rambling essays in criticism represent something of a triumph for his own relaxed, anglicized version of continental historicism, cautiously admitted that 'the historical method is now in the ascendant', affecting 'not only history in the old sense, but philosophy, political

1. From his autobiographical novel, *The Autobiography of Mark Rutherford* (1881) ch. 2.
2. H. R., 'De la littérature des Hébreux, (*Globe* 2 April 1825), p. 467.
3. 'Modern French Historians' (*Westminster Review*, xxxvi, September 1841), pp. 276–7.
4. *Auguste Comte and Positivism* (1865), p. 86.

and social theory, and every other branch of inquiry which has to do with the development of living beings'. 'I will not say', he went on, that the study of literature can be 'made truly scientific'. But literature can be 'treated in a scientific spirit'.[1] A year later, Arnold was dead. He had spent a good deal of his energies for thirty years in denying it all.

The spirit of denial in Arnold's criticism is, on the face of it, the most striking thing about it. He is the great gainsayer of English criticism, the most insistent and professional of nonconformists. His characteristic strategy is, like Pope's Atticus, to 'hesitate dislike'. He delights in sapping confidence. But in all this, paradoxically, he is only behaving in his own manner after the convention of the Victorian intellectual: rude as he is against established literary values, Carlyle and Ruskin were ruder still against established society and morality. Iconoclasm is the strongest and deepest of currents among the Victorian intelligentsia. It was they, after all, who conceived the revolutionary doctrines by which the twentieth century lives and dies, and Arnold in his criticism is just such a spirit of contradiction incarnate. The literary values he recommends are those that the poetry of his day was least able to achieve; his cultural values are everything that cultivated opinion in his own day was not. Both are revolutionary alternatives to the *status quo*; for Arnold, like his contemporary Marx, challenged his own world to suicide and rebirth. The urbanity of his manner is not even superficially a conservative gloss; it was a red rag to a bull in a society that suspected urbanity, it sharpened the challenge.

Arnold's defiance of the Victorian tradition of poetry begins in reaction against himself. In 1849 he had startled his friends with a first collection of poems, *The Strayed Reveller*, where the bright young man just down from Oxford revealed himself as a melancholy romantic in love with solitude. Three years later he issued a new collection of his poems as *Empedocles on Etna,* and in 1853 replaced this drama

1. Leslie Stephen, *Men, Books, and Mountains,* edited by S. O. A. Ullmann (Minneapolis, 1956), pp. 19, 25.

of suicide with the miniature epic *Sohrab and Rustum,* and a preface written during the summer in reply to an anonymous and deprecating review of *Empedocles.*[1] The 1853 preface, written at the age of thirty-one, is the first of Arnold's prose works, and oddly stiff and graceless when we think of the ironic elegance of his later prose. 'It is far less *precise* than I had intended,' he complained in a letter to his old school-friend Clough. 'How difficult it is to write prose.' For the remaining thirty-five years of his life he wrote hardly anything else.

Arnold's criticism measures the distance between his ambition as a poet and his performance. A poet in the tradition of Keats, he seeks in his prose to extricate himself from a romanticism he both loves and despises. Nothing, in the history of criticism, is more familiar than the spectacle of a poet turning in early middle age to justify his achievements and rationalize his failures, as Dryden had done – or, like Baudelaire and Eliot, to explore in prose notions for which, as poets, they felt themselves still unready. Arnold's criticism begins in a more hostile spirit, in self-disgust, and his attack upon the rejected *Empedocles* in the 1853 preface, upon its extravagant subjectivity and its lack of action, is not much less than an attack upon the whole of his brief career as a poet.

The conscientious distaste for his own poetry which is the starting-point of Arnold's criticism began very early, before he had published his first volume of verse. 'What a brute you were', he wrote to Clough in the winter of 1848–9, 'to tell me to read Keats's letters . . . What harm he has done in English poetry. As Browning is a man with a moderate gift passionately desiring movement and fulness, and obtaining but a confused multitudinousness, so Keats, with a very high gift, is yet also consumed by this desire: and cannot produce the truly living and moving, as his conscience keeps telling him. They will not be patient, neither understand that they must begin with an idea of the world in order not to be prevailed over by the world's multitu-

1. *North British Review* (May 1853).

dinousness: or, if they cannot get that, at least with isolated ideas,' and he goes on to condemn the influence upon young writers of Keats, Tennyson, 'yes, and those d—d Elizabethan poets generally'.[1] In October 1852, in a further letter to Clough, he returns to the same point – that the greatest poets may be the worst influences:

Keats and Shelley were on a false track when they set themselves to reproduce the exuberance of expression, the charm, the richness of images, and the felicity, of the Elizabethan poets. Yet critics cannot get to learn this, because the Elizabethan poets are our greatest, and our canons of poetry are founded on their works ... Modern poetry can only subsist by its *contents*: by becoming a complete *magister vitae* as the poetry of the Ancients did: by including, as theirs did, religion with poetry, instead of existing as poetry only, and leaving religous wants to be supplied by the Christian religion. (p. 124)

The demand that poetry help to fill the spiritual void felt and suffered by a faithless age carries us, with surprising suddenness, into the heart of a conviction he spent many years in justifying: that the poet in an open society and in conditions of expanding literacy must, like priests in the age of priests, offer guidance and instruction, and that the language of such poetry 'must be very plain, direct, and severe: and it must not lose itself in parts and episodes and ornamental work, but must press forward to the whole'. No wonder he felt his own poems were worse than useless, a mere addendum to the vicious, or at best irrelevant, tradition of Keats. 'The Scholar-Gipsy', written in 1852, he confessed to Clough 'at best awakens a pleasing melancholy. But this is not what we want.'[2] What we do want – and the 1853 preface might almost be considered a manifesto, if the savour of Arnold's own sense of failure did not hang so thickly over it – is a flat rejection of the poetry of the Romantics and Elizabethans in favour of poems that are 'particular, precise, and firm', dealing with human actions

1. *Letters of Matthew Arnold to Arthur Hugh Clough*, edited by H. F. Lowry (Oxford, 1932), pp. 96–7.
2. ibid., p. 146.

not rooted in one time or place, but which 'most powerfully appeal to the great primary human affections: to those elementary feelings which subsist permanently in the race'. Here, in its grasp of essentials, lay the virtue of the civilization of the Greeks: 'They regarded the whole; we regard the parts.'

The demand is highly reminiscent, and in two ways. It is reminiscent, first, of Coleridge's call, provoked by the 1800 preface, for a new dignity or 'neutrality' of style in contemporary poetry. And secondly, it sounds a little like the defunct seventeenth-century obsession of English poets and critics with the 'heroic poem'; *Sohrab and Rustum* and *Balder Dead*, indeed, are little epics, as oddly isolated in time as those epigones of English pastoral poetry, 'The Scholar-Gipsy' and 'Thyrsis'. But both echoes are accidental: Arnold nowhere shows any sign of having absorbed the Coleridgean aesthetic, and he is evidently conscious only of the classical epic of Homer and Virgil, while remaining noticeably indifferent to such modern experiments as *Paradise Lost*. It was part of the price he paid for rejecting the fashionable historicism of his day that he rarely knew who his own intellectual ancestors were.

In 1857, at the age of thirty-five, Arnold was elected to the Chair of Poetry in Oxford, a position of dignity he held for ten years, with the distinction of being the first incumbent to lecture in English. But to say that is to create a false impression at once: a brilliant poet and man-about-town, still young and contemptuous of academic pedantry, blowing away the cobwebs of Latin scholarship in a mood of intellectual liberation. To realize how wrong all this is, one only has to turn to his inaugural lecture of 1857, 'On the Modern Element in Literature'.[1] It is a lecture against the modern element in literature, in which Arnold seeks an alliance with the classical dons in his audience against the prevailing tide of middle-class romanticism. Oxford University, he declared in the preface to the first series of

1. *Macmillan's Magazine* (February 1869), posthumously collected in the so-called *Essays in Criticism: Third Series* (Boston, 1910).

Essays in Criticism (1865), 'is generous, and the cause in which I fight is, after all, hers'. This is the voice not of modernity and liberation but of neo-conservatism, and perhaps of a candidate for Establishment honours. Arnold might almost be angling for a knighthood. It is true, of course, that the projected alliance between Arnold's New Hellenism and the Old was never effected, and involved too many incongruities ever to be effected; and Arnold may have felt a little ashamed of his Inaugural, with its measured warnings against romantic modernity in favour of ancient classical severity. He did not collect it. Indeed, the first three years of his ensuing Oxford lectures are largely lost (1857–60), and he reappears only in 1860–61, when he delivered three lectures *On Translating Homer* (1861), an attempt to define more closely the qualities of the 'excellent action' of the 1853 preface by means of a summary of the Homeric qualities that any English translator must achieve – rapidity of action, plainness of language, plainness of thought, and nobility – involving himself in controversy with F. W. Newman, whose own version of the *Iliad* (1856) provided Arnold with his whipping-boy. Shortly after, from 1862, he began to publish a series of articles on single authors, which he collected in 1865 under the title of *Essays in Criticism*, for which he wrote, as a provocative opening, 'The Function of Criticism at the Present Time' – the first formal statement of his critical position since the 1853 preface, and logically continuous from it. The 1865–6 lectures *On the Study of Celtic Literature* (1867) were an uninformed attempt to apply racial, anthropological standards to literary studies.

The first series of the *Essays in Criticism* marks the end of the initial stage in Arnold's career as a critic and publicist – the second, indeed, had already begun. The 1860s were perhaps the most controversial of nineteenth-century decades: the religious controversy was taking on a new pugnacity in such debates as that between Charles Kingsley and John Henry Newman. Ruskin half-deserted art-criticism to write *Unto this Last* (1862), and reviewers thought it mad. And in 1862 the Anglican Bishop Colenso of Natal produced a treatise to prove that the Pentateuch 'is not historically true'. It was pre-eminently the age of head-on intellectual collisions, and Arnold met Colenso, as nearly as he ever met any antagonist, head-on. This second phase of his critical career, which carried him far into theology, politics, and educational and social controversy, lasted till the late 1870s, when he returned, for the last few years of his life, to literary studies, including the articles ultimately collected to form the second series of *Essays in Criticism* (1888). The second, and most controversial, phase had confirmed Arnold's intellectual isolation. His attack on Colenso's liberal Christianity had alienated latitudinarian opinion, he had never permanently endeared himself to conservatism, and he now found himself pushed onwards and upwards into that position of exalted independence that accorded so aptly with his temperament. 'Conservatism, like Liberalism, taken alone,' he solemnly assured Eton schoolboys years after, 'is not sufficient, is not of itself saving.'[1]

It is a matter of convenience to consider the first and third phases together, as those in which literary interests predominated. The two series of *Essays in Criticism,* though separated in time by twenty years, are neatly complementary, and their coincidence suggests how little Arnold's critical attitudes evolved. If criticism led him into social interests, which led him in their turn back to poetry, it is not clear that he learnt much that was critically useful in the process. The first and second series of essays are, in outlook, all of a piece: they are contrasted only in subject. In the first series, he considers authors either minor in themselves (Joubert, Maurice de Guérin and his sister Eugénie), or remote from English readers (Spinoza, Marcus Aurelius, Heine). The list of names looks like an appeal to intellectual snobbery, and so it is – these are not authors any English eminent critic had tackled before in literary terms, and they are offered to us now as a cure for intellectual isolationism.

With Arnold, indeed, snobbery enters English criticism

1. 'A Speech at Eton', in *Irish Essays* (1882).

with a vengeance, and it has never been quite eradicated since. The Arnoldian critic invites the reader to enter a charmed circle of connoisseurship, as Johnson and Coleridge had never done, to separate himself from a brute mass of Barbarians, Philistines, and Populace. In 'The Function of Criticism at the Present Time' a programme of connoisseurship is offered, and in a manner of high-bred disdain which is almost as significant as the programme itself. Consider the language of the 1865 preface – and the present passage was not among those excised or subdued in the second edition of 1869:

> One cannot be always studying one's own works, and I was really under the impression, till I saw Mr Wright's complaint, that I had spoken of him with all respect.

Perhaps it is simply bad for people to be invited to lecture at Oxford: at all events, this combination of academic hauteur and lazy man-about-town insolence enlivens, and disfigures, much of his criticism and all of his controversial writings forever after. Both the romantic young poet, and the austere young critic of the 1853 preface, are now dead: the new pose is adult, scintillating, intriguingly decadent: one is, he complains languidly,

> but the last sparkle of flame before we are all in the dark, the last glimpse of colour before we all go into drab – the drab of the earnest, prosaic, practical, austerely literal future.

No one, since Johnson in his *Lives*, had so nearly succeeded in writing a work of criticism that was also a bedside book: the unctuous grace of the *Essays* of 1865 still seduces the reader to answer the call to a 'critical effort' in England that will match the continental. For it is of the first importance that not one of the mediocrities singled out for commendation in the first series is an Englishman. In the mind of this English critic, the grass on the other side of the Channel was always greener. The English Romantics, the staple reading of every literary Englishman, for all that they possessed 'plenty of energy, plenty of creative force, did not know enough' – but Goethe (unlike Byron) did, for his poetry is deeply informed by a 'great critical effort'. The French Revolution was 'a more spiritual event than our Revolution', as French intelligence is superior to mere English common sense, as France herself is 'the country in Europe where *the people* is most alive'. The ensuing attack on the criminal complacency of English society reminds us that the second and social phase of Arnold's interests has already begun.

'The Function of Criticism' establishes itself as a major document not only by embodying a literary programme and a new infectious tone of voice. Like most successful intellectual influences, Arnold provides slogans which give his arguments a memorable, even portable, quality. They are, appropriately, borrowed largely from the French and German, for Arnold is an adapter rather than a coiner of terms. His final, question-begging definition of the function of criticism, 'a disinterested endeavour to learn and propagate the best that is known and thought in the world', lifts a word from an essay of Sainte-Beuve, who had spoken of the critic's task of introducing '*un certain souffle de désintéressement*'. 'Philistine', a word he first uses in the Heine essay,[1] is avowedly borrowed from the German *Philister*; and 'sweetness and light', of later usage, is (curiously enough) borrowed from Jonathan Swift.

But Sainte-Beuve's influence is more thorough-going; his biographical-critical essays, which had begun to appear in French journals in 1824 to continue till his death in 1869, are the source of critical inspiration that Arnold always appealed to, and he twice acknowledged his debt to this 'perfect one' among European critics. It is obvious, indeed, that Sainte-Beuve's *portrait littéraire* is the structural model for an Arnoldian essay in criticism. Here, as in Johnson's *Lives*, most studies begin in biography and end in criticism; but now the two principal components are utterly merged, so that one might seek in vain the moment of separation, and

1. *Cornhill Magazine* (August 1863), reprinted in *Essays in Criticism* (1865).

both subserve a mysterious end superior to biography and critical analysis alike. A Sainte-Beuve portrait has a symbolic function, and his heroes, like Arnold's, are like saints in a secular canon of excellence. And the *portrait* is a pursuit of individual personality which is far more than the sum of biographical details.

The day, the moment, when one hits upon the familiar gesture, the revealing smile, the indefinable blemish, the sad, intimate wrinkle that seeks in vain to hide itself under the already thinning hair – at this moment analysis vanishes into creation, the portrait speaks and lives, you have found the man.[1]

This, on the face of it, is the very ecstasy of historical enthusiasm, and it seems incredible that any critic as bored as Arnold was with historical scholarship should have had any patience with it. But two considerations may have made this doctrine seductive to him, along with the carefully worked *portraits* and *causeries* which it inspired. First, it was French; and second, it was a doctrine not of history but of super-history. Arnold was too discursive an intelligence, and too amateur a scholar, to find any use for the new German tradition of historical research, or for such austere ambitions as Ranke's to rediscover the past 'as it really happened'. Sainte-Beuve's prescription is different from Ranke's in a subtle but important respect. It seeks to re-create the past, not as it was, but as it is for us: 'to see the object as in itself it really *is*'[2], as Arnold defines the critical function, suggests a certain unconcern for the poem as a document in time, 'as it really *was*'. Nineteenth-century historicism on the Continent generated its own special mysticism so fast that it is impossible to draw distinctions between historical scholars and historical re-creators: Ranke himself believed in such mystical realities as the 'inner life' of past political systems as surely as Sainte-Beuve held that 'the man' is more than a sum of

1. Sainte-Beuve, 'Diderot' (*Revue de Paris*, June 1831), collected in *Portraits littéraires* (1844).
2. *On Translating Homer* (1861), Lecture 11. Arnold quotes his own phrase in the first paragraph of 'The Function of Criticism at the Present Time'.

biographical facts. What distinguishes the Arnoldian essay-in-criticism is the eccentric disproportion of fact and re-creation. There is a great deal of icing and not much cake. The essays are usually constructed on a similar plan to Sainte-Beuve – an interpenetration of biography and criticism, often with a brief, generalizing opening – but Arnold's pocket-biographies do not, like Sainte-Beuve's, suggest toil in libraries or a passionate concern for facts. They plagiarize heavily – sometimes upon an essay by Sainte-Beuve. And their manifest purpose lies elsewhere, in directing us, by a series of exemplary and cautionary tales, how (and how not) to behave.

The first, continental series of 1865 teaches us what to be; the second, English series of 1888 teaches us what not. The national antithesis – mainly, but not entirely, a French-English one – is explicit in 'The Function of Criticism', where the ignorance of the English Romantics is essentially an ignorance of continental ideas and poetry: 'this makes Byron so empty of matter, Shelley so incoherent, Wordsworth ... so wanting in completeness and variety.' It is not simply their lack of reading, which was no worse than Sophocles's or Shakespeare's, but the fact that English society since the Puritan Revolution has been rootedly provincial. The very mediocrity of the Continentals selected for praise in the first series establishes the point that the distinction is not one of individual talent but of social maturity. A second-rate Frenchman like Joubert takes pre-cedence over a first-rate English intelligence such as Cole-ridge. Arnold's Joubert is not a figure in history, a largely forgotten author of maxims in Napoleonic France: he is a 'French Coleridge' who, 'with less power and richness than his English parallel, ... had more tact and penetration. He was more *possible* than Coleridge ...' The second series of essays completes the picture. Enthusiastic as some of the praise for the English Romantics may seem here, when quoted out of context, it is too heavily hedged about with qualifications to soften the antithesis, and too condescend-ing in tone to count for much in itself. Keats was 'a great spirit', true, but 'not ripe' for the creation of enduring works such as the *Agamemnon* or *King Lear*; Wordsworth lacks style; Byron emerges as a kind of infant prodigy, Shelley a crazed, angelic clown. This multiple indictment of the English achievement represents no kind of advance in principle upon the twenty-year-old demand, in 'The Function of Criticism', for a period of critical consolidation in English thought. It is a damning judgement in depth of the inadequacy of the whole range of English romanticism.

And yet, between the two series of essays, falls the great body of Arnold's work as a publicist: the educational treatises of the early sixties, the attack upon English social and cultural complacency in *Culture and Anarchy* (1869), and the religious treatises of the seventies such as *St Paul and Protestantism* (1870), *Literature and Dogma* (1873), and its sequel *God and the Bible* (1875). Increasingly irrelevant as it looks to literary concerns, the effort was not discontinuous from Arnold's career as a critic. For Arnold is very Victorian in his refusal to accept formal limitations. Johnson and Hazlitt, even Coleridge, would have thought it improper for a critic to venture so far; but for Arnold it was obvious that poetry and religion are aspects of a wider entity called 'culture', or the total current of ideas in which a given society lives. They are, for Arnold, different versions of human awareness of the human condition, but both T. S. Eliot and Lionel Trilling have surely falsified his purpose in suggesting that he ever sought to substitute poetry for religion. [1] The misunderstanding rests largely on a key passage from 'The Study of Poetry' (1880):

Without poetry, our science will appear incomplete; and most of *what now passes with us* for religion and philosophy will be replaced by poetry [my italics].

It is the sham religion of dogmatic assertion which will be replaced by poetry in this contention, not the true religion of Christian humanism.

1. See Eliot, 'Arnold and Pater' (1930), in his *Selected Essays* (1932), and Trilling, *Matthew Arnold* (New York, 1939), ch. 7.

Arnold's real purpose is to defend what he considered the essentials of Christianity by means of a tactical retreat involving the abandonment of dogma. Colenso's 'weak trifling' against the historical truth of the Pentateuch seemed to him based upon 'a total misconception of the essential elements of the religious problem'. These 'essential elements' are never closely defined: the most that can be said is that for Arnold, as for the young Newman years before, poetry and religion are similar in their humanist emphasis: 'Poetry then is our mysticism,' as Newman had argued in his early, Anglican days, 'and so far as any two characters of mind [the poetical and the mystical] tend to penetrate below the surface of things, and to draw men away from the material to the invisible world, so far they may certainly be said to answer the same end; and that is a religious one.'[1] Poetry and religion are not alternatives or competitors: for Arnold they are twin currents, and he sees their relationship as one of analogy. Each must purge itself to meet the new, continental challenge of criticism: poetry of its subjectivism, its provinciality, its indifference to new ideas; Christianity of its absurd infallibilities, whether the Papal infallibility of the Catholics or the Biblical infallibility of the Protestants, 'the notion that every syllable and letter of the Bible is the direct utterance of the Most High'.

His own role, accordingly, he conceives as one of tactful midwifery, 'to ease a severe transition', as he puts it in *God and the Bible*, towards 'a Catholicism purged, opening itself to the light and air, having the consciousness of its own poetry . . .' – a 'liberal' Christianity, in fact, admitting a ritual whose significance, like that of poetry, is accepted as analogical. The 'liberalism' of Arnold's Christianity is extreme, in the sense that it involves a total rejection of the supernatural; the Incarnation, according to a mock-catechism in his 'Comment on Christmas', is not a historical fact but 'a homage to the virtue of pureness', and the 'kingdom of God' exists not in another world but in an

1. J. H. Newman, 'Prospects of the Anglican Church' (*British Critic*, April 1839).

'ideal society of the future'. Arnold's *religion*, a dogmatic Christian might plausibly complain, is a religion-substitute, whatever his notion of poetry may have been. It is based upon a will to be Christian rather than upon a real conviction of the truth of the Christian story; its motive seems hardly more respectable than that of saving something out of the wreck. It certainly apes Christian observances, like other Victorian religious systems, including Positivism and Marxism. It is a rehabilitation-school for honest doubters, the total sceptic might object, and pseudo-Christian in a sense that is as likely today to disquiet the reverent agnostic as the believer.

Such a religious philosophy would have no place in a history of criticism, were it not for the fact that it brings one closer to a notion of Arnold's aesthetic. He is a critic who disdains theory – which means, of course, not that he lacks theoretical preconceptions, but that they are there only to be guessed at. But his religion-poetry analogy is instructive enough to encourage an account of the Arnoldian aesthetic by inference. The opening passage of 'The Study of Poetry', which heads the second series of *Essays in Criticism* (1888), concluding with the surprising statement that 'the strongest part of our religion today is its unconscious poetry', follows upon a still more surprising chain of argument:

Our religion has materialised itself in the fact, in the supposed fact; it has attached its emotions to the fact, and now the fact is failing it. But for poetry the idea is everything; the rest is a world of illusion, of divine illusion. Poetry attaches its emotion to the idea; the idea *is* the fact.

The most astonishing aspect of this display of Poor Man's Platonism is that Arnold should think it called for so little defence. At least he offers none. The utterly staggering assertion that poetry assumes the real world not to exist is made as casually as if two and two were being added to make four. But the doctrine that poetry is unworldly and evanescent is not just Arnold's – it is Victorian in a more general sense, and .could certainly be paralleled in the writings of Newman and Mill, and traced back to the poems and letters of Keats. It is too incoherent to be dignified by the title of an 'aesthetic'. Unlike the neo-Aristotelianism of Dryden, Pope, and Johnson, and unlike Coleridge's forgotten attempt to create for poetry a unique logical status of its own, the Victorian mind possessed, and sought to possess, no definable doctrine of the nature of art. In this field it despised abstraction. It was insistently obscurantist, as Arnold is here, in all issues of critical theory. Saintsbury's *History of Criticism* (1900) disposed of 'the more transcendental' aesthetic, in his first chapter, as mere 'cloud Junos'. But at least it is clear from such passages that, for Arnold, the essence of poetry lay in its analogical character. The 'unconscious poetry' of Victorian religion refers, of course, to Arnold's view that what many Christians believed to be literally true, for example the Incarnation, was in his view only metaphorically so. 'Poetic', in fact, means 'metaphorical'. The damage done to Christianity by the Pauline Epistles derived, among other causes, from the fact that Paul 'orientalised', or used a language which made no distinction between statement and analogy:

The Hebrew genius has not, like the Greek, its conscious and clear marked division into a poetic side and a scientific side; the scientific side is almost absent; the Bible utterances have often the character of a chorus of Aeschylus, but never that of a treatise of Aristotle. We, like the Greeks, possess in our speech and thought the two characters; but so far as the Bible is concerned, we have generally confounded them...[1]

The Jewish Paul, expressing himself 'by a vivid and striking figure', he claims to have been misinterpreted again and again by the literal Puritan intelligence. The claim anticipates I. A. Richards's distinction of the 1920s between 'emotive' and scientific statements; and most Victorian critics write as if poetic statements belong, indefinably, to some special logical order. But it is one thing to admit the

1. *St Paul and Protestantism* (1870), ch. 1.

force of poetry to be, like liberal Christianity, analogical, and another to show it to be so by the deliberate analysis of individual poems. The oddity of Arnold's criticism is that, while it repeatedly enjoins the reader to choose 'the best, the really excellent' and to adopt 'a high standard and a strict judgement' and to eschew 'the historic estimate and the personal estimate',[1] Arnold is rarely if ever seen doing any of these things himself.

A historical estimate of Arnold must always conclude him to have been the most influential force among the Victorian critics. But if literary description is in question there seems no good reason now for accepting his claims to greatness as a critic. Those who see civilization as a cause rather than a condition of mind will always be attracted to this most insistent and eloquent of its advocates. But to enjoin and encourage men to be critical is no more like being a good critic oneself than to urge men to be good is to be a serious contributor to the study of ethics. Those who see in Arnold's essays evidence of a major critical intelligence should set themselves to consider the following objections. Where, first, in the entire corpus of Arnold's criticism, do we see 'the great critical effort' at work upon any English text – upon a single play of Shakespeare or poem of Milton, Wordsworth, or Keats? The admirers of Johnson, Coleridge, even Hazlitt, can point to demonstrations of critical finesse. The admirer of Arnold's criticism has to accept the word for the deed. Again, Arnold's critical programme of a 'disinterested endeavour' to seek out and advocate the best is not only hopelessly question-begging: it is also hopelessly out of key with Arnold's own achievement. The *Essays in Criticism* and the Biblical reinterpretations are not even remotely disinterested. They are works of passionate partisanship by a skilful, urbane, not always candid controversialist with a zest for opposition. Their virtues, which are considerable, are essentially polemical. If Arnold had seriously tried to be 'disinterested', his career as a critic would not have happened at all. And it is no defence

1. 'The Study of Poetry', op. cit.

to argue that Arnold's passionate partisanship is all in favour of such *désintéressement*. There are Arnoldian values clearly implicit in his preference for French civilization over English, Joubert over Coleridge, Renan over St Paul, Wordsworth over Shelley, and Goethe over both. Those who cannot see such values as especially and distinctively Arnoldian disqualify themselves by their very discipleship from the task of judicious appraisal.

More than that, there is no coherent theory of poetry in Arnold's criticism. This might not matter very much if, as in Johnson, a certain incoherence of ideas were compensated for by vigorous critical demonstration. As it is, Arnold's notion of a poetry purged, like religion, of fact and dealing in analogical truths is explored in vacuous and tautological language. There is a great deal of this kind of thing in the *Essays in Criticism*:

In poetry, as a criticism of life under the conditions fixed for such a criticism by the laws of poetic truth and poetic beauty, the spirit of our race will find . . . its consolation and stay. But the consolation and stay will be of power in proportion to the power of the criticism of life. And the criticism of life will be of power in proportion as the poetry conveying it is excellent rather than inferior, sound rather than unsound or half-sound, true rather than untrue or half-true.[1]

Does this really mean more than that, all things considered, good poems are better than bad poems?

For a critic who enjoyed the benefits of a public career, and who spent a dozen years in writing essays on religious and social questions, Arnold is culpably vague concerning the proper subject of poetry. The 1853 preface is free with advice to poets to be 'particular, precise, and firm' – about what? Arnold's own answer, in this first of his critical essays, is as general, indeterminate, and faint as could well be. The true subject of poetry, he claims, is 'an excellent action' appealing to 'the great primary human affections'. This account, surprisingly, is never enlarged upon in

1. 'The Study of Poetry', op. cit.

151

the religious essays, though an image of perfection emerges in the 'sweetly reasonable' Jesus of *Literature and Dogma* (1873), a figure that combines the virtues of a liberal Protestantism with the Hellenist ethos of Rugby School. It may be – and reference to the poems would, on the whole, support this claim – that an action is 'excellent' to the extent that it recommends such values as loyalty and open-mindedness. But, given Arnold's generous use of such terms as 'good', 'true', 'sound', and 'sweet', it is hardly fair-minded of him to leave us so profoundly in the dark concerning the nature of light.

The deep voids and gaping vaguenesses of Arnoldian criticism are so evident that they call for explanation rather than analysis. It is well worth asking how it happened: Arnold remains in most respects the most seductive of the great Victorian pundits, more variously and wittily intelligent than those great juggernauts Ruskin and Carlyle. His works survive, and for something like their original purpose. He is almost never dull. And the vast contradictions that underlie his programme for the poetry and the civilization of England do not in any way diminish its fascination.

The first impulse of Arnold's criticism, in the 1853 preface, was his own sense of incongruity as the author of poems that 'are not what we want'. This gap remains: we feel certain to the end that Arnold's head and heart are never likely to say the same things. The prophetic Wordsworth of his 'Memorial Verses' of 1850 who 'spoke and loosed our heart in tears' belongs to another and more generous world than that of the sourly qualified praise of the essay of 1879. The poems of the last quarter-century only confirm our image of an incurably romantic poet pushing his own talent hard against the grain. Some impulse more personal than he dared to admit to his readers, and perhaps even to himself, must have driven him on. His long career as an Inspector of Schools, and his failure to win a post or sinecure more consonant with his dignity, may have embittered him more than he knew. One biographer has already found 'a shadowy personal significance' in *Sohrab and Rustum*,[1] where 'the strong son is slain by the mightier father', and the hint is worth pursuing to explain the paradox of his prose. The great themes of the poems are of solitude and isolation in the midst of men ('The Scholar-Gipsy', 'Thyrsis', the Marguerite poems), most fittingly portrayed in *Sohrab and Rustum*, where the young Sohrab seeks his father through the world and meets him only in mortal combat. Arnold's father was also his headmaster, Thomas Arnold of Rugby, himself a propagandist for the classical tradition in English schooling; and Arnold's fast-fading, self-questioning career as a young romantic poet may have found its apt model, at the age of thirty, in the Persian fable of the young warrior who dies at the hand of the very father he has long sought out, while his dying injunction to Rustum reads like Arnold's injunction to his own society to revive for itself the classical mode:

> Do thou the deeds I die too young to do.
> And reap a second glory in thine age. (ll. 775–6)

And old Rustum's answer, not less aptly, seems to acknowledge the hopelessness of the task:

> And the great Rustum drew his horseman's cloak
> Down o'er his face, and sate by his dead son. (ll. 858–9)

1. Trilling, op. cit., ch. 4.

CHAPTER 8

HENRY JAMES

THE three decades between Arnold and Eliot (*c.* 1890–1920) defy easy generalization. It is the age of the aesthetes, such as Pater, Wilde and the young W. B. Yeats, with their self-conscious attempt to demoralize criticism (in a peculiarly literal sense) by belittling the importance of meaning; but it includes the birth of an intensely moralistic tradition of novel-criticism in the reviews and prefaces of Henry James, and the triumph of motive-analysis in the *Shakespearean Tragedy* (1904) of A. C. Bradley (1851–1935). Bradley's achievement, which can now be seen to have transformed Shakespearean studies in a permanent sense, continued in later collections of essays and papers, *Oxford Lectures on Poetry* (1909) and *A Miscellany,* and along with an earlier commentary on *In Memoriam* (1901), it was continuously informed by a rare intellectual probity and a concern for descriptive truth.

And all the while, in a less original key, the triumph of historical criticism is completed in the works of academic journalists such as George Saintsbury, Arthur Quiller-Couch, and Edmund Gosse, and with the establishment of chairs in English literature at Oxford and Cambridge around the turn of the century. Edwardian criticism is an odd compound of these several elements – the aesthetic, the moralistic, and the biographical. But then the quality of the age is confused and eclectic, heartily indifferent to dogmatic consistency, and delightedly aware of the variety of uses to which literature can be put. The immense mass of critical essays and literary histories of George Saintsbury (1845–1933), for instance, is built upon the assumption that no critical law is ultimately worth observing through thick and thin. Obviously the tradition in which he writes is, in one sense, continuous from the biographical tradition of Sainte-Beuve:

The essential qualities of literature, as of all art, are communicated by the individual, they depend upon idiosyncrasy.

But, paradoxically,

biographical and anecdotic detail has, I believe, much less to do with the real appreciation of the literary value of an author than is generally thought ... If they are not allowed to shoulder out criticism altogether, there can be no harm in them.[1]

Such unconfident historical criticism is already vulnerable in its sheer lack of principle: biography has turned to gossip, and gossip is now defended on the ground by which gossip can always be defended – that it is amusing for its own sake. This is a whole world away from the serious Victorian enthusiasm that had once seen in history a key to all knowledge, and though literary history has enjoyed a few belated triumphs, as in the works of R. W. Chambers (1874–1942) and C. S. Lewis (1898–1963), it found it difficult, in the early twentieth century, to recover from the lack of confidence occasioned by late Victorian disparagement. Before T. S. Eliot and I. A. Richards were schoolboys, the ground for anti-history was being prepared by academics who could find no better excuse for information than Saintsbury could find, and by ninetyish aestheticians with an open contempt for the human values of literature. The ground for Modernism was already being cleared.

In this complicated story, the criticism of Walter Pater (1839–94) occupies an ambiguous position: it is almost as moralistic as Arnold's and James's, and we are rarely allowed to forget for long that Pater was an Oxford don of serious Christian inclinations. But the doctrines which, in all seriousness, he offers are fatally trivializing to the intellectual status of poetry, and no good critic could afford to swallow them. For Pater, the content of literature is an embarrassing necessity, 'mere matter' and 'nothing with-

---

1. *Essays in English Literature 1780–1860* (1890), pp. xii, xxviii–ix.

out the form', which is, ideally, 'an end in itself'. 'All art constantly aspires towards the condition of music'[1] is a slogan bound to reduce descriptive criticism to the level of unfalsifiable statements, for analysis only flourishes where content is seriously regarded and where the text is respected by critic and reader as a common point of reference. Pater is a tentative, unsystematic critic, and as a professional academic philosopher of the Hegelian period his interests often converge, as in his *Imaginary Portraits* (1887), on the links between belief and personal temperament. This means that contradictory statements could easily be found. In the later essay on 'Style', for instance, in *Appreciations* (1889), he looks more like a disciple of Arnold than an ancestor of Wilde, 'the distinction between great art depending immediately, as regards literature at all events, not on its form, but on the matter'.

Pater's uncertain attack was quickly reinforced. Oscar Wilde (1854–1900), in a few flimsy essays on critical issues, popularized anti-history in epigrams that turned the historical sense on its head and had no difficulty in making it look old-fashioned. 'All bad poetry springs from genuine feeling'[2] – the fallacy is not plausible enough to be worth exposing, but its vogue in the nineties and after suggests how close the critical tradition came to total collapse.

The monumental exception lies in the criticism of Henry James (1843–1916), the American expatriate who, in a rare and even unique degree, continued to see literature intensely as a human and moral concern, and who dared to apply his critical talents, with immense seriousness, to the analysis of the novel. The revolution was extraordinarily

1. 'The School of Giorgione' (*Fortnightly Review*, October 1877) collected in the second edition of *The Renaissance* (1877).

2. From the dialogue 'The Critic as Artist'. There is surviving evidence of Wilde's early, conventional historicism in the prize-essay *The Rise of Historical Criticism* (Hartford, Conn., 1905), probably written at Oxford in 1879, which is full of the usual Victorian enthusiasm: 'Historical criticism . . . is part of that complex working towards freedom which may be described as the revolt against authority . . .' See facsimile in Stuart Mason, *Bibliography of Oscar Wilde* (1914), p. 471.

sudden and complete. The English novel had been obliged to wait an extravagantly long time – well over a hundred years – for a body of criticism to match its own dignity. It is even more surprising to find how suddenly and how powerfully the first mood of critical curiosity made itself felt. As late as 1884, Henry James, already a middle-aged novelist, called the English novel 'undiscussed': twenty years later he discussed it so thoroughly in eighteen prefaces for the New York edition of his *Novels and Tales* (1907–9) that one is left asking what critical instrument peculiar to the novel he has failed to use. No critical revolution can ever have been so total as that represented by the New York prefaces. It is as if the horseless carriage had been invented at one stroke as a race-track model. Novel-criticism in English does not grow, as the art of analysing poetry grows, painfully, over the three centuries that separate us from Dryden. It just happens; for whatever importance we attach to the mid-Victorian reviews of novels by George Eliot, G. H. Lewes, and Walter Bagehot, it is as clear today, as it was to James himself, that they were written without an assured technique and without an assured audience.

And yet a silent need there must have been to meet the 'contemporary deluge' of novels, as James called it in 1899: the novel, by the eighties, was self-evidently the pre-eminent literary form in England, and still longer and more firmly established in France and Russia. Critics like Arnold, Pater and Wilde who looked elsewhere did so out of a deliberate, fastidious denial of the taste of their own time and place. James, an older man and a provincial American in origin, looked firmly to the present. Admitting all the sophistication of his criticism, it was a characteristically naïve decision. For the first time since Fielding – that curious false-starter among critics of the novel – an English-speaking novelist writes memorably of his art.

The publication of James's notebooks in 1947 has established what was never worth doubting, that this art was deeply conscious and articulate from the start. Almost from the beginning, from the age of thirty-five until his death,

James soberly set down his rational choices as he worked, and consciously and articulately made up his mind on paper. It is in these notebooks, from the year 1878 onwards, that novel-criticism as we know it was born. Every novel and every story was willed into existence in an almost uniquely self-conscious sense, and the eighteen prefaces he wrote at the end of his career, in his mid-sixties, knowingly celebrate an accomplished career. Those who believe good criticism to take its rise most naturally from the failure of a creative life should be directed here, where the balance between criticism and creation seems almost designedly perfect. Certainly the dominant tone of James's criticism is not, like that of Dryden's, apologetic. James's prefaces are in no sense self-defensive. They are modestly confident, paradoxically buoyed up by a respect for the ultimate obscurity of all great works of art. Indeed, as James early emphasizes, his early novels were so remote from his elderly recollection as to seem to him almost the work of another man.

Notebooks apart – and they must always remain apart, inevitably unique, studio-talk rather than analysis – James's criticism falls into three stages. Its scope is not wide, since James concentrated his critical energies as a professional from the start. Almost all his criticism is about contemporary authors, almost all are English, American, and French, and the great majority are novelists. First come the early reviews written from the age of twenty-one, some as early as a decade before his final settlement in Europe in 1875; at which early age, he tells us later, 'the verb *to contribute* took on at once to my ears a weird beauty of its own,'[1] and he contributed articles to the newly established *Nation* and elsewhere on any sort of book – including an attack on Dickens's *Our Mutual Friend* (1865).[2] His first review, indeed (October 1864), appeared only a few months

1. 'The Founding of the *Nation*' (*Nation*, New York, 8 July 1915), reprinted in his *American Essays*, edited by Leon Edel (New York, 1956).
2. *Nation* (21 December 1865), reprinted in *The House of Fiction*, edited by Leon Edel (1957). See Edel and Dan H. Laurence, *A Bibliography of Henry James* (revised edition, 1961), pp. 289f.

after his first story, and he collected some of them early as *French Poets and Novelists* (1878). Secondly, there is the magnificent central phase that opens with a manifesto-like 'The Art of Fiction' (1884),[1] a review of a published lecture of this title by Walter Besant, and followed by major essays on Trollope (1883), R. L. Stevenson (1888), Maupassant (1888), Zola (1903), and Balzac (1905); while the early, deeply generous tribute to Hawthorne in the English Men of Letters volume (1879) may be added here, and late reviews such as 'The Younger Generation' on Conrad, Arnold Bennett, and Hugh Walpole.[2] Thirdly, there are prefaces of 1907–9, composed in a single, confined period of preparation for the collected edition of his works. They are so nearly a total statement of his view of the novel that it is convenient to consider them at once, adducing evidence from the earlier reviews and essays as they contribute to the total argument.

The New York prefaces occurred half-accidentally, arising out of a publisher's contract. In 1904–5 James revisited his native America for the first time in twenty years, and arranged the terms of a definitive edition of his fiction with Scribner's of New York during the visit. Perfectionism prompted a revision of the novels, and the impulse to write prefaces at all may have taken its rise from a desire to explain the case for revision in the light of the genesis of each work. They must have been written mainly in the course of 1906–7, though James did not complete them all, or even know how many there were to be, until the appearance of the twenty-four-volume edition was well advanced. In a letter to Grace Norton, probably written as late as the beginning of 1908, he promises twenty-three volumes, and fifteen prefaces only, adding that the latter were 'difficult to do – but I have found them of a jolly interest'. The revising

1. *Longman's Magazine* (September 1884), collected with many of the following essays in *Partial Portraits* (1888) and *The House of Fiction*, above.
2. *The Times Literary Supplement* (19 March and 2 April 1914), revised as 'The New Novel' in his *Notes on Novelists* (1914).

of the text of his fiction and the proof-reading were bad enough, but the prefaces were 'the real tussle'; he dictated them, according to his secretary Theodora Bosanquet, every morning over many weeks, in the long, luminous style of his last period. James may have surprised himself with the wealth of his own theoretical interests, and the design surely grew under his hands as he wrote: why else should so methodical a genius set down so much of critical interest in a series of eighteen overlapping and interrelated essays, when their interest so far exceeds the merely prefatorial? There is a hint of missed opportunity in the letter to W. D. Howells (17 August 1908):

They ought, collected together,. . . . to form a sort of comprehensive manual or *vademecum* for aspirants of our arduous profession. Still, it will be long before I shall want to collect them together for that purpose and furnish *them* with a final Preface,

a hint usefully taken up years later by R. P. Blackmur in his collected edition of the prefaces, *The Art of the Novel* (1934). As a manual of novel-writing they are, inevitably, hopelessly disorganized, since each novel and each group of tales dictates its own set of critical questions. Besides, the very choice of stories for the New York edition now seems capricious. Six novels – *The Europeans* (1878), *Confidence* (1880), *Washington Square* (1881), *The Bostonians* (1886), *The Other House* (1896), and *The Sacred Fount* (1901) – were omitted altogether from the collection, and accordingly have no preface. The case of *The Bostonians*, rejected by Scribner's on prudential grounds, is especially regrettable, and was openly regretted by James himself. Chaotic, then, the material admittedly is, but one ought to feel grateful for what there is. At all events, the nine novels and the nine groups of tales which together compose the New York edition provide material assorted enough to call out most of James's resources as a critic.

James's object in his criticism, as it develops, is ambitious and clear: it is to create from nothing an English tradition in the criticism of the novel. And he is very certain that no such criticism exists: in 'The Art of Fiction' of 1884 he complains that

only a short time ago it might have been supposed that the English novel was not what the French call *discutable*. It had no air of having a theory, a conviction, a consciousness of itself behind it – of being the expression of an artistic faith, the result of choice and comparison ... There was a comfortable, good-humoured feeling abroad that a novel is a novel, as a pudding is a pudding, and that our only business with it could be to swallow it.

And in the previous year he had noticed, in the essay on Trollope, that in English terms

it is rather dangerous to be explicitly or consciously an artist – to have a system, a doctrine, a form.

The English novel, then, unlike the French, was not discussable, but James set out to make it so. His own account of what it means to discuss or criticize – 'to appreciate, to appropriate, to take intellectual possession' – fits the eighteen prefaces, but in a rather unusual sense. It is not just that the novels so discussed are James's own, as the plays of Dryden's prefaces are Dryden's plays. James's prefaces are only doubtfully self-criticism, after all, for he sees his own stories distantly, through a nostalgic haze. The first of the novels, *Roderick Hudson* (1876), was already thirty years old when he came to revise it, and though the first part of each preface is concerned with reconstruction and recollection, 'the story of one's story', time has thrown the author himself now into the role of a mere reader, now into that of the elderly sage whose past life, as he reads and revises, returns irresistibly over the passage of the years. There are stories which, he admits in the preface to *The Reverberator*, 'become in the highest degree documentary for myself', and there are moments of passionate evocation as the greatest of all American tourists in Europe seems to see, smell, and touch the cities of his early manhood. 'There are pages of the book', he wrote of *The Portrait of a Lady* (1881), which had been partly composed in Venice, 'which, in the reading over, have seemed to make me see again the bristling curve of the wide Riva . . . The Venetian footfall and the Venetian cry – all talk there, wherever uttered, having the pitch of a call across the water – come in once more at the window'; and of *The Tragic Muse* (1890) he writes: 'I catch again the very odour of Paris, which comes up in the rich rumble of the Rue de la Paix.' James's great critical effort begins as a labour of love, his remembrance is in itself 'a great romance'.[1]

And the evocation is useful, in a double sense: first, it sets the stage for isolating the novel's point of departure, its 'germ'; and second, it serves to remind one, as James seeks to do, that the artist himself must entertain no arrogant certainty that he can reconstruct the work of his own past as it once grew under his hands. The author is a privileged, uniquely well-informed reader of his own works – but he is a reader too, with a reader's due uncertainties. The very form of the novel, indeed, forbids any possibility that he can ever feel certain to have said everything: 'The private history of any sincere work, however modest its pretensions, looms with its own completeness in the rich, ambiguous aesthetic air, and seems at once to borrow a dignity and to mark, so to say, a station.'[2] The professional critic has something to learn in humility from James's fastidious uncertainties:

The sunk surface as here and there, beyond doubt, refused to respond: the buried secrets, the intentions, are buried too deep to rise again . . .[3]

The disclaimer reminds us of neo-critical theories that urge the critic not to waste time over the author's intention,[4] but

1. Letter to A. C. Benson (24 February 1895); *Henry James: Letters to A. C. Benson*, edited by E. F. Benson (1930), p. 5.
2. *The Art of the Novel*, edited by R. P. Blackmur (New York, 1934), p. 4 (preface to *Roderick Hudson*).
3. ibid., p. 11.
4. W. K. Wimsatt and Monroe C. Beardsley, 'The Intentional Fallacy', *Sewanee Review*, liv (1946), reprinted in Wimsatt, *The Verbal Icon* (Lexington, Kentucky, 1954).

the resemblance is only superficial. For James is perceptive enough to see that mere impossibility does not rule out endeavour, and that no species of criticism is ever likely to enable us utterly 'to take intellectual possession'. There are kinds of criticism that lead to within shouting distance of the work, and kinds that lead further and further away; and James is clear that 'the buried secrets, the intentions' of the novelist are what his imaginary novelist, Vereker, in 'The Figure in the Carpet' (1896) called 'the thing for the critic to find'. This story, from James's middle period, insists with frankness on the propriety of historical criticism. It is the naïve narrator who protests that the critic

was like nothing ... but the maniacs who embrace some bedlamitical theory of the cryptic character of Shakespeare. To this he replied that if we had had Shakespeare's own word for his being cryptic, he would at once have accepted it.[1]

Even the Baconians, then, are right in principle, though of course idiotic in the particular case: good poems really are what poets mean them to be, whatever they may be besides. It is important to recognize that the ironic force of the story lies not, as some have supposed, in any assumption that Vereker's secret is not worth having – there is no hint of this in the notebooks, and it is explicitly denied in the preface – but in the narrator's simple-minded attempt to discover the novelist's secret in any way except by a careful reading of the novels. Each interview takes him further away from the intelligence of the dead genius – whereas a 'close or analytic appreciation' might have led him straight to the secret. The story repeats James's protest against the lack of effective novel-criticism in England, and against what he calls 'this odd numbness of the general sensibility'. 'How strangely and helplessly among us all', he exclaims in his preface to the story, 'what we call criticism ... is apt to stand off from the intended sense of things.'[2] On the histori-

1. 'The Figure in the Carpet', ch. 5; in his *Embarrassments* (1896).
2. *The Art of the Novel*, edited by R. P. Blackmur (New York, 1934), pp. 227, 228, 229.

cal issue, then, James is simply a romantic critic, as intently concerned with the creative art as Coleridge himself. It is true that design may, in this view, grow under the artist's hands, but it is not less the artist's design because he modifies it in the course of creation. The characters of *The Portrait of a Lady* (1881), he remarked, behaved as if they were in search of an author, and answered their novelist as he worked 'that if I would trust them, they would show me' what the heroine Isabel Archer was to do; and he urges his readers, in the preface to *The Ambassadors* (1903), never to underestimate 'the energy which [a story] simply makes for itself'. Coleridge's theory of the organic form of works of art seems only just around the corner, though there is no evidence of a direct debt. Some of James's analogies, certainly, sound startlingly familiar: in 'The Art of Fiction' he had called the novel

a living thing, all one and continuous, like any other organism, and in proportion as it lives will it be found, I think, that in each of the parts there is something of each of the other parts.

The central obsession of the prefaces is the issue of 'form', obsessional because based upon the intractable paradox that stories never fit their author's purposes simply, like pints in pint pots. The perfectionist in James accepted the challenge: art, he proudly concluded in his preface to *The Golden Bowl* (1904), 'is nothing if not exemplary'. Without form, novels are mere 'fluid puddings', as he called the novels of Tolstoy and Dostoyevsky: 'form alone *takes,* and holds and preserves, substance.'[1] He dreamed of himself, incongruously, as a ruthless technician of the novel – 'art should be as hard as nails' and the artist 'an absolutely Roman father'[2] – and summoned up French novels whose morality shocked him to teach the English novel a sense of technical competence. And still the paradox defeated him: you cannot pin

1. Letter to Hugh Walpole (19 May 1912); *Letters of Henry James,* edited by Percy Lubbock (1920), 11, 246.
2. Letter to A. C. Benson (26 February 1895); *Letters to A. C. Benson* (1930), p. 7.

down life (that echoing word in the prefaces) like a butterfly upon a board. All art, ultimately, has this element of falsity, pretending to a tidiness that is quite unreal:

Really, universally, relations stop nowhere, and the exquisite problem of the artist is eternally but to draw, by a geometry of his own, the circle within which they will happily *appear* to do so. He is in the perpetual predicament that the continuity of things is the whole matter, for him, of comedy and tragedy; that this continuity is never, by the space of an instant or an inch, broken, and that, to do anything at all, he has at once intensely to consult and intensely to ignore it.[1]

This is screwing the problem up to a high pitch, and it is not obvious that 'the continuity of things', or causality in human relations, is 'the whole matter' in a novel. It counts for very little in some novelists, like Fielding; though it is an indispensable part of all novels that aspire to psychological truth, the only kind James ever wanted to write. Such novels, inevitably, are something of a cheat, in an absolute sense; but James insisted that the cheat must at least be professionally contrived, 'only by delicate adjustments and an exquisite chemistry, so that there will at the end be neither a drop of one's liquor left nor a hair's breadth of the rim of one's glass to spare'. A novel, at its technical best, is a 'successfully *foreshortened* thing',[2] selecting from 'clumsy Life' and 'the fatal futility of Fact'[3] what is revealing and significant – 'life being all inclusion and confusion,' as he put it in the preface to *The Spoils of Poynton* (1897), and art 'all discrimination and selection'. It is in this sense, as he explains at length in the same preface, recounting how he had heard its 'germ' at a London dinner-table,

1. Preface to *Roderick Hudson*; *Art of the Novel*, p. 5.
2. Preface to *The Tragic Muse*; ibid., p. 87. Cf. his account of the even more stringent demands of form made by the drama, which 'needs a masterly structure. It needs to be shaped and fashioned and laid together', like packing a coffer: 'it closes perfectly, and the lock turns with a click; between one object and another you cannot insert the point of a penknife' (*Views and Reviews* (1908), pp. 181–2).
3. Preface to *The Spoils of Poynton*; *Art of the Novel*, pp. 121–2.

that life is a nuisance: it does not know where to stop.

A fruitful confusion of terms, of which James nowhere seems conscious, emerges at this point: for life is not just an untidy aggregation of facts in James's criticism: it is also, as in the stories themselves, a moral imperative. From the ardent young Roderick Hudson to the tentative Strether of *The Ambassadors* (1903), James's heroes make their bid for Life and meet defeat at its hands, and are yet justified in the attempt: 'Live all you can; it's a mistake not to. It doesn't much matter what you do in particular as long as you have your life. If you haven't had that, what *have* you had ...?' This is Lambert Strether's advice to little Bilham, approvingly quoted by James in his preface to the novel. The ambiguity is significant. James's fascination with form and his tragically agnostic vision meet in verbal ambiguity at this point: life is supremely worth the telling, for it is all that we have.

And yet its essential complexity remains, to the end, a technical challenge. James developed the technique known now as 'the central intelligence' – the technique of viewing the action of a novel through the eyes of a character whose subtlety of mind equals or almost equals that of the novelist himself – as early as *Roderick Hudson*, though his account of Rowland Mallet in his preface of thirty years after is surely, as analysis, predictive of his later years:

The centre of interest throughout *Roderick* is in Rowland Mallet's consciousness, and the drama is the very drama of that consciousness – which I had of course to make sufficiently acute in order to enable it, like a set and lighted scene, to hold the play.

This 'most polished of possible mirrors', as he calls Mallet when he returns to the subject in the preface to *The Princess Casamassima* (1886), is to be set 'right in the middle of the light' or the thick of the action. The technique is genuinely new, for previous 'central intelligences', such as some heroines of Jane Austen and George Eliot, had been protagonists too. But James's fascination with problems of perspective in the novel carried him beyond this technique into the far more intricate design of multiple vision, as in *The Golden Bowl* (1904), which

abides rigidly by its law of showing Maggie Verver at first through her suitor's and her husband's exhibitory vision of her, and of then showing the Prince, with at least an equal intensity, through his wife's; . . . these attributions of experience display the sentient subjects themselves at the same time and by the same stroke . . .

By the new century, even the subtleties of the technique of a central intelligence had come to seem limiting and mechanical.

The extent of James's revolution in the criticism of the novel is difficult to overstate. Before he wrote, few or none of the familiar assumptions of twentieth-century novel-criticism were current; and James not merely made them current but even added many of the delicate qualifications which a pioneer might ordinarily be expected to leave to his successors. It was James who, in the deceptively mandarin prose of his prefaces, made us look for a total and unifying meaning in novels by identifying the biographical points of departure of his own; it was James who taught us to see such significances as organized part by part, and to study the interrelations of those parts; it was James who defined the role of morality in the novel as having nothing to do with 'special precept' or the demands of social conformity, and James who pointed to the inevitable falsity of fiction as well as to its essential truth. And – as if this were not enough – it was James who first convincingly explored the technical problems of the novel in English, though his demonstration lacks comprehensiveness and omits many a familiar academic issue such as the place of the narrator and the virtues of the first-person singular. And all this is effected with no Arnoldian imperatives, no open injunction but that of 'life' itself, and no obtrusive aspiration to legislate for other novelists. His private name for the New York prefaces, a '*vademecum*', proves after all to be not quite a joke; for with all proper reservations concerning their lack of sustained argument and neatly formulated principles, they may to this day serve the patient reader very well as that.

CHAPTER 9

THE EARLY TWENTIETH CENTURY

T. S. Eliot

THE question sounds eminently reasonable, but remains unanswerable: what is revolutionary in the criticism of T. S. Eliot? Everyone –except apparently Eliot himself– can see that the critical tradition of the whole English-speaking world was turned upside down by the trickle of articles and lectures – there has never, strictly, been a critical book – issuing from his pen since the First World War. But the nature of his influence as a critic has always been felt to be mysterious and indefinable. E. M. W. Tillyard, in his history of the Cambridge English School, has told how the essays in *The Sacred Wood* (1920), when they first appeared, 'made me uncomfortable, and I knew they could not be ignored'.[1] Disciples – even enemies – have hardly succeeded in identifying what is new and special in Eliot's criticism, though they have been loud both in praise and censure. The most discreet of major English critics, he has practised evasion and reticence with determined skill. In his earliest period, positions were tentatively stated and argument disarmed by a certain irony; in his middle years, argument was openly spurned; and in the later years, since the Second World War, he elaborately pretended never to have been a major critic at all. Altogether, his critical career might have been planned as a vast hoax to tempt the historian into solemnities for the sport of Philistines.

The key to Eliot's reticence as a critic surely lies in the relationship between his criticism and his poetry. In a sense, his criticism is a smoke-screen to the rest of his career. It misleads as much as it reveals about the quality of his poems,

1. *The Muse Unchained* (1958), p. 97.

and the smoke-screen grows thicker as the years pass. By the 1950s Eliot's determination to hide himself from the devotees of his poetry by means of critical red-herrings had grown so obvious as to suggest a possible motive: the intense love of privacy, perhaps, of a fastidious New Englander whose poetry has led him into the indignity of spiritual self-exposure. One fears something of the kind as early as a Harvard lecture of 1932, where he attempted to disarm analysis of *Ash-Wednesday* (1930), a poem intimately tracking the path of a religous conversion, by suggesting the addition to the poem of a Byronic motto:

> But the fact is that I have nothing planned,
> Except perhaps to be a moment merry . . .[1]

The mask of the sage slips at such moments of embarrassing whimsy, to reveal the face of an injured piety.

The formal properties of Eliot's criticism, at least, are clear enough, and may be summarily described. An Eliot essay is a statement of an attitude, a *prise de position*, an evaluation. It docs not even pretend to be biographical, in the sense that an Arnold essay so pretends: Arnold's claim to be a disciple of Sainte-Beuve gives way, with Eliot, to a frankly unhistorical insistence upon the immediacy of certain poets here and now, and Eliot hardly ever stoops to purvey information. Secondly, 'relevance' refers to modern poets rather than to modern readers, and Eliot commits himself openly to this object in the 1935 lecture on Milton:

> Of what I have to say I consider that the only jury of judgement is that of the ablest poetical practitioners of my own time.[2]

Thirdly, Eliot eschews close analysis in favour of general judgements; his taste and techniques were formed decades before the New Criticism of the thirties, and he never practises the 'close analysis' characteristic of that school. These are hardly arguable statements about Eliot's criti-

1. *The Use of Poetry and the Use of Criticism* (1933), pp. 30–31.
2. 'A Note on the Verse of John Milton', *Essays and Studies*, XXI (1935), reprinted on his *On Poetry and Poets* (New York, 1957), p. 157.

cism. They go a very little way, however, towards describing what an Eliot essay is like. To do that would require a more impressionistic account, leading to statements that might prove highly debatable, since the rhetoric of his criticism is opaque enough to leave a good deal in doubt. What does seem clear is that Eliot is Arnold's successor in terms of the audience he expects for criticism: a minority audience, aware of itself as a cultural leadership, and peculiarly vulnerable, like Arnoldians, to the seductions of intellectual snobbery. It might be unfair to attribute to Eliot himself the stock-market approach to literary values that characterizes a good many of his followers; but certainly, in this regard, Eliot finishes what Arnold began. A price-scale of values for an intellectual élite among the dead poets, of a kind that would certainly have puzzled Dryden, Johnson, and Coleridge, is part of the Eliot inheritance, however little he may like it. But the object of Eliot's criticism is not just an Addisonian ambition to correct taste: more narrowly, it is the correction of taste with a view to influencing his own future readership and audiences. The real parallel among our classic critics lies not in Addison but in Dryden, and an Eliot essay – though not openly prefatorial and self-justifying, like most of Dryden's criticism – serves a comparable purpose.

Thomas Stearns Eliot (1888–1965) was born in St Louis, Missouri, of New England family, and was educated at Harvard, Oxford and Paris. At the beginning of the First World War he settled in London, and soon accepted British citizenship, renouncing (as Henry James never did) the liberal ideals of American society. The famous preface to *For Lancelot Andrewes* (1928), in which he declared himself 'a classicist in literature, an Anglo-Catholic in religion, and a royalist in politics', was evidently designed to burn all boats and set a term to boyhood and youth. His conversion to Christianity seems to date from the late twenties, after the appearance of *The Waste Land* (1922), and only *The Sacred Wood* (1920), among his critical writings, is innocent of the neo-scholastic tinge. But Eliot's rejection of liberalism, or the cult of individual man, certainly dates from the years before 1914 and from his early association with Ezra Pound and T. E. Hulme – even, perhaps, from hearing Irving Babbitt's Harvard lectures against romanticism. The originality of his essay 'Tradition and the Individual Talent',[1] with which his critical career effectively begins, lies not in its anti-liberalism but in its application of that fashionable doctrine to the immediate critical situation. It is so evidently an unofficial manifesto of Eliot's criticism, or an account of the principles the young critic planned to bring to bear upon English poetry, that its implications deserve to be studied before looking at Eliot's career as a critic in detail.

'Tradition and the Individual Talent' is not the kind of essay that invites open discussion. Its tone is drily pontifical, and Eliot's distaste for debate and free speech is firmly suggested in the rhetorical properties of the essay. It asks not to be examined – which is a very good reason for examining it. The deliberate perversities of Eliot's use of language are part of the Arnoldian minority-appeal of the essay: the reader is invited from the start to enter where only a few will follow by a denial of a popular 'fallacy': 'we dwell with satisfaction upon the poet's difference from his predecessors, ... endeavour to find something that can be isolated in order to be enjoyed.' This prepares the reader for a redefinition of key-terms – 'tradition' does not mean 'a blind or timid adherence' to the successes of a former generation, but

it involves, in the first place, the historical sense, which we may call nearly indispensable to anyone who would continue to be a poet beyond his twenty-fifth year; and the historical sense involves a perception, not only of the pastness of the past, but of its presence; the historical sense compels a man to write not merely with his own generation in his bones, but with a feeling that the whole of the literature of Europe from Homer, and within it the whole of the literature of his own country, has a simultaneous existence and composes a simultaneous order ...

1. *Egoist*, October – December 1919 (in two parts), reprinted in *The Sacred Wood* (1920) and *Selected Essays* (1932).

And this 'historical sense' is 'what makes a writer tradi-tional'. But it is an odd historical sense that denies chrono-logy and conceives of the past both as 'the timeless and the temporal'; it might have been franker, one begins to feel as the essay proceeds, to call it 'the anti-historical sense'. It is a tribute to the fading power of historical studies that Eliot, like Arnold, seeks to maintain a façade of historicism behind which to develop a doctrine of poetry very like Arnold's own - the poetry of the past existing as a 'simul-taneous order' and inviting study not for what it meant to the poet and his first readers, but for what it means to the practising poet of our own day - 'the object as in itself it really is', in Arnold's words, where 'really' aptly suggests a certain contempt for previous judgements.

Contempt for historical criticism is confirmed in Eliot's argument as it develops: poets do not express themselves in poetry, but escape from themselves by 'a continual extinct-ion of personality'; so that historical criticism, by implicat-ion, is convicted of looking for the wrong things. It looks to the poet and his historical situation, whereas the poem itself points away from both towards some ideal of impersonal truth: 'Honest criticism and sensitive appreciation is direct-ed not upon the poet, but upon the poetry', for ultimately, the individuality of the poet is irrelevant, his business being 'not to find new emotions, but to use the ordinary ones'. Again the Arnoldian echo, this time from the 1853 preface, where Arnold demands poems about 'those elementary feel-ings which subsist permanently in the race'. 'Romantic', as in Babbitt and Hulme, is here a term of abuse, and Words-worth's formula 'emotion recollected in tranquillity' is rejected as inexact, on the grounds that 'poetry is not a turning loose of emotion, but an escape from emotion; it is not the expression of personality, but an escape from per-sonality'. The wary reader, undazzled by so much confi-dent assertion, may still ask why such a view should lead him to conclude that 'to divert interest from the poet to the poetry is a laudable aim'. It would be an odd escape-story that omitted first to describe the prison, and how the captive managed to get out of it.

What Eliot calls 'the historical sense', then, can be grouped among other attacks upon the historiography of literature in the age that followed Arnold. But Eliot's real historical sense is not to be dismissed: it is far finer than Arnold's, who often seems to live and think in a strait-jacket of mid-Victorian enlightenment. There are plenty of passages in *The Sacred Wood,* and even later, notably in *The Use of Poetry and the Use of Criticism,* that make one wonder what a delicately intuitive historian of literature was lost in Eliot. In the early essays, attacks on the historical principle, and examples of acute historical judgement, coexist oddly in the same passage, like 'the timeless and the temporal':

If we write about Middleton's plays we must write about Middleton's plays, and not about Middleton's personality,

he writes in the essay on Middleton in *For Lancelot Andrewes* – but only, it becomes clear as the essay proceeds, because we do not know enough about Middleton's life and cannot do anything else. Who, without prompting, could guess that Eliot could be as relativistic a critic as the following passage suggests? (It is from the 1936 essay on Tennyson's *In Memoriam*):

Innovation in metric is not to be measured solely by the width of the deviation from accepted practice. It is a matter of the historical situation: at some moments a more violent change may be necessary than at others. The problem differs at every period.

This does not make *In Memoriam* sound like part of a 'simultaneous order': if only the tone were not so coldly judicial, it might almost be Sainte-Beuve. And yet, Eliot might plead, this is merely a technical question: on the subject of poetry he remains sceptical of historical proof:

If poetry is a form of 'communication', yet that which is to be communicated is the poem itself ... The poem's existence is somewhere between the writer and the reader.... Consequently the problem of what a poem 'means' is a good deal more difficult than it at first appears.[1]

Any tastes Eliot had towards historical inquiries into poetry – and they may easily have been strong – were frustrated by an ideological conviction that poetry is not in an absolute sense communication at all. The lecture 'Shakespeare and the Stoicism of Seneca', read before the Shakespeare Association in 1927, is an elaborate and outrageous joke against the historical method:

I propose a Shakespeare under the influence of the stoicism of Seneca. But I do not believe that Shakespeare was under the influence of Seneca. I propose it largely because I believe that after the Montaigne Shakespeare ... and after the Machiavelli Shakespeare, a stoical or Senecan Shakespeare is almost certain to be produced. I wish merely to disinfect the Senecan Shakespeare before he appears. My ambitions would be realized if I could prevent him, in so doing, from appearing at all.

Eliot's critical convictions cannot be said to evolve in any very striking sense. His alleged change of heart over Milton between 1935 and 1947 is more like a tactical withdrawal under fire; his growing scepticism, as he aged, over the utility of criticism – any criticism – certainly modifies his tone of voice, but hardly his deepest convictions about literature. Correspondences pop up oddly, decades apart, in his writings: thoughtful readers of the 1919 essay 'Tradition and the Individual Talent' will know just where they are in his poem 'The Dry Salvages' (1941):

It seems, as one becomes older,
That the past has another pattern, and ceases to be a mere sequence –
Or even development...

Eliot did not have to become older to learn that the past is not a mere sequence. It is all in *The Sacred Wood*. Still, preoccupations change where theologies do not, and if there are few Eliot juvenilia and no dramatic changes in front, the

1. *The Use of Poetry and the Use of Criticism* (1933), p. 30.

mass of his five hundred essays, reviews and published lectures still falls comfortably enough into three periods, not unlike the Arnoldian dialectic of the two literary periods separated by an intermediate decade of social interests. Eliot's career evolved in a broadly similar way: from the first, pre-Christian decade (1919–28) of literary preoccupation, mainly with sixteenth and seventeenth-century dramatists and poets in *The Sacred Wood* (1920), *Homage to John Dryden: Three Essays* (1924), and *For Lancelot Andrewes* (1928); through a second decade of social and religious criticism (1929–39) following on his conversion and his final break with 'modernism', in *Dante* (1929), *Thoughts after Lambeth* (1931), *After Strange Gods* (1934); to the post war Olympian period, which marks a certain renewal of interest in critical (especially dramatic) issues, though hardly in the concentrated form of the first decade. It already seems clear – and not only for such reasons as this abrupt analysis may suggest – that any serious estimate of Eliot as a critic must depend upon the early essays. Stiff, sly, and pompous as their language sometimes is, they are none the less even-tempered, conscientious, and exploratory, and Eliot's frigid distaste for debate is less evident here, and less damaging, than in his later writings. Reshaped as *Selected Essays* in 1932, and since enlarged, the early essays are a nearly complete monument to his genius as a critic.

The appearance of *The Sacred Wood* in November 1920 seems at first to have startled hardly anybody, and the book made its way easily in the world. Most of the seventeen essays had already appeared in a variety of journals. The reviewer in *The Times Literary Supplement* (2 December 1920) noted with approval the dry, precise manner of the young American critic so different from the flowery Edwardian mode of current literary journalism: Eliot, he wrote, 'does not try to write prose-poetry about poetry, to make his criticism the poor relation of poetry' – though he was mildly shocked by what still seems Eliot's worst contribution to the style of English criticism, the glancing insult which attacks too abruptly to admit reply:

He tries to annoy them [admirers of Meredith] by slipping in contemptuous remarks about Meredith which cannot be refuted because they say nothing except that Mr Eliot despises Meredith and those who admire him.

Eliot's habit of killing off his literary and theological enemies in a parenthesis, like the hero of an E. M. Forster novel – '(not that Montaigne had any philosophy whatever)'[1] – was rather charitably interpreted, by the same reviewer, as 'a malice the more insidious because unconscious'. The design and unity of *The Sacred Wood* seems to have passed unnoticed, even by later idolators of Eliot. This is probably because everyone now reads these essays (or most of them) as they stand depleted and engulfed in later and larger collections, the attacks upon the impressionistic Edwardian school (Arthur Symons, George Wyndham, Charles Whibley, and others) in 'The Perfect Critic', and 'Imperfect Critics' being omitted from *Selected Essays* (1932) as ungracious or out of date. In his 1928 preface to *The Sacred Wood*, Eliot claimed that 'what coherence they [the essays] have, is the problem of the integrity of poetry, with the repeated assertion that when we are considering poetry we must consider it primarily as poetry and not another thing'. This claim to aesthetic detachment is not much more convincing than Arnold's – Eliot's criticism is partisan from the start, and increasingly so with the years. What unites the essays is not any doctrine of the 'integrity' of poetry, but of its availability. Eliot behaves towards the dead poets of Europe with all the casual skill of a shoplifter in a department store. He knows what he wants and what he can use, and he seizes upon it as coolly as if no established scale of values already existed among the English poets. He arrives at his views by a process of unhurried irreverence, gently defining what he means (and, very characteristically, what he does not mean), and concluding with judgements which are readily felt to be radical and vaguely momentous: Marlowe's verse, when he died, was moving 'towards this intense and serious

1. 'Shakespeare and the Stoicism of Seneca', in *Selected Essays* (1932), p. 129.

and indubitably great poetry which, like some great painting and sculpture, attains its effects by something not unlike caricature'; Jonson's plays represent 'a part of our literary inheritance craving further expression. . . . There is a brutality, a lack of sentiment, a polished surface, a handling of large bold designs in brilliant colours, which ought to attract about three thousand people in London and elsewhere'. This last appeal to minority-values is uncharacteristically frank – in general, only the most masterly and refined rhetorical analysis could explain how much contrives to be suggested in these essays, as against how relatively little is openly stated, and how powerful and 'insidious' (as *The Times* put it) is the youthful irreverence that inspires them. The title – presumably an afterthought – suggests a revealing metaphor. The 'wood', no doubt, is the sacred grove of Nemi, near Rome, described in fine romantic detail by Sir James Frazer[1] in the first chapter of *The Golden Bough* (1890). Even as late as imperial times, Frazer tells us,

in the sacred grove there grew a certain tree, round which at any time of the day, and probably far into the night, a grim figure might be seen to prowl. In his hand he carried a drawn sword, and he kept peering warily about him as if at every instant he expected to be set upon by an enemy. He was a priest and a murderer; and the man for whom he looked was sooner or later to murder him and hold the priesthood in his stead. Such was the rule of the sanctuary. A candidate for the priesthood could only succeed to office by slaying the priest, and having slain him, he retained office till he was himself slain by a stronger or a craftier.

This 'rule of succession by the sword', by which a runaway slave might make his bid for a precarious liberty, provides a key to the unity of Eliot's first critical essays. A youthful poet turns critic to justify his own place in the line of succession, to stake a claim. He is priest and murderer. Perhaps the metaphor is doubly suggestive: Eliot, the new priest of

1. In an early article Eliot names Frazer (with Henry James and F. H. Bradley) as one of the three principal intellectual influences of his life. See his 'Lettre d'Angleterre', no. 3 (*Nouvelle Revue Française*, XI, 1 November 1923).

the 'tradition', inherits by a kind of critical massacre, belittling the rights of dead poets to historical existences and boldly plundering their remains.

The succession was swift. *The Waste Land,* when it appeared in 1922, was quickly hailed as the poem of a whole war-sick generation; in the same year Eliot became founder-editor of his journal *Criterion,* which he ran until the outbreak of the Second World War; and in 1926, before the age of forty, he delivered the Clark lectures in Cambridge on the Metaphysical poets. By then he was famous and acclaimed, especially among the young, and the leader of a literary cult.

The plunder of the new priest-king, in the essays of the twenties, is various, but mainly Elizabethan in *The Sacred Wood,* Metaphysical and Restoration in the collections that follow. The Renaissance emphasis is in itself a little surprising: in a literary sense Eliot is so much the child of Arnold (in theology and politics, of course, they stand almost as far apart as the distance between Right and Left) that one might have expected him to echo Arnold's youthful horror of 'those d—d Elizabethans'. But it is still possible to guess why he did not. In the first place, though a Franco-phile like Arnold, he shared none of Arnold's distaste for English civilization as such. In criticism and in poetry Eliot is a British patriot, though the England he loves is a happy self-deception of pomps and royalties, noble houses like the Wilton of Sir Philip Sidney and his sister, a Church Established:

> Elizabeth and Leicester
> Beating oars
> The stern was formed
> A gilded shell
> Red and gold . . .[1]

Only those who insist upon reading Eliot as total irony will deny the note of infatuation with an age which British nationalists are irresistibly led to glorify. James Anthony

1. *The Waste Land* (1922), ll. 279–83.

Froude, upon whose mid-Victorian historical extravaganzas this passage (according to Eliot's own note) is based, may have been a thought too Protestant for his taste, but surely not too patriotic. And secondly, Eliot sees in the Elizabethans and their successors qualities invisible to Arnold. Arnold thought them responsible for the confused and fragmentary quality of English romanticism: Eliot, very characteristically, sees them not as historical influences at all, but simply as a school where the apprentice-poet can learn his craft. And in this cause he is ready to make an alliance with the Devil himself. The more outrageously out of fashion the poet, indeed, the better Eliot seems to like the notion of finding a use for him: Tennyson and Swinburne are respectfully handled, for example, Shelley and Keats not. More characteristically, Eliot joins and leads a vogue already under way, such as the late Victorian and Edwardian vogue for Donne which had culminated in Grierson's edition of 1912. Essays like 'The Metaphysical Poets' and 'Andrew Marvell' (1921) aptly explain by justification techniques Eliot was already using in verse: the 'telescoping of images and multiplied associations' which, in Donne and the dramatists of his age, is 'one of the sources of the vitality of their language'; and the famous phrase by which he sums up the peculiar essence of Marvell's Horatian Ode, 'wit, a tough reasonableness beneath the slight lyric grace', might be an account of the central style of *The Waste Land*.

The celebrated hint in the first of these essays – it is hardly elaborate enough to be called a theory – of a 'dissociation of sensibility',[1] of thought from sensation, is best studied in this

1. The phrase, which has proved the most successful of all Eliot's adventures in critical jargon, is mysteriously echoic. F. W. Bateson (*Essays in Criticism*, 1 (1951), has suggested a source in Rémy de Gourmont, who twenty years before had suggested that Laforgue died before he could '*dissocie[r] son intelligence de sa sensibilité*'. Eric Thompson, in a reply (ibid., 11 (1952)), suggests F. H. Bradley as a source. Goethe is another possible candidate, and there is no doubt that Eliot was acquainted with Goethe as a poet and critic at an early stage in his career, as his Hamburg Lecture of 1955, 'Goethe as the Sage', suggests. See *Winckelmann und sein Jahrhundert* (1805), from the section 'Antikes':

light: that of Eliot's own poetic ambitions in the twenties. It identifies a breach he sought to heal:

A thought to Donne was an experience; it modified his sensibility ... [But] in the seventeenth century a dissociation of sensibility set in, from which we have never recovered; and this dissociation, as is natural, was aggravated by the influence of the two most powerful poets of the century, Milton and Dryden.

Eliot's majestic historical sense suddenly reveals two systems of vast correspondences, a poetical tradition tragically split beyond a point where romanticism could help. But his own use of the theory seems out of touch with the theory itself. We should have expected Milton and Dryden to be judged as equal offenders: but in fact Milton is ignored until 1935 and then lightly dismissed, Dryden celebrated in an early essay of 1921 as a mentor for poets of today and tomorrow:

In the next revolution of taste it is possible that poets may turn to the study of Dryden. He remains one of those who have set standards for English verse which it is desperate to ignore.

In other words Dryden, for all his 'commonplace mind', is useful as a verbal quarry for Eliot and poets like Eliot. Milton is not.

Eliot's two lectures on Milton,[1] like his essays on poetic drama, overlap the second period of political and theological interests, and even the third, exhausted phase of critical activity. They take tone and colour from the fact that they are belated. Both are written in a convoluted style of qualification and reservation that grows more complex with the years, a style in total contrast to the blank assertions of his colleague Ezra Pound, whose *Literary Essays* (1957)

'*Noch fand sich das Gefühl, die Betrachtung nicht zerstückelt, noch war jene kaum heilbare Trennung in der gesunden Menschenkraft nicht vorgegangen.*' (Emotion, thought, were not yet fragmented, and that scarcely remediable split in the healthy abilities of men had not yet occurred.) But 'feeling' in Eliot's language (as Mr Thompson insists) refers to sensation rather than to emotion.

1. Delivered in 1935 and 1947, and collected in *On Poetry and Poets* (New York, 1957) and, in part, in *Selected Prose of T. S. Eliot*, edited by John Hayward (Penguin Books, 1953).

he was later to edit; and it is only by a narrow margin that the first lecture can be called an exercise in the qualified rejection of Milton, or the second one of qualified assent. By the thirties, negatives and limiting judgements settle thickly upon the prose of Eliot – 'by this I do not mean to say that . . .' 'perhaps', 'somewhat'. Argument advances crabwise: the Milton of the first lecture is called 'a very great poet indeed', but 'a bad influence'. But to be a bad influence is not necessarily 'a serious charge'. But Milton's poetry 'could *only* be an influence for the worse, upon any poet whatever', and the twentieth-century poet too must struggle against it. And then, startlingly, Eliot shows his hand:

The kind of derogatory criticism that I have to make upon Milton is not intended for such persons who cannot understand that it is more important, in some vital respects, to be a good poet than to be a *great* poet . . .

It is Eliot's rooted assumption that criticism is an aid to his own career as a poet, rather than any intuition of a 'dissociation of sensibility', that governs his choices here. A good poet is one who, like Dryden, is useful to later 'poetical practitioners'; a great poet, such as Milton, may lack the merits of the salvageable. The faint retraction embodied in the second Milton lecture changes little in critical terms, though Eliot seems aware that such Christian Miltonists as Charles Williams and C. S. Lewis, whom he quotes, have respectabilized Milton as a theologian in the intervening decade. Milton as an ally against a godless age is a possibility which evidently takes him by surprise, but he is eager to accommodate himself to the new rules of play: 'It is probably beneficial to question the assumption that Milton was a sound Free Churchman and member of the Liberal Party.' It is all rather like a game of musical chairs played out to liturgical music.

The Sacred Wood, then, though it remains the nub of Eliot's achievement as a critic, offers only elusive hints concerning his system of values, and few certainties beyond an intuition of his egoistical purpose in using criticism as 'a by-product of my private poetry-workshop'[1] with the object of judging and rejecting the work of the past by the standards of his own immediate needs as a poet. Certainties followed, in the second decade (1929–39), but they were of a kind to alarm his disciples and darken a reputation in an age even more starkly controversial than the 1860's. It is easy now to see that the bright young people of the twenties, for whom a volume of Eliot's poems, and even *The Sacred Wood*, had talismanic force, had failed to note the illiberal echoes in Eliot's first works. They are faint, but they are there: the contrast posed between a heroic past and a decadent present, the distaste for argument, the contempt for cosmopolitanism, the references easily interpreted, rightly or wrongly, as anti-Semitic. And, in any case, the bright young people of the twenties can hardly have known then that the next decade would find them Marxists. Looking back, one can see as inevitable a schism between master and disciples which left the disciples with a sense of angry betrayal, and the master with some sense of relief. Eliot, like Arnold, preferred to walk by himself.

Eliot's second period opens with a delightfully disarming prelude, the monograph *Dante* (1929), a frankly amateurish, enthusiastic introduction to Dante for readers who possess little Italian, and the kind of book that no one could dislike. Eliot's love for Dante, infectiously suggested, looks literary rather than neo-scholastic, a poet's rather than a convert's enthusiasm. An ensuing pamphlet, *Thoughts after Lambeth* (1931), collected, like *Dante*, in the *Selected Essays* of 1932, is a sensible and moderate comment on the Anglican conference of 1930, but sets its face firmly against humanism in its conclusion:

The World is trying the experiment of attempting to form a civilized but non-Christain mentality. The experiment will fail; but we must be very patient in awaiting its collapse; meanwhile redeeming the time: so that the faith may be preserved alive through the dark ages before us ...

1. 'The Frontiers of Criticism' in his *On Poetry and Poets* (New York, 1957), p. 117.

The echoes of *Ash-Wednesday* (1930) are overpowering, and even the ultimate direction of *The Waste Land* (1922) seems clearer as the story of Eliot's later development unfolds. The Harvard lectures of 1932–3, reluctantly published as *The Use of Poetry and the Use of Criticism* (1933) – 'another unnecessary book', he sourly calls it in the preface – is a sketchy, occasionally suggestive survey of poets as critics from Sidney to I. A. Richards, but the shades are falling. This is the Lenten period of his career, to stretch his own metaphor. Eliot is already half bored with poetry, and more than half bored with criticism, and intensely bored with his own role as poet-critic. 'The sad ghost of Coleridge beckons to me from the shadows,' he concludes glibly, after repeating the vulgar fallacy that 'poets only talk when they cannot sing'. And there is worse to come.

After Strange Gods (1934), a collection of three lectures delivered at the University of Virginia in 1933, a few months after Hitler's accession to power, was published in 4,500 copies (now exceedingly difficult to come by), and never reprinted. It is the oddest of Eliot's books, and certainly the most difficult to justify. Perhaps it is a fulfilment of the promise made in a footnote in the *Use of Poetry* (p. 137n.), where after quoting Jacques Maritain on 'the unconcealed and palpable influence of the devil' on many writers of the time, Eliot adds solemnly: 'With the influence of the devil on contemporary literature I shall be concerned in more detail in another book.' The promise rings ominously, especially when the eye travels to a footnote opposite: 'The Roman and Communist idea of an index of prohibited books seems to me perfectly sound in principle.' The austere subtitle to *After Strange Gods* – ' A Primer of Modern Heresy' – strikes a certain inquisitorial chill, and refusals to discuss grow ever more explicit and insistent. 'I refuse to be drawn into any discussion ...' is a phrase from the *Use of Poetry* (p. 35n.) often echoed by Eliot in the thirties and after. 'In our time,' he proclaimed in the preface to *After Strange Gods,* controversy seems to me, on really fundamental matters, to be futile. It can only usefully be practised where there is common understanding. It requires common assumptions ... The acrimony which accompanies much debate is a symptom of differences so large that there is nothing to argue about. ... In a society like ours, worm-eaten with Liberalism, the only thing possible for a person with strong convictions is to state a point of view and leave it at that.

The lectures that follow take as their starting-point the fifteen-year-old essay 'Tradition and the Individual Talent', and we are made to understand the neo-conservative seduction of a word which, in the early essay, seems strikingly and deliberately incongruous. Eliot's poetic tradition had nothing to do with a historical sequence: his political tradition has. There is praise for the tradition of the Old South and for the resurrectionist group of neo-agrarians such as John Crowe Ransom and Allen Tate, for old New England, for 'stability', 'unity of religious background' ('reasons of race and religion combine to make any large number of free-thinking Jews undesirable'), 'orthodoxy'. The two lectures that follow are a diatribe against free inquiry and the sinister effects of the modern movement where 'morals cease to be a matter of tradition and orthodoxy', and against the novels of George Eliot, Hardy, Joyce, and D. H. Lawrence – Lawrence who suffered a 'deplorable religious upbringing' which gave him 'his lust for intellectual independence' and left his vision 'spiritually sick' (pp. 63, 65). With this book, offered not as literary criticism but as an attack upon a wider range of views then currently fashionable, Eliot's tragic break with the dominant impulses of his age was declared total and permanent.

The third period of Eliot's activity as a critic, since the Second World War, is profoundly anti-climactic. There is little attempt to renew the anti-liberal controversies of the thirties, but his return to literary issues seems only half-convinced. *Notes towards the Definition of Culture* (1948) only palely reflects a pre-war concern for intellectual values in a stable society. *Poetry and Drama* (1951) and *The Three Voices of Poetry* (1953) suggest a spark of enthusiasm for a poetic drama which has its roots deep in the Elizabethan essays of *The Sacred Wood*; but the despairingly high ideal of achieving a 'musical order' in language 'without losing that contact with the ordinary everyday world with which drama must come to terms', as in Shakespeare's last plays, is, on his own telling, unattainable, and his later plays are distinguished flops. The dominant tone of his last essays and lectures is sarcastic and irritable, and the target is usually the very criticism his own examples created. Like a startled Frankenstein, Eliot recoils from the monster he has created, wearily disclaiming responsibility: 'I fail to see any critical movement which can be said to derive from myself,' as he told a Midwestern audience in 1956. [1] There is not much twentieth-century criticism which does not stand condemned by its chief ancestor in this late effusion of despair, for all the many polite evasions ('I do not mean that they are bad books'): the scholarly tradition of 'explanation by origins', as in J. L. Lowes's study of Coleridge, *The Road to Xanadu* (1927); excesses of subtlety provoked by Joyce's *Finnegans Wake* (1939) and Eliot's own works; biographical criticism; non-biographical criticism practised by Richards and Empson as verbal analysis, or 'the lemon-squeezer school of criticism'. Finally we arrive full-circle to the very position that Eliot, in the suppressed anti-Edwardian essays of *The Sacred Wood*, had youthfully condemned: an elderly, dilettante, 'appreciative' criticism whereby the critic may 'help his readers to *understand and enjoy*'. Anyone old enough to have observed the march of English criticism continuously for fifty years might be justified in murmuring: 'This is where we came in.'

These, then, are the three voices of T. S. Eliot the critic: first, the youthful, exploratory enthusiasm of the twenties, where an almost ideal balance between poetic and critical activity is realized; second, an abortive career of social and religious advocacy in frankly obscurantist causes; and third, a bold but exhausted attempt to recover the creative urge, followed at once by denial and desperation. The imposing

1. 'The Frontiers of Criticism', ibid., p. 117.

sense of a vast critical intelligence that emerges, especially in the twenties, is not of a sort that can be defined and codified, and the question with which this chapter began must remain unanswered. Eliot made English criticism look different, but in no simple sense. He offered it a new range of rhetorical possibilities, confirmed it in its increasing contempt for historical processes, and yet reshaped its notion of period by a handful of brilliant intuitions. It is not to be expected that so expert and professional an observer of poetry should allow his achievement to be more neatly classified than this.

I. A. Richards

The most elementary mistake one could make about the criticism of I. A. Richards (b. 1893) – it is also one of the commonest – is to suppose that he pioneered a school of twentieth-century criticism of which Eliot is a member. The dates alone forbid such a notion: Eliot is the older man by five years, and his first, and best, critical work, *The Sacred Wood* (1920), appeared before Richards had published at all. Richards is simply the most influential theorist of the earlier century as Eliot is the most influential of descriptive critics; and, as so often, practice anticipates theory. Still, Richards has his own, independent achievement as an aesthetician which could have happened almost as readily if Eliot had never existed; and he is inescapably a part of this story by virtue of the techniques of analysis that he inspired.

Richards's claim to have pioneered Anglo-American New Criticism of the thirties and forties is unassailable. He provided the theoretical foundations on which the technique of verbal analysis was built. The fact, on the whole, has proved an embarrassment to the New Critics; Richards's theories are appallingly vulnerable, and have been under expert fire from philosophers and psychologists for many years; and further, his own books since the twenties have grown increasingly eccentric. He is one of those unfortunate thinkers whose later works tend to discredit not only themselves and their author, but earlier books as well. Only his influence on descriptive criticism is in question here, however, and not the total range of his aesthetic.

After reading Moral Science at Cambridge, Richards was abruptly invited, in the summer of 1919, to lecture on critical theory in the infant Cambridge School of English. The decision was momentous: Richards's major books, which all appeared in the twenties, were based upon his experience of Cambridge audiences, and his own influence upon the teaching of English there was massive and lasting. His interest in psychology was already wide-ranging, eclectic if unprofound, and it is through his agency that the new science first impinged directly and powerfully on English criticism. Its relevance to literary studies emerges clearly enough in his first book, *The Foundation of Aesthetics* (1922), a collaboration with two friends of undergraduate days, C. K. Ogden and James Wood – a characteristic attempt to define 'beauty' by studying its effects on the audience of art. In *The Meaning of Meaning* (1923), Ogden and Richards created a new jargon in semantics with their positivistic distinction between the 'symbolic' use of language in science and its 'emotive' use in poetry, and in his first work of strictly literary aesthetics, *The Principles of Literary Criticism* (1924), Richards continued to explore alone the 'emotive' language of poetry, culminating in *Practical Criticism* (1929), which disclosed the results of lecture-room experiments conducted in Cambridge by means of analysis of texts stripped of all evidence of authorship and period. With this book, which is very far from being his last, Richards's period of major influence ends; he spent less and less time in Cambridge, lectured in China, experimented in Basic English with Ogden, and in 1939 settled in the United States as a Harvard professor.

Richards, like Ogden, is extravagantly polymath, and his work straddles such distinctions between kinds of criticism as I have tried to maintain here, besides scores of other interests. Primarily, of course, he is a theoretical critic, like Coleridge; and, like Coleridge, he has indulged in literary analysis only as illustration of a method. The analogy does not carry us far. Coleridge was a literary man to the tips of his fingers who sacrificed every interest to an obsessive love of poetry: Richards is, of all the major English critics, the one most difficult to visualize with a book of verse in his hands. His interest in poetry seems abstracted to the point where all English poetry is reduced to the role of an illustration of an aesthetic principle or a mass of data to provide experiments towards a theory of communication. And his criticism is not only more abstract than Coleridge's: it is also violently opposed in tone. Both men write as amateurs, and both (in their intensely English way) are naïvely proud of their amateur status, as if the run of a gentleman's library and a few bright ideas were bound to be more fruitful than the soul-destroying concentration of the specialist. But Coleridge's amateurishness is fervent and affectionate: Richards's is callowly iconoclastic, and his language seems designed to trade upon the fashionable anti-romanticism of Cambridge between the wars. He dismisses the past even more cavalierly than Eliot. The first chapter of the *Principles*, 'The Chaos of Critical Theories', is an all-but-total dismissal of the 'almost empty garner' of all European criticism before Richards: 'a few conjectures, a supply of admonitions, many acute isolated observations, some brilliant guesses ...' The stage is set for the insinuation of an assumption implicit everywhere in Richards's criticism: that the findings of experimental science are intellectually impressive as the findings of no other kind of inquiry can be, and that literary criticism must equip itself with experimental weapons. Criticism, for Richards, is pre-Baconian, and the object of his own aesthetic is to hurry it forward, with the help of the new psychology, towards the happy condition where the critic can use laboratory techniques and make falsifiable assertions.

The oddity of this programme is obvious enough, but it is no odder than its application in detail. We should expect such a programme to insist upon poetry as a communication between poet and reader ('the arts are the supreme form of the communicative activity'), since any attempt to harness psychology to the service of criticism is bound to insist upon poetry as a strictly analysable *human* activity, like Wordsworth's 'man speaking to men'. The realities of psychology are exclusively human. But, by a baffling contradiction, Richards does just the reverse. He shrugs off the formidable prospect of a psychological school of criticism in direct descent from the biographical criticism of the Victorians. Perhaps, in the twenties, the mantle already looked too threadbare to be worth picking up, and Richards is certainly a pundit acutely aware of the power of intellectual fashion. The almost total absence of psychological criticism – there are, of course, isolated examples such as *A Psychoanalytic Study of Hamlet* (1922) by Freud's disciple Ernest Jones – is the most astonishing negative fact of all English criticism in the earlier twentieth century, at least on the British side of the Atlantic. The escape must have been a very narrow one: even at this distance, it looks like an impossible paradox. At the very moment when psychology was respectabilizing itself as a science, and at the very moment when the most influential of English critics – himself a man of some psychological training – was seeking to respectabilize criticism in a similar sense, criticism abandoned its traditional interest in poets in favour of an elaborate pretence that poems are autonomous, self-sufficient artefacts. Richards dismisses the prospect so airily that one is hardly given time to take breath and start an argument. In the fourth chapter of the *Principles*, at the very point in the book where the doctrine that communication is the artist's 'principal object' is proclaimed, Richards adds unequivocally:

Whatever psycho-analysts may aver, the mental processes of the poet are not a very profitable field for investigation. They offer far too happy a hunting-ground for uncontrollable conjecture ... Even if we knew far more than we do about how the mind works, the attempt to display the inner working of the artist's mind by the evidence of his work alone must be subject to the gravest dangers. And to judge by the published work of Freud upon Leonardo da Vinci or of Jung upon Goethe, ... psycho-analysts tend to be peculiarly inept as critics.

This is highly unconvincing as a general proposition. To generalize from two instances is an obvious absurdity, and to object that psycho-analytical conjecture must in any special sense be 'uncontrollable' is false, since such criticism would be as subject as any other descriptive kind to the demand for evidence ('Show me *that* in the poem'). In any case, why should the critic limit himself to 'the evidence of the work alone'? Of course Richards's disinclination, so soon after his announcement of a communication-theory, to view communications only from the poet's end may indeed have its practical justification. He is passionately drawn to the world of the experimental sciences: 'only the simplest human activities', he exclaims regretfully in the first chapter of the *Principles*, 'are at present amenable to laboratory methods'; and there is no doubt that readers of poetry are easier to dragoon into laboratories than poets are. Most poets, after all, are dead, and those who are alive are notoriously difficult to pin down. But any lecture-room will offer a ready supply of readers, and you may mount experiments on their ability to read, and classify the results, with convenience and confidence. There is only one practical difficulty: some readers are better informed than others, and Richards shared the modish prejudice of the years between the wars against historical information. It is at this point that the experiment called 'practical criticism' was conceived.

Richards proposes three objectives in *Practical Criticism* (1929): to document 'the contemporary state of culture', to create a new kind of reading-habit 'for those who wish to discover for themselves what they think and feel about poetry' (apparently by mounting similar experiments upon themselves), and to reform the teaching of literature. With these objects he distributed to his Cambridge audiences largely modernized texts of unfamiliar poems, with invitations to comment freely. A selection of these comments, which he calls 'protocols', forms the substance of the book, followed by an analysis of characteristic errors and suggestions for educational reform.

Richards's own conclusion from his experiment is that the

state of literacy is outrageously low. His guinea-pigs were well above average – 'I see no reason whatever to think that a higher standard of critical discernment can easily be found under our present cultural conditions' (p. 5) than at Cambridge University. And yet, according to his own analysis, ten kinds of failure crippled the responses by his protocol authors, ranging from failure to understand the plain sense to sentimentality, inhibition, and doctrinal adhesions. It is not easy, however, to share Richards's sense of despair. The failure of his pupils might be thought implicit in the test he offers them, for there is no reason to think that any poetry was ever written for the purpose to which Richards applies it here. This is a view he comes near to admitting, with damaging force, in his introduction: 'The precise conditions of this test are not duplicated in our everyday commerce with literature' (p. 5). This is a sizeable understatement. It seems more natural to suppose that all but the simplest poems exist in traditions which dictate in some sense the significance of the poem, and that poems torn from their historical context tend to mean some other thing, or to descend into the merely meaningless. If this is so, then *Practical Criticism* and its record of failures in response is not an indictment of English education – justly indictable as that may be on other grounds – but an impressive body of evidence to suggest that unhistorical reading is bad reading.

Such unhistorical reading, however, encouraged by Richards as an 'experiment' though never recommended as an ideal, is promoted to the ultimate ideal of analysis in the 'New Criticism' which arose in England in the late twenties, spread to the United States in the years before the Second World War, and showed signs of dominating academic criticism, especially in America, after 1945. John Crowe Ransom's *The New Criticism* appeared in 1941, two years after Richards had settled in the United States, and fixed upon anti-historical criticism the sad epithet of 'new' which has inevitably grown less appropriate with every passing year. By the late thirties it already looked characteristically American – so much so that it is easy to forget its largely British origins. The conflict in the United States, indeed, over the historical element in criticism has always been more dramatic than in England: partly because in America the scholarly conservatives were more conservative; and partly because the special needs of American universities genuinely call for an emphasis on techniques of analysis and explanation of texts – a need which the historical critics had tended to overlook, and which the New Critics seemed eager to supply.

None the less, there can be no doubt that the neo-critical tradition takes its rise in the England of the twenties. Eliot stands rather loosely to the movement, part pioneer, part sceptic; Richards provides a ramshackle aesthetic to build upon, and the example of a criticism that is 'practical' rather than pedantically historical; and the first neo-critical analysis occurs in a 'word-by-word collaboration' between Robert Graves and the American poetess Laura Riding, *A Survey of Modernist Poetry,* a reasoned defence of some post-1918 poetry published in London in 1927. The account of Shakespeare's 129th sonnet there was, according to Richards's own account, William Empson's model in his *Seven Types of Ambiguity* (1930), and ushers in an account of Richards's greatest disciple.

William Empson

The Graves-Riding analysis of 'Th' expense of spirit in a waste of shame' illustrates most of the assumptions and tactics of Empson's later analyses in *Seven Types.* In their view, many modern poems, notably those of e. e. cummings, are only spuriously difficult by virtue of their eccentric spelling and punctuation: 'They are too clear, once the plain reader puts himself to work on them. Braced as they are, they do not present the eternal difficulties that make poems immortal ...' (p. 75). A Shakespeare sonnet is genuinely difficult, and a line like

Mad in pursuit and in possession so

represents 'a number of interwoven meanings' (Graves-Riding make no special play with the term 'ambiguity'). The analysis is only partly vitiated by a naïve faith in the absolute authority of spelling and punctuation in the pirated 1609 text of the Sonnets, and it is still in principle historical enough to claim that 'Shakespeare's punctuation allows the variety of meanings he actually intends'. What counts for more is the richly seminal doctrine that 'difficulty' is chief among the poetic virtues:

If we choose any one meaning, then we owe it to Shakespeare to choose at least one he intended and one embracing as many meanings as possible, that is, the most difficult meaning. It is always the most difficult meaning that is the most final (p. 74).

And the account that follows notes both properties of structure ('the very delicate interrelation of the words of the first two lines') and verbal ambiguities too ('the double meaning of *waste* as both "expense" and "wilderness"').

The authority for naming the Graves-Riding *Survey* as Empson's inspiration is Richards himself. Born in 1906, William Empson came to Magdalene College, Cambridge (Richards's own college) in 1925 to read mathematics, a year after the appearance of Richards's *Principles of Literary Criticism*. In 1927, the year when the *Survey* appeared, he

switched over for his last year to English. As he was at Magdalene, this made me his Director of Studies. He seemed to have read more English Literature than I had, and to have read it more recently and better, so our roles were soon in some danger of becoming reversed. At about his third visit he brought up the games of interpretation which Laura Riding and Robert Graves had been playing with the unpunctuated form of 'The expense of spirit in a waste of shame'. Taking the sonnet as a conjuror takes his hat, he produced an endless swarm of lively rabbits from it and ended by 'You could do that with any poetry, couldn't you?' This was a Godsend to a Director of Studies, so I said, 'You'd better go off and do it, hadn't you?' A week later he said he was still slapping away at it on his typewriter. Would I mind if he just went on with that? Not a bit. The following week there he was with a thick wad of very illegible typescript under his arm – the central 30,000 words or so of the book.[1]

Empson's first and most influential book, in fact, *Seven Types of Ambiguity*, was first drafted in two weeks by a twenty-one-year-old undergraduate. It appeared in 1930 and again, heavily revised and with some brutally concessive notes, in a second edition of 1947. There have been only three books of criticism since, and two very slim volumes of neo-Metaphysical verse written in the thirties. The first critical books represent a sort of ebb-and-flow between the two chief preoccupations of the New Criticism: between verbal, and structural (or 'organic') analysis. *Seven Types* divides the 'difficulty', provocatively rechristened 'ambiguity', of Graves and Laura Riding (or 'any verbal nuance, however slight, which gives room for alternative reactions') into seven types representing 'stages of advancing logical disorder'. The tensions in question here are essentially those between words. With the second critical book, *Some Versions of Pastoral* (1935), his interest shifts to the total meaning of whole works, with many evidences of powerful Marxist and Freudian influence. Empson has often insisted that his Marxism in the thirties and later – at least until the Communist revolution in China in 1949, which he witnessed – was more serious than his writings reveal, and *Some Versions* assumed the class-analysis of society and the ideal status of the 'proletariat'; though he frankly admits, in his first chapter, that the book is 'not a solid piece of sociology'. Pastoral, for Empson, is one of the conventions out of which ambiguity may arise, since it consists in 'simple people expressing strong feelings in learned and fashionable language' by 'putting the complex into the simple'. Again, he divides into the magical number of seven: first, proletarian literature as it may some day evolve, the modern proletarian standing in for the traditional shepherd – a manifesto for a Socialist literature, this, and Empson's unique

1. *Furioso* (New Haven, Spring 1940), quoted in Stanley E. Hyman, *The Armed Vision* (New York, 1948), p. 294.

excursion into legislative criticism – followed by the sub-plots of drama, a Shakespearean sonnet, Marvell's 'Garden', the Adam of *Paradise Lost*, Gay's *Beggar's Opera* (an urban pastoral), and *Alice in Wonderland* ('The Child as Swain'). Marxism and criticism meet (though in a paradoxical and self-defeating sense) in Empson's theory that irony may function as a device for reconciling ruler and ruled – in which case, one should have supposed, it ought to be condemned as a popular opium. Marx is more consistently, though not much more plausibly, employed in the analysis of Shakes-peare's 73rd sonnet, where the 'bare ruined choirs' are held to suggest the decay of the feudal, monastic order in the face of Elizabethan capitalism. The Freudian influence is prominent mainly in the last chapter, in the analysis of *Alice*, where Empson (in defiance of Richards's sanction) boldly sets out to 'use psycho-analysis where it seems rele-vant', and proceeds to interpret the book, through a wealth of unconscious sexual symbolism, as a neurotic form of the pastoral in which 'child-becomes-judge':

The symbolic completeness of Alice's experience is I think import-ant. She runs the whole gamut [of sexual experience]; she is a father in getting down the hole, a foetus at the bottom, and can only be born by becoming a mother . . . (pp. 272–3).

The circle is complete. Empson, at first a disciple of Richards in his rejection of biographical criticism, seems poised here on the edge of a species of biographical exegesis more inti-mate than anything practised by the Victorians. He pauses, indeed, to praise Ernest Jones's Freudian analysis of *Hamlet*.

With his third book, *The Structure of Complex Words* (1951), largely a collection of revised articles published in the thir-ties and forties, Empson returns to verbal analysis of an even more rigorous kind than that of *Seven Types*. Key-words are now distinguished and tested. It all seems further from Rich-ards than ever, though the dedication courteously calls him 'the source of all ideas in this book, even the minor ones arrived at by disagreeing with him'. But there is nothing minor about Empson's attack on 'the simple Emotive theory' of the language of poetry which, as Empson notices, 'would make most literary criticism irrelevant, let alone the sort of verbal analysis that most interested me' by appearing to dismiss poetry as not strictly significant. Empson now approaches historicism for the second time, but from a different, linguistic angle: he invents a set of symbols to apply to the senses of key-words listed in the *Oxford English Dictionary* – a linguistic form of historical criticism to which the nineteenth century, if only for lack of sufficient tools, never submitted. And finally, since his return to England from China and his appointment as Professor of English at Sheffield in 1953, Empson has produced *Milton's God* (1961), a magnificently vituperative attack on Christianity in terms of a paradoxical defence of *Paradise Lost*, which he enlarged in 1965 in reply to numerous objections. The book changes all the known rules of Milton scholarship. It is a justification, not of God's ways but of the poet's, by an atheist who finds the Christian ethic 'horrible and wonderful', like a Kafka novel. There follows a stream of articles, mainly on Shakespeare, Milton, and the novel, in which Empson's powerful if amateur biographical and psychological interests re-emerge. 'I think a critic should have an insight into the mind of his author,' he wrote in brave disregard of fashion in 1955, 'and I don't approve of the attack on "The Fallacy of Intentionalism".' [1]

Empson did not invent the technique of verbal analysis which dominated critical fashion in the forties and fifties; but he was the first to systematize it, and he popularized much of its characteristic jargon ('ambiguity,' 'irony', 'tension'). And the technique cannot reasonably be dismissed as a passing phase, as the ageing Eliot tried to do in his sneer about 'the lemon-squeezer school of criticism'. [2] Verbal nuance, or 'ambiguity', is a significant fact of poetry, and it is arguable that the property of poetry to suggest more than it states is what makes it what it is – the final distinction between poetry and mere 'verse' which both Words-

1. From a letter to *Mandrake* (autumn 1955); see p. 162n., above.
2. 'The Frontiers of Criticism'; see p. 185, above.

worth and Coleridge had pursued, and which the Victorians later abandoned as a hopeless quest. That English criticism should have had to wait some three hundred years – until the 1920s – for such a crucial discovery suggests how laborious and fumbling our early aesthetics were, and how immature the study still is: by the mid twentieth century, English criticism is still in some respects barely adolescent. But to say all this is not to deny the rashness of some of Empson's examples, or the dangers and limitations of his method in the hands of others. For verbal analysis has one great limitation: it is appropriate only to brief examples (usually short poems); and Empson's *Complex Words,* where he proceeds by a rigorous selection of key-words, only doubtfully adapts the technique to longer works such as epics and novels. Preciosity, too, remains a constant menace, though it is not unavoidable, and the analyses of some of Empson's followers in England and America point to a new and terrifyingly uncritical kind of Alexandrianism. To all such dangers Empson himself is only occasionally prone. The quality of his mind is too animated to drown itself in a mass of gratuitous detail. Of all the English critics, he is the most variously ingenious, and the readiest to make a fool of himself in public. His mind sparks off original ideas with startling rapidity – it is not really surprising to learn that *Seven Types* was drafted in two weeks. Lavishly self-indulgent to his own theories, he precariously treads a borderline between brilliance and absurdity. He cares almost as little as Coleridge about accurate quotation, overstates by force of habit, and exultantly reveals his own past howlers in errata lists and footnotes to later editions. The ironic element in his criticism – Empson's own ambiguity – ultimately defies analysis, Empsonian or other, but only the most unwary of his reviewers has ever been foolish enough to doubt his fervent dedication to poetry. 'When it was done,' Empson wrote of his *Complex Words,* 'I felt *Nunc dimittis*; I was free, I was ready to die.'[1] This is, at first sight, oddly dedicated language. But to look steadily at Empson's critical achievement is to see clearly in retrospect

1. *Mandrake,* op. cit.

that passion as well as ingenuity has played its part, and that the mind that produces the endless swarm of lively rabbits would have tired long ago if it had no better motive than to show off.

F. R. Leavis

The most influential British-born critic of the early twentieth century, however, was the less original and more predictable F. R. Leavis (b. 1895) – the only native critic of the age, perhaps, to penetrate in his influence (as Arnold once did) below the intellectual élite who actually read criticism, and to enter by indirections into British schoolroom teaching. His influence on the teaching of English was profound in schools; in the universities he succeeded in making himself a major controversial figure, and there were once few departments of English in the Commonwealth which did not boast, or conceal, at least one disciple. And yet the nature of his achievement seems to have escaped serious analysis, perhaps because, in the hurly-burly of charge and counter-charge as to whether Leavis's criticism is good or bad, it has not occurred to anyone to ask very seriously what it is.

The classic view of Leavis is that his criticism belongs to the school of verbal analysis, and that, in consequence, it is an eccentric British counterpart to the American New Criticism. This is the conclusion of Stanley E. Hyman, in his *The Armed Vision* (1948), who finds that Leavis's quarterly *Scrutiny* (1932–53) contains 'some of the sharpest close reading of our time', and that his own criticism is 'at its best when technical and exegetical' (p. 273). And Laurence Lerner, in a valedictory article on *Scrutiny* published soon after its demise,[1] labelled Leavis a child of I. A. Richards, a 'practical critic' employing the analytic techniques of *Practical Criticism*: 'The achievement of *Scrutiny* is, in a way, peculiar to the twentieth century: it is the building up of a body of practical criticisms, of substantiated literary

1. 'The Life and Death of *Scrutiny*', *London Magazine* (January 1955).

judgements, that has surely no equal in extent and quality.'
Scrutiny, he continues, set out from the beginning 'to apply
their methods [i.e those of Eliot, Graves, Richards,
Middleton Murry, and the American New Critics] not
sporadically but systematically, over the whole field of English Literature', and the Scrutineers proceeded by ' a minute
and brilliant examination–by a scrutiny–of actual passages.'

There is remarkably little evidence, it must be said at
once, either in Leavis's books or in the files of *Scrutiny* itself,
for the substantial legend that Leavis was a verbal analyst.
I know of only one example of anything like an extended
analysis on seemingly neo-critical lines in Leavis's own
books – that of Matthew Arnold's sonnet on Shakespeare in *Education and the University* (1943): and even there
Leavis's purposes lie well outside those one would normally
attribute to Richards and Empson. The analysis is offered
as an example, merely, of how spurious much familiar an-
thology-poetry is, and in no sense as analysis for its own sake.
But there are interesting reasons why observers have been
so easily misled. In the first place, Leavis's criticism had
an undeniable air of contemporaneity in the thirties: the
New Criticism is presumably new, Leavis is undoubtedly
new, therefore Leavis is a New Critic – so the unconscious
argument may once have run. Again, he chose, when he
founded his review in 1932, to entitle it *Scrutiny*, and it was
easy to assume that the Leavis school scrutinized 'actual
passages' – the more so because they always encouraged
liberal quotation. The title was more probably suggested by a
series of articles 'Scrutinies' in Edgell Rickword's monthly
(later quarterly) *Calendar of Modern Letters* (1925–7) which
gave rise to two collections under similar titles edited by
Rickword, and to an admiring selection, *Towards Standards
of Criticism* (1933), edited by Leavis. Again, Leavis himself
occasionally talked as if he believed in verbal analysis – however much a comparison with the criticism of Empson, or of
American New Critics such as Cleanth Brooks and John
Crowe Ransom, would show that he did not practise it; he
seems, in principle at least, a critic eager not to stray from

his text. 'No treatment of poetry', he writes in the introduction to *Revaluation* (1936) 'is worth much that does not keep very close to the concrete: there lies the problem of method ... In dealing with individual poets the rule of the critic is, or should (I think) be, to work as much as possible in terms of particular analysis – analysis of poems or passages – and to say nothing that cannot be related immediately to judgments about producible texts.' That sounds very like the Richards-Empson tradition in criticism, and no doubt that tradition genuinely influenced Leavis to the extent that he always felt a compulsion to appear to play the game according to the new rules. But Leavis instantly makes it clear that he does not consider mere analysis as the real object of the critic: the critic's discipline of confining himself to 'producible texts', he goes on, 'while not preventing his saying anything that he should in the end find himself needing to say, enables him to say it with a force of relevance and an edged economy not otherwise attainable'.

Leavis's concern with verbal analysis, then, is relatively superficial, perhaps a strategy to placate a school whose method – being only a method – may have seemed to him too trivial to argue with and too fashionable to attack. His real concern lies with what he calls the thing he 'finds himself needing to say', and this characteristic object defines the difference between *Scrutiny* and the New Criticism well enough. The run of New Critics, ultimately, feel no compulsion to assert anything as critics; their business lies in discrediting one method (the historical and biographical) and in instituting another, a form of analysis from which, relatively speaking, history and biography have been self-consciously excluded. Their convictions are often shadowy and (one suspects) probably uninteresting. Leavis is all passionate conviction.

Leavis's career as a critic begins in discipleship to Eliot. One might even say that its total progress can be traced in terms of his alienation from this influence; though it might be more accurate to argue that it is Eliot that has moved, and Leavis who has stood four-square by the critical attitudes which his master represented in the 1920s. He bought a copy of *The Sacred Wood*, he tells us in a late essay, at the moment when it appeared, when he was twenty-five, and 'for the next few years I read it through several times a year, pencil in hand'.[1] But like most disciples, he is embarrassed to describe the nature of Eliot's influence as a critic: 'it was a matter of having had incisively demonstrated, for pattern and incitement, what the disinterested and effective application of intelligence to literature looks like, what is the nature of purity of interest . . .' The last phrase, it must be conceded, points to a radical misunderstanding of Eliot's early criticism and its close relationship to Eliot's career as a poet. But for Leavis the misunderstanding was fruitful.

Leavis's first independent book of literary criticism, *New Bearings in English Poetry* (1932), opens frankly with an acknowledgement of the same debt: 'How little I suppose these considerations to be original the book will make plain: it is largely an acknowledgement, vicarious as well as personal, of indebtedness to a certain critic and poet.' In *New Bearings* Eliot's poems, up to and including *Ash-Wednesday*, are explained (but hardly 'verbally analysed') and justified, with Pound and Hopkins sharing pride of place as moving spirits of poetic modernism; other late Victorians, W. B. Yeats, and the Georgians are summarized and dismissed in language which Leavis never again equalled in ironic potency. The next book, *Revaluation* (1936), a collection of *Scrutiny* essays predetermined for book form, follows closely upon *New Bearings* as part of a single plan: 'the planning of the one book was involved in the planning of the other. An account of the present of poetry, to be worth anything, must be from a clearly realized point of view . . . [which] must have been determined and defined as much in relation to the past as to the present.' *Revaluation*, in fact, is a backward exploration into literary history to rediscover those poetic qualities already extolled in Eliot, Pound, and Hopkins. They are identified in the Metaphysicals and

1. *The Common Pursuit* (1952), p. 280.

momentarily in Pope and missed, on the whole, in the poetry of the Romantics.

In the early forties Leavis's concern shifted towards the novel, a form which, in its substantial moral preoccupations, has suited the implacably moralistic bent of his mind better than any but a few poets; and in 1948 he collected a group of essays under the title of *The Great Tradition: George Eliot, Henry James, Joseph Conrad*. The great tradition in English fiction, in this account, has been the tradition of serious moral concern – Leavis calls such novelists 'significant in terms of the human awareness they promote; awareness of the possibilities of life' (p. 2). It begins in Jane Austen – a novelist whom his wife, Q. D. Leavis, had already treated in a group of articles in *Scrutiny* (1942–4), unfortunately never realized as a book – and passes through George Eliot, James, and Conrad to D. H. Lawrence, whom Leavis reserved for a separate study in 1955. But, after *The Great Tradition*, the quality of his interests regrettably shifted from literary criticism to literary politics. His attacks upon the 'cultural establishment' of the British Council and the BBC, and indeed upon anyone who appeared to qualify his achievement, however mildly, took on an air of strident self-justification, and the study of Lawrence, though it contains passages of the old perception, shows a falling off in power to organize material. The later career of Leavis, indeed, suggests a corruption of an unusual kind. Unlike Eliot, he never retreated. But he remained in the same position so obstinately that one suspected he was there at all only out of force of habit, and his vehemence often seemed out of all proportion to the contradictions under attack, while his absolute refusal to admit honest errors of judgment sapped the confidence of some of his most serious admirers. The tailpiece entitled 'Retrospect 1950', appended to a new edition of *New Bearings* (1950), suggests how a reasoned confidence in the real excellence of *Scrutiny* could harden into a cultish worship of revealed truth:

I may say that this placing of Auden [as 'adolescent'] has been enforced in *Scrutiny* by detailed criticism in more than half a dozen reviews, coming from half a dozen different hands. The dismissal of Spender (once in conventional esteem the Shelley of the Poetic Renaissance), Day Lewis, MacNeice, George Barker, Dylan Thomas, has also been done critically in *Scrutiny*. My brief placing reference to Empson and Bottrall has also its due backing there in a number of reviews by different hands. (p. 227 n.)

This is peculiarly self-deceived, and we are entitled to object that support of a *Scrutiny* view by a *Scrutiny* reviewer is, in itself and without further evidence, no evidence for anything. Such in-group complacency looks all the more dangerous when we turn to the files of *Scrutiny* itself and observe the gross inferiority of disciples to master, and the alarming glibness of most reviews of modern poetry that appear there. And self-deception seems still more serious when we turn up, in the Epilogue to *New Bearings,* the passage so evasively defended in the Postscript of 1950. The 1932 'placing' of Ronald Bottrall reads:

There is another young poet [besides Empson] whose achieved work leaves no room for doubt about his future. Mr Ronald Bottrall's development has been remarkably rapid and sure – it is convincing – and his published volume, *The Loosening and Other Poems*, establishes him as a very considerable poet indeed . . .

Is it conceivable that any review, whether in *Scrutiny* or anywhere else, could provide 'due backing' to such judgment? The quality of *New Bearings* is hardly affected by such bad prophecies, and prophecy, in any case, is not the business of criticism. But Leavis believed so passionately in the defence of 'values' by the correct 'placing' of individual poets in a hierarchy of excellence – it is part of his inheritance from *The Sacred Wood,* fiercely formalized – and was so convinced that these values were embattled and in imminent danger of extinction, that a simple *peccavi* became a tactical impossibility for him. To give way on one point would have seemed like surrendering along an entire front.

And as honest admissions of error grew to be impossible, so could claims always to have been right, and right first, be gently extended back into the past. *Scrutiny*, a well-connected journal in the thirties with an eye to rising reputations in London as well as Cambridge, had become by 1963, when it was reprinted with a retrospect, 'an outlaws' enterprise' (vol. xx, p. 1), and Leavis's late account of his early debt to Eliot is a further example of the creation of myth. As early as the mid-1920s Eliot was a publicly acclaimed poet and critic, hailed by London reviewers and others as the poet of the new generation and lectured on by Richards at Cambridge; and nobody, in consequence, could doubt that *New Bearings*, when it first appeared in 1932, was other than a work of late discipleship in a familiar cause. Three years earlier Leavis, in the *Cambridge Review*, had already written of 'the vogue that Mr Eliot enjoys, and suffers from'.[1] But by the 1950 Retrospect to the postwar edition of *New Bearings* that vogue is forgotten, and the claim is of a lonely struggle against 'the indignant resistance of the academic and literary worlds' (p. 217) in the martyred cry of a pioneer. That such a claim could be made in print, and in defiance of abundant published evidence of Eliot's early acclaim, shows how far mandarin confidence can reach in the protected little world of a clique.

Leavis fought his war for 'values' with a persistant air of heroism. But the cause itself remains something of a mystery, except by inference, since he always refused to commit himself to general positions. It is the central paradox of his achievement that, while it challenges the reader with its apparent severity and fierce discrimination, it refuses to discuss the standards by which it proceeds. And it is known why Leavis always declined to talk of ultimate principles: his refusal is not a diplomatic evasion, or a sophisticated awareness of the defects of verbal definitions, but arises out of a firm conviction that the critic must remain available to readers of all doctrinal persuasions, that he has a duty not to show his hand. The title of a late collection of essays, *The Common Pursuit* (1952), derives from Eliot's 'The Func-

1. Leavis, 'T. S. Eliot: a Reply to the Condescending', *Cambridge Review* (8 February 1929); see George Watson, 'The Triumph of T. S. Eliot', *Critical Quarterly*, vii (1965), pp. 333f.

tion of Criticism', 'one of those essays of Mr Eliot which I most admire', as Leavis confesses in the preface: 'The critic ... should endeavour to discipline his personal prejudices and cranks – tares to which we are all subject – and compose his differences with as many of his fellows as possible in the common pursuit of true judgment.' Once again, Leavis is a more Eliotian critic than Eliot himself, and the discipline must have cost him something in personal reticence, as well as in terms of whatever causes he privately supported. The independence of pre-war *Scrutiny* of the fashionable – almost compulsory – Marxism of the day is striking evidence of Leavis's determination that the critical pursuit should remain common to all intelligent men. A 1937 article by one of his followers on the directors of the Left Book Club dared to chide them for their failure to achieve 'a stricter maintenance of the standards they profess' – an article later defended, in an editorial note, as representing 'the considered point of view held by *Scrutiny*';[1] and another anonymous note defines the nature of Leavis's outward political independence: 'If *Scrutiny* could make it more difficult for intelligent persons to invoke the Webbs on Russia as Mr [Boris] Ford does, we should feel that a useful function had been performed.'[2] Political independence is not a virtue in itself; but this kind of actively critical independence looks better, in retrospect, than the aberrations of most critics and poets in the days when German and Russian collectivist ideas were fashionable.

One can only guess, then, from his evident admiration for J. S. Mill, George Eliot, Henry James, Conrad, and D. H. Lawrence, at the exact nature of Leavis's radical agnosticism, and wonder whether the critical pursuit can be carried as far as he insists before doctrinal splits threaten its coherence. Doctrinal reticence, indeed, involved Leavis in controversies all the more personal and vindictive for the failure of either side to identify points of principle in the

1. H. A. Mason, 'Education by Book Club?' (*Scrutiny*, December 1937); note (March 1938), p. 428.
2. *Scrutiny* (March 1938), p. 428.

Scrutiny attitude. Even the technical and linguistic pre-suppositions of his criticism, such as his repeated insistence on the need for 'concreteness', 'specificity', and the 'realization' of feeling in poetic language, do not cease to be uncertain because they are passionately held, and his lofty indifference to inquiries that would lead beyond a few well-trodden assumptions makes it hard to guess whether neglect of evidence is innocent or wilful. I have already described the inflation of his own role in establishing Eliot's early reputation, which was established before Leavis published a word on the matter; but the case is not isolated. In 1948, for example, in *The Great Tradition*, Dickens is largely excluded from a title to greatness, but *Hard Times* is singled out, with a characteristic assertion of originality, for an accolade; and the assertion is repeated in *Dickens the Novelist* (1970), where the acceptance of Dickens as the supreme English novelist is achieved with very slight admission of a change of heart. Hailing *Hard Times* as a masterpiece, Leavis goes on to ask:

Why has it not had general recognition? To judge by the critical record, it has had none at all. If there exists anywhere an appreciation, or even an acclaiming reference, I have missed it. (p. 187)

But the search of the critical record cannot have been thorough: indeed it is doubtful if it ever began. For the acclaiming references are there, in Ruskin's *Unto this Last* and in Bernard Shaw's introduction to the novel in 1912. Simple forgetfulness, one might conclude, since it is hard to credit that Ruskin and Shaw went unread. But so much forgetting, and of such a convenient order, creates a consistent pattern of self-acclaim where the manner of remembering leaves the critic himself, in his own admiring recollection, the first in every field and the hero of every occasion.

The charges against Leavis's criticism, then, remain serious: a continuous instinct for self-importance in defiance of evidence; a disregard, especially in later work, for the delicate complexity of literary judgment; and a lack of knowledge which often looks like a disinclination to find out. In scholarly terms he remains rootedly a British provincial, moved by no perceptible foreign influences except the usual twentyish fixation with France and, in his later years, the nineteenth-century Russian novel. The principal effect of his writings has been conservative: among the last of the Victorians to survive and remain vocal, he succeeded in delaying the extinction of a peculiarly English and nineteenth-century brand of moral criticism for longer than some emancipated spirits between the wars either expected or desired. The effect, it is true, was pedagogic rather than broadly literary; much as Leavis and his followers employed the word 'academic' as a term of contempt, no race of men were ever more exclusively academic than they. His was a bold, aggressive conservatism, a familiar sound in any epoch in lecture-halls and Common Rooms, and it provides an apt conclusion to this history. The analytical revolution begun by Dryden is triumphant and complete. Such confident claims for the significance of literary criticism in the life of the mind and even in the world of affairs, rash as they may have been, surely represent a climax of confidence and a point of change. They could only have happened at all in a society where the claims of literary analysis are so widely accepted that criticism, far from needing to defend its right to exist, is in some danger of being mistaken for a way of life.

CHAPTER 10

THE MID-CENTURY SCENE

THIS book is a history, not a manifesto, and the historian who discourses upon the present inevitably describes less accurately than he could wish, approving and condemning more rashly. To describe the scene in English criticism since Eliot's shift of interest away from literature in the 1930s is open to every historian's peril. The terrain is unmapped, and must for the time being remain so. The subject, at the best, is an untidy one, and every attempt to make it look tidy must suffer from some distortion and suppression of evidence. And, of course, it is vast, for no other literary tradition – not even the French – attributes so much importance to the role of the critic as the English today, and certainly no linguistic area can rival the English-speaking world in the wealth of its critical activity or in the intensity of its literary debates.

The story is complicated further by the emergence of the United States in the thirties as a vastly productive centre of literary criticism, and especially of academic criticism. The experience has been a unique one. No other European literature has ever been subject to such a sudden access of energy as the English at the hands of the American. One is abruptly reminded that less than one quarter of all native speakers of English now live in the British Isles, and that a large majority of them now live in North America. And yet the American influence on British criticism since the thirties – like the less noticed, but not less remarkable, influence in the opposite direction – has not been all of a piece. Happily enough, there is no characteristically British critical tradition in the mid twentieth century, and no American either. Those who think otherwise are generalizing on evidence which is either partial or out of date. Americans who complain of a special British tone in London literary periodicals are usually found, on interrogation, to be talking about 'Bloomsbury' – and Bloomsbury is all but dead, and was never the whole story; and Englishmen who think that the quality of American criticism can be identified with the last plump Ph.D. thesis they have glanced at are wildly underestimating the variety of literary scholarship in the United States. There are no national traditions in English criticism today, on either side of the Atlantic. There does, however, exist a variety of critical schools, and they are largely Anglo-American schools. We might group them under three headings – the Moralists, the New Critics, and the Historians – remembering always that criticism since the Second World War has tended to stir these elements together and to defy category; and it will often be found useful, in discussing all three in turn, to forget that the Atlantic Ocean exists at all.

The Moralists

Most English critics before Arnold and Ruskin assumed that all good poetry is morally edifying, and that (as Johnson had insisted in his preface to Shakespeare), 'it is always a writer's duty to make the world better'. But there is a tradition in twentieth-century criticism stemming from Arnold which is distinct from all previous moral theories of literature. The difference may be simply stated: Johnson, like other Renaissance and eighteenth-century critics, took it for granted that everyone is more or less agreed about the difference between right and wrong, and that the moral duty of the poet lies simply in observing a recognized code: 'justice', he goes on confidently, as if he were speaking for all Christendom, 'is a virtue independent on time or place.' Modern moralism, by contrast, is more often agnostic, exploratory, and self-consciously élitist. Its tone is not that of the common preacher anticipating assent: it is more often embittered and embattled. Its very dogmatism is based upon the uncertainty of its dogma and the difficulty of finding an audience. Johnson does not have to raise his voice: the modern moralist tends to shout, like D. H. Lawrence (1885–1930) in the last decade of his life, indicting the sanctions of White Protestant societies, whether British or American, in his *Studies in Classic American Literature* (1923) or in the essays posthumously collected as *Phoenix* (1936). So does Lawrence's disciple John Middleton Murry (1889–1957), who in a spate of books, and in his periodical the *Adelphi,* always proclaimed that criticism 'depended on values – a delineation of what is good for man'.[1] George Orwell (1903–50), too, used such authors as Dickens and Kipling to flay the infantilism and dictator-worship of the British literary Left; and F. R. Leavis, whose criticism has been discussed at length in a previous chapter, offers an unusually pure example of critical moralism. The vast school of Shakespearean criticism inspired since 1930 by G. Wilson Knight has ambitiously interpreted dramatic characters as if they represented philosophical ideas. And there is a brilliant and eccentric American example in the dissident figure of Yvor Winters (1900–68), a critic with a strikingly homegrown air about him whose work, uniquely among critics of this kind, looks independent of Arnoldian influence, bluntly and unfashionably insisting through the thirties and forties that the critic's business is to assert what the 'best poems' are, and that any poem, being 'a statement in words in which special pains are taken with the expression of feeling',[2] ought to make plain sense, even if written by Hopkins or T. S. Eliot.

The moralists are the prophetic figures in modern criticism. They most readily excite discipleship. Their influence may even extend to matters of conduct; in some cases, indeed (as in Lawrence and Orwell) the critical interest is a late extension of some wider moral or political purpose.

1. J. Middleton Murry, *Selected Criticism 1916–57*, edited by Richard Rees (Oxford, 1960), p.viii (quoted from Murry's journal).

2. *In Defense of Reason* (New York, 1947), p. 363. This collection represents most of Winters's critical work over more than fifteen years.

They are self-righteously non-professional, they tend (however scholarly in themselves) to despise scholarship, they are prone to conspiratorial theories of 'Establishments' and, however well established themselves, insist upon being regarded as outcasts. George Orwell, aggressively drinking his tea from his saucer in the BBC canteen, may be taken as the eternal model of the modern English moralist. The influence of such men stands highest in an age which, like the thirties and forties, is avid for moral certainties of a new kind. In the fifties, in an atmosphere notably less assertive and more tentative, it tended to dilute itself with uncertainties and, even in the act of spreading, to lose confidence and force. It now seeks intermixture with history, with sociology, and with politics, as in such latter-day moralists as Richard Hoggart (b. 1918) and Raymond Williams (b. 1921); and such studies of 'the cultural situation' and its antecedents as Hoggart's *The Uses of Literacy* (1957), or Williams's *Culture and Society 1780–1950* (1958), and its sequel *The Long Revolution* (1961), seem as much scholarly as prophetic in their quiet, hesitant insistence that the truth is an object of study rather than a preserve of the right-minded: 'Issues much more difficult than those I have directly treated were being approached' in *The Uses of Literacy*, as Hoggart gently assures us in his conclusion. '. . . These are issues I am not qualified to pursue. In order to be able to till my own part of the field I felt I could reasonably take for granted a general agreement on certain assumptions, an agreement sufficient to allow me to use, without closer definition than emerges from the detailed illustrations, words such as "decent", "healthy", "serious" . . .' The concern for culture as a cause to be defended, and the assumption that the concern is proper to an educated minority, place Hoggart in the tradition of Arnold. But the very explicitness of his language, his readiness to name and even to question 'certain assumptions', suggest a loss of confidence, a new open-mindedness, a prospect of growth. Moralism is as common today as ever it was in English criticism. But it

lacks its former certainty, whatever its underlying dog-
matisms, and its influence, though widespread, is now less
sharp and less sure than once it was.

The New Critics

The origins of the so-called New Criticism have already
been described in the first work of Robert Graves and
William Empson where, even before 1930, both verbal and
structural analysis was practised, and the characteristic search
for what Graves had called 'the most difficult meaning'
was accepted as the ultimate object of good reading. But
neither Graves nor Empson is noticeably anti-historical; and
neither is the most distinguished and original of American
Empsonian critics, Kenneth Burke (b. 1897). Their successors among the American New Critics decidedly are, and
the final character of the New Criticism is hardly defined
until its translation to the United States in the late thirties.
In its American form, indeed, the New Criticism had something like the character of a school. Its pioneer, John
Crowe Ransom (b. 1888), who taught English at Vander-
bilt University in Tennessee from 1924 to 1937, and later at
Kenyon College in Ohio, bequeathed to such pupils as Allen
Tate (b. 1899) and Robert Penn Warren (b. 1905) a neo-
conservative veneration for the Old South and its coherent
social values which may owe something to the Eliot of *After
Strange Gods*. In the American New Critics, contempt for late
nineteenth-century values is general: not only for historical
criticism and its accompanying pedantries, but for agnostic
enlightenment, democratic optimism, industrialism, and
such international ideals as Marxism. It is a frankly reactionary movement, and the word 'New' must always
have held for it an air of pleasing paradox.

The Aesthetic Movement of Pater and Wilde had tended
to belittle the study of the origins of poetry, and Eliot's
famous remark that a 'poem's existence is somewhere
between the writer and the reader'[1] is clearly intended to

1. *The Use of Poetry and the Use of Criticism* (1933), p. 30.

foster a similar scepticism. But it is hardly until the thirties that any general attack is mounted upon the whole concept of historical criticism, and hardly until the forties, when New Critics began to fill major posts in universities in the United States, that anti-historical manifestoes became fashionable. The influential college anthology *Understanding Poetry*, edited by Cleanth Brooks and Robert Penn Warren, which appeared in New York in 1938, condemned in its preface the use of poetry for any purpose beyond itself, whether historical or moralistic, and declared itself 'conceived on the assumption that if poetry is worth teaching at all, it is worth teaching as poetry'. The same anti-cognitive enthusiasm reveals itself sharply in other documents, even in the scholarly handbook that synthesizes so much of the school, René Wellek and Austin Warren's *Theory of Literature* (1949). 'I should like to think that criticism has been written, and may be again, from a mere point of view,' wrote Allen Tate in 1955, in the preface to his collection *The Man of Letters in the Modern World*, and neo-critical studies such as Warren's account of 'The Ancient Mariner'[1] or Brooks's assemblage of analyses entitled *The Well Wrought Urn* (1947) are strikingly indifferent to historical probability. 'If literary history has not been emphasized,' wrote Brooks in his preface, 'it is not because I discount its importance, or because I have failed to take it into account. It is rather that I have been anxious to see what residuum, if any, is left after we have referred the poem to its cultural matrix.' On a similar principle, one is inclined to reflect, Peer Gynt sought a kernel to his onion, and found that when he had peeled and peeled away he was left with nothing but his tears. For all poetic meaning may be reasonably referred to its historical setting, and to argue as if the value of poetry could lie in what is 'left' after historical interpretation has done its work is to argue away the very existence of what is sought.

The fullest accounts of the doctrines of the New Criticism appeared as late as 1946–9 in two articles in the *Sewanee*

1. Reprinted in his *Selected Essays* (New York, 1958).

Review by W. K. Wimsatt and Monroe C. Beardsley, 'The Intentional Fallacy' and 'The Affective Fallacy', both collected in Wimsatt's *The Verbal Icon* (1954). Two of the assumptions of romantic criticism are held up to the light in these articles, and pronounced fallacious. 'The design or intention of the author is neither available nor desirable as a standard for judging the success of a work of literary art,' as Wimsatt and Beardsley protest in the first; and as for the second, 'the Affective Fallacy is a confusion between the poem and its results. . . . It begins by trying to derive the standard of criticism from the psychological effects of the poem, and ends in impressionism and relativism.' But these manifestoes, though richly symptomatic of the New Criticism, are late to appear, and suffer from the over-confidence of a movement already victorious. The real merits of the school are not to be studied in its attempts to theorize. It is rootedly pragmatic and particular, a way of teaching rather than a formal doctrine, and based upon an urgent impatience with academicism rather than upon any coherent principle. In American universities in the thirties and forties it must have felt like a clean wind.

But a reaction was already forming under the leadership of Ronald S. Crane in the late thirties in the Chicago School of neo-Aristotelians which, employing a more formidable scholarship and a less popular style, insisted upon a return to questions of design and structure by whatever method and upon whatever assumption seemed appropriate to the particular case. The Chicago view, according to Crane himself, was 'pluralistic and instrumentalist', insisting that 'we must accord to critics the right of free choice as between different basic methods'. This programme makes the Chicago critics look more eclectic than in fact they were. They represent a heresy of the New Criticism – still neo-critical, after all, in their interest in structural analysis, as in Crane's exemplary account of the plot of *Tom Jones*, and diverging from the orthodoxy of the New Criticism only in two minor respects: in their slightly more tolerant attitude to historical data; and in their attacks upon what Crane called the neo-critical 'impoverishment of poetic theory' through an incessant search for irony, tension, and paradox. But these are family quarrels. For Crane, too, accepts such neo-critical slogans as 'poetry as poetry and not another thing'.[1] The Chicago School may, in its day, have shaken a little of the confidence of the New Criticism. But only in a radically anti-historical atmosphere in English studies could it ever have achieved a reputation for historical criticism.

The Historians

There is no such thing as an historical school of criticism in early twentieth-century English, if 'school' means something coherent or reasonably homogeneous. Literary history, since its birth in eighteenth-century England in the works of the Wartons and of Johnson, never had such a shamefaced air as in the half-century after the First World War. The confident Victorian tradition of literary history, embodied in such a figure as Leslie Stephen and in an enterprise like his *Dictionary of National Biography* (1885–1909), had already passed its zenith by the time chairs of English were founded in Oxford and Cambridge, around the turn of the century, though in the United States and in Scotland literary history survived longer and, in America at least, provoked a more extreme reaction. Even as historical a critic as George Saintsbury could not think of any principled defence of an art he practised voluminously for half a century, and vast, composite enterprises like the *Cambridge History of English Literature* (1907–16) or the *Oxford History of English Literature* (1945–) have, on the whole, an exhausted air, while the Pelican *Guide to English Literature* (1954–61), edited by Boris Ford and belonging rather to the anti-historical reaction, can hardly be said to attempt a narrative scheme at all. The old, free narrative tradition of Thomas

1. Quoted approvingly from Eliot in *Critics and Criticism*, edited by Crane (Chicago, 1952), p. 83. Four of Crane's major essays, including 'The Concept of Plot and the Plot of *Tom Jones*' and 'The Critical Monism of Cleanth Brooks', appear in this symposium.

Warton, Hazlitt, Saintsbury, and Oliver Elton became simply defunct in England, though Americans like Hardin Craig, and David Daiches, a Scot, still practise an art which, in its unpretentious way, must always have had a broadly educative function and which once aspired to something more.

And yet, to peer closer, two strands seem visible in the complex pattern of largely academic historiography as it has been practised on both sides of the Atlantic. The one is largely Christian, the other largely Marxist and ex-Marxists The Christian tradition is essentially British – Anglican, indeed – and has powerful medieval affinities, emerging from the ruck of late Victorian editing of medieval texts into an astonishingly clear light with such good academic critics as W. P. Ker (1855–1923) in his *Epic and Romance* (1896) and *The Dark Ages* (1904); or his pupil R. W. Chambers (1874–1942), who succeeded him to the Chair at University College, London, in 1922. A devoted Anglican, he sought to establish a sense of continuity between modern England and its medieval, Catholic past; and the novelist-critic Charles Williams (1886–1945) and his friends Dorothy Sayers (1893–1957) and C. S. Lewis (1898–1963) continued in that task. Lewis's *The Allegory of Love* (1936), largely written in his early agnostic days, and his volume on the sixteenth century published as part of the Oxford History of English Literature in 1954, may stand as models of unexpected vigour in the decaying tradition of literary history, for they successfully unite a polemical energy hardly inferior to Orwell's with an unfashionable respect for such virtues as formal excellence and decorum, and for such defunct forms as the Christian epics of Spenser and Milton. The Ker–Chambers–Lewis tradition in historical criticism, though it never came near to holding the centre of the stage in its own day, and though it attracted little disinterested enthusiasm, still contrived to define itself in a hostile atmosphere and to make itself known.

The Marxist tradition in modern English, on the other hand, has been overwhelmingly American, for the flirtation of the British intelligentsia with Marxism in the era of the Spanish Civil War was too transient, and too stubbornly English and moralistic, to create a genuine Marxist school of letters. The American outcome, though no doubt heretical too by strict political standards, bears the evidence of Marxist influence more deeply etched into its character. Much of it, paradoxically, is ex-Marxist and even anti-Marxist; but the weight and seriousness of social concern is felt even in the later writings of such critics as Edmund Wilson (1895-1972) and Lionel Trilling (b.1905), whereas the postwar criticism of British ex-Marxists like W. H. Auden and Stephen Spender bears little or no scar of past political wars.

All Marxist criticism is inevitably historicist, and in a special sense, since it judges all contemporary literature in relation to its political effect, and all past literature in relation to its social setting. It is, like much nineteenth-century criticism, rootedly relativistic. No Marxist critic could write an essay called 'The Intentional Fallacy'; no Marxist critic could reasonably belong to the Aesthetic Movement or to the New Criticism, and none holds views individualistic enough to qualify (in the special sense in which I have been using the term in this chapter) as a Moralist. And yet, of course, all good critics have an intensely individual quality, including Wilson and Trilling, and the description of Marxist only fits them in a loose sense. It was from his Princeton professor Christian Gauss, so Edmund Wilson tells us in the dedication to *Axel's Castle* (1931), that he learned that 'literary criticism ought to be a history of man's ideas and imaginings in the setting of the conditions which have shaped them'. This is a programme any Victorian would have approved, and Wilson's study, in this first book, of Yeats, Valéry, Eliot, Proust, Joyce, and others must have provided thousands with an eminently serviceable introduction to the modern movement, remarkable for its unambitious clarity and for its tolerance (especially in its opening chapter defining Symbolism) of some unexpectedly bourgeois values:

Each [Symbolist] poet has his unique personality; each of his moments has its special tone. . . . And it is the poet's task to find, to invent, the special language which will alone be capable of expressing his personality and feelings.

Wilson's talents as a critic are, in the noblest sense, journalistic, and have been expanded in a mass of reviewing of an unusually weighty and reflective kind: talents for summarizing invitingly and intelligently, and for quick, simple definition of complex historical movements. Exceptionally, he is not an academic, and his style lacks the deadening pressure of qualification which even so committed a critic a Lionel Trilling feels bound, at times, to admit into his prose. Trilling's passionate sense of history – a symptom, perhaps, of his political interests in the thirties and forties – raises itself again and again to the level of a moral concern, and his name belongs almost as readily to the class of Moralists as it does here. His first book, aptly, was a study of Matthew Arnold (1939), and is full of an intense concern for questions of society and of class, while his essay of 1942, 'The Sense of the Past', later collected in *The Liberal Imagination* (1950), is the most effective of all historicist answers to the New Critics. As Trilling insists, the New Critics 'forget that the literary work is ineluctably a historical fact, and . . . that its historicity is a fact in our aesthetic experience'. This quality of the 'pastness' of poems, as Trilling calls it, dignifying a term used a generation before by Eliot in 'Tradition and the Individual Talent', is offered now as a prime object of critical study, for 'it is only if we are aware of the reality of the past as past that we can feel it as alive and present'.

Such intelligent compromise offers to reconcile the functions of critic and historian, so oddly divorced in the years between the two world wars. The revival of respect by critics for the historical process, and by literary historians for critical discrimination, is a marked symptom of English criticism both in Britain and in the United States since 1945. By the 1950s both Marxism and the New Criticism had failed and had been seen to have failed: the future lay somewhere beyond dogma. And a wise eclecticism is the best thing that could happen to our critical tradition, reminding us that it was only by an historical accident that literary critic and literary historian were ever set at odds with each other. Anyone, indeed, who supposes that there is one method apt to every critical adventure must be vastly underestimating the immense variety of the thousands of documents called English literature. There *could* be no one way, in the nature of things, and the search for absolute certainties by critics between the wars was bound to end in failure. And yet their failure has proved more significant than their success could ever have been. For poetry, by its uniquely ambiguous status, resists interpretation by any single criterion, and the good critic is one who perceives that it is only because he knows as much as he does that he is able to discriminate and judge.

SELECT BIBLIOGRAPHY
OF MODERN EDITIONS AND STUDIES
The place of publication is noted, unless it is London,
following the short title

I · FIRST PRINCIPLES
Histories

Four comprehensive histories of (or including) English criticism
have already appeared, though one was never completed. George
Saintsbury, *A History of English Criticism* (Edinburgh, 1911),
extracted from his earlier *History of Criticism and Literary Taste in
Europe*, 3 vols. (Edinburgh, 1900–4), is a genial Victorian survey
that goes as far as Arnold and Pater. The second, J. W. H. Atkins's
unfinished *English Literary Criticism*, 3 vols. (Cambridge, later
London, 1943–51), is a more detailed and less readable history
based upon principles similar to Saintsbury's and completed to
about 1800. The third book, René Wellek, *History of Modern
Criticism*, 4 vols. (New Haven, 1955–), is an encyclopaedic account
by a Czech-American scholar of all Western literary criticism,
including Russian and American, since about 1750, and the
fourth, *Literary Criticism: a Short History* (New York, 1957), is a
755-page 'argumentative history' by two American New Critics,
W. K. Wimsatt and Cleanth Brooks, both of classical criticism
and of English criticism since the sixteenth century. A fifth book of
considerable but patchy distinction, T. S. Eliot's Harvard lectures of 1932–3, *The Use of Poetry and the Use of Criticism* (1933).
mainly on 'the criticism provided by the poets themselves' (p.32),
may also be cited here, as well as David Daiches, *Critical Approaches
to Literature* (1956), which describes itself as being concerned,
not with 'the history of criticism as such', but with 'methodology',
or 'the varying ways' in which literature can be discussed.

Anthologies

Among the most useful anthologies of criticism are *Loci Critici*,
edited by George Saintsbury (Boston, 1903); *The Great Critics*,
edited by J. H. Smith and E. W. Parks (New York, 1932, enlarged
1939); *A Calendar of British Taste from 1600 to 1800*, edited by
E. F. Carritt (1949); *Criticism: the Major Texts*, edited by W. J.

Bate (New York, 1952); and the twin volumes *Literary Criticism: Plato to Dryden*, edited by Allan H. Gilbert (New York, 1940), and *Pope to Croce*, edited by G. W. Allen and H. H. Clark (New York, 1941); and *English Critical Texts, 16th to 20th Century*, edited by D. J. Enright and E. de Chickera (1962). Hugh Sykes Davies's Pelican *The Poets and their Critics* (1943), enlarged as 2 vols. (1960–62), marshals critiques of the major English poets, and R. W. Stallman, *The Critic's Notebook* (Minneapolis, 1950) provides extracts from theoretical and controversial criticism, mainly of the twentieth century, under abstract headings.

Studies

On the 'access of doubt' in English criticism in the 1950s, T. S. Eliot's *On Poetry and Poets* (1957), including the 1956 lecture 'The Frontiers of Criticism', is primary evidence, as well as Helen Gardner, *The Business of Criticism* (Oxford, 1959), which includes her earlier *Limits of Literary Criticism* (Oxford, 1956), and John Holloway's collection *The Charted Mirror* (1960), which includes the 1956 broadcast 'The New "Establishment" in Criticism'. Northrop Frye, *Anatomy of Criticism* (Princeton, 1957) is an ambitious and original attempt to revive the study of the literary kinds; Graham Hough, *An Essay on Criticism* (1966) clarifies the principal kinds of criticism in the mid-century; and George Watson, *The Study of Literature* (1969) analyses the historical status of literary argument and its relations with other humane studies.

The Three Kinds of Criticism

LEGISLATIVE CRITICISM

Most Elizabethan criticism was collected by G. Gregory Smith in his *Elizabethan Critical Essays*, 2 vols. (Oxford, 1904), to which must now be added new editions of Puttenham's *The Arte of English Poesie*, edited by Gladys D. Willcock and Alice Walker (Cambridge, 1936); Abraham Fraunce's *The Arcadian Rhetorike* of 1588, edited by Ethel Seaton (Oxford, 1950); and Richard Wills's *De re poetica* of 1573, edited by A. D. S. Fowler (Oxford, 1958), the last two for the Luttrell Society. There is a *History of Literary Criticism in the Renaissance* (New York, 1899) by J. E. Spingarn; see also Wilbur S. Howell, *Logic and Rhetoric in England 1500–1700* (Princeton, 1956). Sidney, *An Apology for Poetry* (1595) has been edited by Geoffrey Shepherd (1965) with an extensive introduction and commentary, notably on the intellectual sources of Renaissance Platonism.

THEORETICAL CRITICISM

Much of seventeenth-century criticism was collected by J. E. Spingarn in his edition *Seventeenth-Century Critical Essays*, 3 vols. (Oxford, 1908–9), and further extracts, mainly theoretical, will be found in *Critical Essays of the Eighteenth Century 1700–25*, edited by W. H. Durham (New Haven, 1915), and *Eighteenth-Century Critical Essays*, edited by Scott Elledge, 2 vols. (Ithaca, 1961). There is no comprehensive history of English literary aesthetics; see E. F. Carritt, *Philosophies of Beauty from Socrates to Robert Bridges* (Oxford, 1931), and Samuel H. Monk, *The Sublime: a Study of Critical Theories in Eighteenth-Century England* (New York, 1935) and, for a study of Locke's influence, Ernest L. Tuveson, *The Imagination as a Means of Grace* (Berkeley, 1960).

DESCRIPTIVE CRITICISM

René Wellek, *The Rise of English Literary History* (Chapel Hill, 1941), traces the art of historical description from the Middle Ages to Thomas Warton. For the groundwork of the literary antiquaries, see David C. Douglas, *English Scholars 1660–1730* (1939, revised 1951); and for an account of the Battle of the Books, R. F. Jones, *Ancients and Moderns* (St Louis, 1936) and R. S. Crane in his *Idea of the Humanities*, vol. i (Chicago, 1967). Augustus Ralli, in his *History of Shakespearean Criticism*, 2 vols. (Oxford, 1932), has traced one aspect of the story.

For editions and studies of individual descriptive critics since Dryden, see below.

2 · JOHN DRYDEN

Dryden's prose was first collected by Edmond Malone as *Prose Works*, 4 vols. (1800), and much of the criticism was re-edited by W. P. Ker as *Essays*, 2 vols. (Oxford, 1900). The first complete edition of the criticism is by George Watson, *Of Dramatic Poesy and Other Critical Essays*, 2 vols. (1962, Everyman's Library). For a compilation of quotations, see *The Critical Opinions of Dryden; a Dictionary*, edited by John M. Aden (Nashville, 1963), and for an analytical index of terms, based on the Everyman edition, H.

James Jensen, *A Glossary of Dryden's Critical Terms* (Minneapolis, 1969). The complete works were edited by Sir Walter Scott in 18 vols. (1808) and revised by George Saintsbury (1882–93); there is a Californian edition in progress, edited by E. N. Hooker and H. T. Swedenberg (Berkeley, 1956–).

The best general studies of Dryden are Johnson's Life in his *Lives of the English Poets* (1779–81), Scott's (1808), George Saintsbury's *Dryden* (1881), and D. Nichol Smith's Clark lectures, *Dryden* (Cambridge, 1950). For biography, Malone's life in his edition of Dryden's prose, above, has been supplemented by J. M. Osborn's *Dryden: some Biographical Facts and Problems* (New York, 1940, revised Gainesville, 1965), and Charles E. Ward, *The Life of Dryden* (Chapel Hill, 1961). Studies of Dryden as a critic include W. P. Ker's introduction to his edition of the *Essays*, above; Louis I. Bredvold, *The Intellectual Milieu of Dryden* (Ann Arbor, 1934); Frank L. Huntley, *The Unity of Dryden's Dramatic Criticism* (Chicago, 1944) and *On Dryden's Essay on Dramatic Poesy* (Ann Arbor, 1951); H. T. Swedenberg, *The Theory of the Epic in England, 1650–1800* (Berkeley, 1944), and Robert D. Hume, *Dryden's Criticism* (Ithaca, 1970).

Rymer and Dennis

Rymer's *Critical Works* have been edited by Curt A. Zimansky (New Haven, 1956), and Dennis's by E. N. Hooker, 2 vols. (Baltimore, 1939–43).

3 · THE AUGUSTANS

For a brief general study, see R. S. Crane, 'English Neo-classical Criticism: an Outline Sketch' in *Critics and Criticism Ancient and Modern,* edited by Crane (Chicago, 1952).

Pope

The volume of the Twickenham edition of the poems of Pope (General Editor, John Butt) containing the *Essay on Criticism* was among the last to appear; meanwhile George Sherburn's edition of the *Correspondence,* 5 vols. (Oxford, 1956) has brought new material to light concerning Pope's literary relationships, along with J. M. Osborn's edition of Joseph Spence, *Observations, Anecdotes and Characters,* 2 vols. (Oxford, 1966). The best account of Pope is still Johnson's in the *Lives* (1779–81); George Sherburn, *The Early*

Career of Pope (Oxford, 1934) and R. K. Root, *The Poetical Career of Pope* (Princeton, 1938) should also be consulted, as well as William Empson's essay '"Wit" in the *Essay on Criticism*' in his *Structure of Complex Words* (1951), reprinted in *Essential Articles for the Study of Pope*, edited by Maynard Mack (Hamden, Conn., 1964, enlarged 1968).

Addison

The Milton papers of 1712 were revised and collected in the year of Addison's death as *Notes upon the Twelve Books of Paradise Lost* (1719), and have since been edited by Edward Arber (1868), Albert S. Cook (Boston, 1892) and, with other essays on literary subjects, by Donald F. Bond in *Critical Essays from the Spectator* (Oxford, 1970), where the text is modernized from his edition of the *Spectator*, 5 vols. (Oxford, 1965). Addison's *Letters* were edited by Walter Graham (Oxford, 1941). There are studies of Addison in Johnson's *Lives* (1779–81) and in Macaulay's *Essays* (1843); the standard *Life* is by Peters Smithers (Oxford, 1954, revised 1968). There are critical essays by C. S. Lewis in *Essays on the Eighteenth Century Presented to David Nichol Smith* (Oxford, 1945) and C. D. Thorpe, 'Addison's Contribution to Criticism' in *The Seventeenth Century: Studies by R. F. Jones and Others* (Stanford, 1951).

Fielding

The Wesleyan edition of the *Works*, edited by W. B. Coley, Fredson T. Bowers, M. C. Battestin and others (Middletown, Conn., 1967–) is now in progress; meanwhile, *The Criticism of Fielding*, edited by Ioan Williams (1970), collects much of his literary essays and prefaces, giving precedence to inaccessible items such as play-prefaces, letters and essays from his first newspaper, the *Champion* (1739–41). The standard lives of Fielding are by Wilbur L. Cross, *The History of Henry Fielding*, 3 vols. (New Haven, 1918) and by F. Homes Dudden, *Fielding: his Life, Works and Times*, 2 vols. (Oxford, 1952); and there is a study of the criticism by F. O. Bissell, *Fielding's Theory of the Novel* (Ithaca, 1933). See also W. L. Renwick, 'Comic Epic in Prose', *Essays and Studies* xxxii (1946); Ronald S. Crane, 'The Concept of Plot and the Plot of *Tom Jones*', in *Critics and Criticism*, edited by Crane (Chicago, 1952); and the section on Fielding in Ian Watt, *The Rise of the Novel* (1957), especially pp. 241f.

4 · SAMUEL JOHNSON

The complete works of Johnson are being edited by Allen T. Hazen, J. H. Middendorf and others (New Haven, 1958–), including *Johnson on Shakespeare,* edited by Arthur Sherbo, 2 vols. (New Haven, 1968), with an index of words and phrases glossed by Johnson and an introduction by Bertrand H. Bronson. There are one-volume selections of the works by Mona Wilson (1950, Reynard Library) and R. W. Chapman (Oxford, 1955). The 1765 prefaces to Shakespeare, together with the 1756 *Proposals* and some notes, were collected by Walter Raleigh as *Johnson on Shakespeare* (Oxford, 1908, revised 1925) and, with fewer notes but three additional items, by W. K. Wimsatt (1969, Penguin). The best complete edition of the *Lives of the English Poets* is still by G. Birkbeck Hill, 3 vols. (Oxford, 1905). The *Letters* were magnificently edited by R. W. Chapman, 3 vols. (Oxford, 1952).

Apart from the early lives of Johnson by Mrs Thrale (1786), John Hawkins (1787) and James Boswell (1791) – the last of which should be consulted in the edition of G. Birkbeck Hill revised by L. F. Powell, 6 vols. (Oxford, 1934–50) – there are modern studies by Walter J. Bate, *The Achievement of Johnson* (New York, 1955) and James L. Clifford, *Young Samuel Johnson* (New York, 1955), on the first forty years (1709–49), as well as *New Light on Dr Johnson,* edited by F. W. Hilles (New Haven, 1959), including an article by Hilles on the Life of Pope. W. K. Wimsatt has written two studies of Johnson's language, *The Prose Style of Johnson* (New Haven, 1941) and *Philosophic Words* (New Haven, 1948), as well as a lecture on the 1755 *Dictionary* collected in Hilles, above. There is an essay by T. S. Eliot, 'Johnson as Critic and Poet' (1944) collected in his *On Poetry and Poets* (1957); and specialist studies include Jean H. Hagstrum, *Johnson's Literary Criticism* (Minneapolis, 1952), G. J. Kolb, *Dr Johnson's Dictionary* (Chicago, 1952), and Arthur Sherbo, *Johnson, Editor of Shakespeare* (Urbana, 1956).

For the rise of literary history, see under I, above. Early Shakespeare criticism, including Morgann on Falstaff, is collected by D. Nichol Smith in *Eighteenth-Century Essays on Shakespeare* (Glasgow, 1903, revised Oxford, 1963); Morgann is edited by Daniel A. Fineman (Oxford, 1972); and there is a rich mine of information in Bishop Percy's *Letters,* edited by D. Nichol Smith, Cleanth Brooks and others, 5 vols. (Baton Rouge, 1944–57). Whiter is fully discussed by F. P. Wilson in his 1941 lecture 'Shakespeare and the Diction of Common Life', expanded in his *Shakespearian and Other Studies*

(Oxford, 1969); and his *Specimen* is now edited, enlarged with Whiter's unpublished notes, by Alan Over (1964).

5 · WORDSWORTH AND COLERIDGE

Wordsworth's 1800 preface, with other essays and much of Coleridge's *Biographia*, was edited by George Sampson (Cambridge, 1920), and the preface with its subsequent revisions and additions has been meticulously edited by W. J. B. Owen in *Anglistica* (Copenhagen), ix (1957); there is now a collection which includes the 1809–10 *Essays upon Epitaphs* etc., as *Literary Criticism of Wordsworth*, edited by Paul M. Zall (Lincoln, Nebraska, 1966), and a full study by W. J. B. Owen, *Wordsworth as Critic* (Toronto, 1969).

Coleridge's works are now being collected for the first time (General Editor, Kathleen Coburn) (1969–) in the Bollingen series, beginning with the *Watchman* and the *Friend*; and there is a useful one-volume section edited by Stephen Potter in the Nonesuch Library as *Select Poetry and Prose* (1933, enlarged 1950). The *Shakespearean Criticism* (mainly lectures of 1811–12) was edited by T. M. Raysor, 2 vols. (Cambridge, Mass., 1930, revised for Everyman's Library, 1960); the 1811–12 lectures alone have now been edited as *Coleridge on Shakespeare* by R. A. Foakes (1971); and the *Miscellaneous Criticism* (mainly the lectures of 1818), edited by Raysor, appeared in 1936. *Coleridge on the Seventeenth Century*, edited by R. F. Brinkley (Durham, N.C., 1955), assembles critical comments under author-headings. The *Biographia Literaria* was edited by John Shawcross, 2 vols. (Oxford, 1907) and by George Watson in Everyman's Library (1956, revised 1960). The *Notebooks* are being edited complete for the first time by Kathleen Coburn, 11 vols. (1957–) in the Bollingen series, and the *Collected Letters* by E. L. Griggs, 6 vols. (Oxford, 1956–71).

The standard life of Coleridge is E. K. Chambers, *Coleridge: a Biographical Study* (Oxford, 1938, revised 1950), while Humphry House's Clark lectures, *Coleridge* (1953) reconsider his personality and his poetry. J. L. Lowes, *The Road to Xanadu* (Boston, 1927, revised 1930), studies the relation between his poetry and his reading. I. A. Richards, *Coleridge on Imagination* (1934) has now appeared with comments by Kathleen Coburn (Bloomington, 1960). See also M. H. Abrams, *The Mirror and the Lamp: Romantic Theory and the Critical Tradition* (New York, 1953); J. A. Appleyard, *Coleridge's*

Philosophy of Literature (Cambridge, Mass, 1965); George Watson, *Coleridge the Poet* (1966).

6 · LAMB, HAZLITT, DE QUINCEY

For general studies of romantic criticism, see under 5, above; and for an anthology, *English Critical Essays* (*Nineteenth Century*), edited by Edmund D. Jones (Oxford, 1916) (World's Classics).

Lamb

The works of Lamb have been edited by E. V. Lucas, 7 vols. (1903–5, revised in 6 vols. 1912), as well as the *Letters*, 3 vols. (1935); and the *Criticism* has been collected in one volume by E. M. W. Tillyard (Cambridge, 1923). The *Specimens of English Dramatic Poets* were edited by Israel Gollancz, 2 vols. (1893). The best general studies are by E. V. Lucas, *Life of Lamb* (1905, revised 1921), and Edmund Blunden, *Lamb and his Contemporaries* (Cambridge, 1933). See also R. C. Bald, 'Lamb and the Elizabethans', in *Studies in Honor of A. H. R. Fairchild* (Columbia, Missouri, 1946).

Hazlitt

The *Complete Works* were exhaustively edited by P. P. Howe in 21 vols. (1930–4). There is no good one-volume selection of the criticism, but the *Characters of Shakespear's Plays*, the *Lectures on the English Poets*, the *Lectures on the English Comic Writers*, *Table Talk*, and *The Spirit of the Age* have all appeared in World's Classics (1901–24). The standard lives are by P. P. Howe, *The Life of Hazlitt* (1922, revised 1928), and Herschel Baker, *William Hazlitt* (Cambridge, Mass., 1962), and there is a respectful analysis of Hazlitt's critical theory by Elisabeth Schneider in *The Aesthetics of Hazlitt* (Philadelphia, 1933, revised 1952), and another by Roy Park, *Hazlitt and the Spirit of the Age* (Oxford, 1971); as well as two candid Victorian portraits by Leslie Stephen in the second series of his *Hours in a Library* (1876), and by George Saintsbury in his *Essays in English Literature 1780–1860* (1890).

De Quincey

The works were edited incomplete by David Masson in 14 vols. (Edinburgh, 1889–90), and the *Literary Criticism* by Helen Darbishire (Oxford, 1909). The *Recollections of the Lake Poets* have been edited by David Wright (1970, Penguin) and by Edward Sackville-West (1948), who has also written a critical biography, *A Flame in Sunlight* (1936). As with Hazlitt, there are Victorian studies by Leslie Stephen in the first series of his *Hours in a Library* (1874), and by George Saintsbury in his *Essays in English Literature 1780–1860* (1890).

7 · MATTHEW ARNOLD

The complete prose works are being edited for the first time by R. H. Super (Ann Arbor, 1960–), and this now includes an edition of the first series of *Essays in Criticism*, with the Celtic lectures, etc., as *Lectures and Essays in Criticism* (1962), as well as *Culture and Anarchy* and *Friendship's Garland*, etc. (1965). There is a one-volume selection of *Poetry and Prose* edited by John Bryson in the Reynard Library (1954), as well as a collection of *Essays, Including Essays in Criticism 1865, On Translating Homer,* etc. (Oxford, 1914) and *Selected Prose*, edited by P. J. Keating (Penguin, 1971). Some of the letters were edited by G. W. E. Russell, 2 vols. (1895), and the *Letters to A. H. Clough* (Oxford, 1932) and the *Note Books* (Oxford, 1952) have both been edited by H. F. Lowry. *Culture and Anarchy* has been edited by J. Dover Wilson (Cambridge, 1932), and *Five Uncollected Essays* by Kenneth Allott (Liverpool, 1953).

There is a critical biography by Lionel Trilling, *Matthew Arnold* (New York, 1939, revised 1955), and a study of both poetry and criticism by E. K. Brown, *Arnold: a Study in Conflict* (Chicago, 1948). T. S. Eliot's view can be consulted in the 1930 essay 'Arnold and Pater' in his *Selected Essays* (1932), and in his *The Use of Poetry and the Use of Criticism* (1933). John Holloway's *The Victorian Sage* (1953) includes a study of Arnold's language of persuasion, and his *The Charted Mirror* (1960) a general assessment. There is a study of Arnold's controversial phase in William Robbins's *The Ethical Idealism of Arnold* (1959).

8 · HENRY JAMES

There are studies of the aesthetic movement in Graham Hough, *The Last Romantics* (1949) and in Frank Kermode, *Romantic Image* (1957). Oscar Wilde's criticism has been edited by Richard Ellmann as *The Artist as Critic* (New York, 1969). James's prefaces have been collected as *The Art of the Novel,* edited by R. P. Blackmur (New York, 1934), the *Notebooks* were edited by F. O. Matthiessen and Kenneth B. Murdock (New York, 1947), and some of the letters by Percy Lubbock in 2 vols. (1920). There are numerous overlapping editions of James's critical essays, including *The Art of Fiction*, edited by Morris Roberts (New York, 1948), *The House of Fiction*, edited by Leon Edel (1957), and *Selected Literary Criticism*, edited by M. Shapira (1963). Three of his literary exchanges have been collected: *Letters to A. C. Benson and Auguste Monod*, edited by E. F. Benson (1930); *James and R. L. Stevenson*, edited by Janet A. Smith (1948); and *James and H. G. Wells*, edited by Leon Edel and G. N. Ray (1958). There is a study of the criticism by Morris Roberts, *James's Criticism* (Cambridge, Mass., 1929), and of the prefaces by Leon Edel, *The Prefaces of James* (Paris, 1931) whose biography, 5 vols. (Philadelphia, 1953–71) is now complete.

9 · THE EARLY TWENTIETH CENTURY

There is a survey of twentieth-century criticism, British and American, in Stanley E. Hyman, *The Armed Vision* (New York, 1948, abridged and revised 1955), and of the theoretical aspects of the New Criticism, especially in Eliot and Richards, in Murray Krieger, *The New Apologists for Poetry* (Minneapolis, 1956). John Crowe Ransom's *The New Criticism* (Norfolk, Conn., 1941) is an important historical source, especially on Richards, Empson, Eliot and Winters. A symposium by the Chicago Critics, *Critics and Criticism Ancient and Modern*, edited by R. S. Crane (Chicago, 1952), contains articles on Richards, Empson, and the American New Critics by Crane, Elder Olson, and others; and Crane's *The Language of Criticism and the Structure of Poetry* (Toronto, 1953) returns to the attack.

Eliot and Others

The Pelican *Selected Prose of Eliot*, edited by John Hayward (1953), offers a wide selection from Eliot's criticism in all periods. Early commendations of Eliot as poet and critic include I. A Richards, *Science and Poetry* (1926) and *Principles of Literary Criticism* (enlarged 1926, with appendices); and Edmund Wilson, *Axel's Castle* (New York, 1931). There is a hostile reaction in Yvor Winters, 'Eliot or the Illusion of Reaction' collected in his *Anatomy of Nonsense* (Norfolk, Conn., 1943), *In Defense of Reason* (New York, 1947) and *On Modern Poets* (New York, 1959). Eliot is defended in Seán Lucy, *Eliot and the Idea of Tradition* (1960) and Northrop Frye, *T. S. Eliot* (Edinburgh, 1963, in *Writers and Critics* series). *Criterion*, which

SELECT BIBLIOGRAPHY

Eliot edited 1922–39, now has *Indexes* by E. A. Baker (1967). See Donald Gallup, *Eliot: a Bibliography* (1952, revised 1968).

There is a study of I. A. Richards in Jerome P. Schiller, *Richards' Theory of Literature* (New Haven, 1969). *Scrutiny* (1932–53) has been reprinted with an index, 20 vols. (Cambridge, 1963), followed by *A Selection from Scrutiny*, edited by Leavis, 2 vols. (Cambridge, 1968). For a comment on Leavis see Lionel Trilling in his *A Gathering of Fugitives* (Boston, 1956).

INDEX

Abrams, M. H., 227
Aden, John M., 223
Addison, Joseph, 16f., 58–62, 225
Aeschylus, 149
Aesthetic Movement, 149, 154f., 229
Affective Fallacy, 132 and n., 214
Allen, G. W., 222
Allott, Kenneth, 229
ambiguity, 192f.
Ancients and Moderns (Battle of the Books), 32, 34, 58, 223
Andrewes, Lancelot, 170, 173, 175
Appleyard, J. A., 227–8
Arber, Edward, 225
Ariosto, Lodovico, 98
Aristotle, 3, 7, 34, 149; in Addison, 61, 62; in Chicago School, 214; in Coleridge, 115–16; in Fielding, 68; in Johnson, 78; in Lamb, 124–5; in Pope, 53f.; in Wordsworth, 117
Arnold, Matthew, 3, 8, 9, 11, 12, 13, 15, 17f., 27, 64 and n., 134–53, 154, 169, 198, 209, 211, 218, 229; and Eliot, 169f.; Leavis on, 199
Arnold, Thomas, 153
Atkins, J. W. H., 2, 221
Aubrey, John, 49
Auden, W. H., 13, 202–3, 217
d'Aunois, Mme, 85
Austen, Jane, 64, 115, 166, 202

Babbitt, Irving, 171, 172
Bacon, Francis, 3n., 32, 49, 163
Badawi, M. M., 114
Bagehot, Walter, 157
Baker, E. A., 231
Bald, R. C., 228
Balzac, Honoré de, 159
Barker, George, 203
Bate, Walter J., 221–2, 226
Bateson, F. W., 111, 179n.
Battestin, M. C., 225
Baudelaire, Charles, 9 and n., 29, 137
Beardsley, Monroe C., 132n., 162n., 214
Beaumont, Francis and John Fletcher, 35, 40n., 42 and n.
Bennett, Arnold, 159
Benson, A. C., 162n., 164n., 230
Benson, E. F., 162n., 230
Berkeley, Bishop, 83
Besant, Walter, 159
biography, 50, 67–8, 83f., 143f. 195
Bissell, F. O., 225
Blackmore, Sir Richard, 20
Blackmur, R. P., 160, 162n., 163n., 229
Bloomsbury Group, 125, 209
Blunden, Edmund, 228
Boerhaave, Herman, 85 and n.
Boileau, Nicolas, 54, 77
Bond, Donald F., 57n., 59–61n., 225
Bosanquet, Theodora, 160
Boswell, James, 5, 73f., 226

DATE DUE
